Social Work and Human Relations

Social Work and Human Relations

H.Y. Siddiqui

Rawat Publications
Jaipur • New Delhi • Bangalore • Guwahati • Kolkata

ISBN 978-81-316-0745-9

Published by
Prem Rawat for **Rawat Publications**
Satyam Apts, Sector 3, Jawahar Nagar, Jaipur 302 004 (India)
Phone: 0141 265 1748 / 7006 Fax: 0141 265 1748
E-mail: info@rawatbooks.com
Website: www.rawatbooks.com

New Delhi Office
4858/24, Ansari Road, Daryaganj, New Delhi 110 002
Phone: 011 2326 3290

Also at *Bangalore, Guwahati* and *Kolkata*

Typeset by Rawat Computers, Jaipur
Printed at Chaman Enterprises, New Delhi

This book is dedicated to all my students
and my grandchildren,
Saiyra Sana Siddiqui,
Zahir Collins Siddiqui, and
Senan Collins Siddiqui.

Contents

Preface xi
Acknowledgement xiii

1 **Introduction** **1**
Understanding Relationships 6
Embedded Self-View of Relationships 9
Human Relations: Definition and Nature 10
Laws of Relationships 12
Importance of Relationships 15
Case Studies 18
Intervention Strategies 21

2 **Social Work and Human Relations** **23**
Problem of Definition 23
Global Definition of Social Work 27
Case Studies **34**

3 **Human Relations: Theories and Concepts** **39**
THEORIES 41
Theory of Social Exchange 43
Theory of Interdependence 43
The Theory of Self and Others Orientation 45
The Theory of Interpersonal Cognition 48

	Theory of Attachment	49
	CONCEPTS	52
	Emotional Energy	52
	Emotional Intelligence	52
	Anxiety	53
	Betrayal	53
	Intrapersonal Conflict	54
	Conflict and Change	55
	Control	56
	Dependence Regulation	57
	Depression	58
	Parenting Styles	58
	THERAPIES	59
	Behavioural Couples Therapy	59
	Cognitive Behavioural Couples Therapy	60
	Integrative Behavioural Couples Therapy	60
	Emotionally Focused Therapy	60
	Family Systems Therapy	61
4	**The Self-Concept**	**63**
	Different Facets of Self-Concept	65
	Theories of Self-Concept	69
	Concepts	70
5	**Family Relations**	**76**
	The Spousal Relationship	76
	Parent-Child Relationship	85
	Sibling Relations	92
6	**Conflicts in Relationships**	**96**
	Conflict	96
	Factors Causing Problems in Relationships	98
	Communication and Conflict in Family	102
7	**Working with Families**	**107**
	Family Structure	108
	Communication	108
	Domestic Violence	108

Extramarital Affairs or Betrayals 109
Gender Roles 109
Ethical Issues 109
Process of Working with a Family 109

8 Working with Individuals 114
First Stage: Establishing a Contract 115
Second Stage: Assessment 116
Third Stage: Preparing a Client to Face and Accept the Reality 123
Fourth Stage: Listening to the Client Version of the Problem 124
Fifth Stage: Developing an Explanation 124
Sixth Stage: Finding a Solution 125
Terminating/Referral 126

9 Working with Groups 127
Set the Routine 127
Monitoring 128
Analysing the Relationship Patterns in Group 130
Group Conflict 131

10 Working with Communities 133
Concepts Relating to Community 134
Communities and its Environment 136
Community Activists/Leaders 138
Major Community Concerns 138
Professional Approach 143
Other Methods of Entry into the Community 144
Developing a Community Profile 146
Determining Community Needs 147
Programme Planning 148
Mobilizing Peoples Participation 148

11 Social Action: Dealing with Macro Realities 155
Globalization of Economy 160
Marginalization of State 162
Growth of Social Iniquities 163
Problem of Governance 164

	Continuation of Absolute Poverty: Economic and Human Dimension	165
	Environmental Issues	168
	Inadequate Health Care	168
	Human Rights Violation	170
	Gender Inequality	170
	Child Abuse	172
	Political Participation	178
	The Advocacy Process	179
12	**Skills of Facilitating Relationships**	**182**
	Skills in Rapport Building	183
	Communication Skill	184
	Listening	189
	Observation	190
	Analytical Thinking	190
	Empathy	191
	Self-Control	192
13	**Techniques of Facilitating Relationships**	**195**
	Assessment of Individuals	196
	Family Assessment	202
	Assessment of Groups	211
	Assessment of Communities	212
	Assessment of Organizations	214
	Computerized Assessment	217
14	**Rethinking Social Work in India**	**218**
	References	225
	Index	251

Preface

Social work in India has become well known after completing nearly eight decades of its existence in India. There are so many departments and schools of social work that have been added in the last two decades. The exact number remains a mystery. Numbers, as the believers in qualitative method of research believe, do not reveal the truth. One has to look beyond the facade of numbers and words, both verbal and written, to discover truth or come closest to discovering a logical explanation of an event – past or present. Therefore, when we come across a sufficiently large number of students, being educated to practice professional social work, to deal with a variety of problems in society, is it logical to assume that social work education has the knowledge and a system to pass on the knowledge, and to generate skills, for practitioners to deal with these problems. And then when you examine the issue a little closely, you are shocked to discover that both the assumptions are not exactly true if they are not exactly false. The overall quality of social work education in the country is declining so rapidly, as Pathak (2000) noted, that it should be a matter of concern for those associated with it. The reasons for decline though are not difficult to ascertain. To begin with, professional social work education being so culturally sensitive and multidisciplinary in nature, is still being carried out with the help of academic text, written in a very alien cultural context and delivered by persons not having enough practice experience, to students without any undergraduate academic background to receive it. To make the matter even worse, it is now being offered through a distance mode as well. Contextualizing social work practice in India Narayan (2008) suggests, social work must incorporate multidimensional analyses of structural disadvantage, and this must be at the forefront of social work thinking at whatever level the social worker is practicing. Octavia Hill, considered a pioneer in discovering a novel method of working with the poor, said that her major goal was to help people to become capable of helping themselves and become independent of any help. It can be carried out by having a caring relationship. In her opinion each case and each situation must be individualized. Everyone should be respected and given their privacy and independence (see Kendall, 2000).

No wonder then, the very definition of the subject remains as ambiguous as its practice in the country, though some may say, globally. The current text offers a new perspective, for both its education and practice in India. It provides a new definition of social work, which unifies its practice at different levels – individual, group, community and society – offers a definite expertise area – human relations, which all social workers will possess as their core expertise. In the modern day society a profession needs very specific skills to qualify as a profession, which its members acquire through specialized education and training. The text is an effort to achieve the same.

H.Y. Siddiqui

Acknowledgement

Writing a book requires various inputs and hence contributions by many persons are needed, apart from the author. It is not possible to mention all the names yet I take this opportunity to thank every one who helped in making it possible. To begin with, in making the decision about what to write, the audience is very important, since the very purpose of a book is lost if no body is there to read it. I am grateful to all my students and colleagues who showed considerable interest in my earlier texts encouraging me to write more. My colleagues in Hyderabad and Delhi helped in discussing the chapters at different stages and finalizing these. I am grateful to the department of social work in Maulana Azad National Urdu University in Hyderabad and Jamia Millia Islamia, New Delhi for their whole-hearted support. Rawat Publications as usual provide the final touches and I am grateful to their staff for doing a great job.

H.Y. Siddiqui

1

Introduction

The human relationships can be compared to the flow of blood that keeps the human body functioning efficiently, similarly relationships keep an individual, group, family, community and finally society functioning smoothly. Social workers provide help to people individually, in groups and to a community through the medium of relationship alone. Relationships by both clients and social work are increasingly seen in procedural, legal and administrative terms. However, research studies examining both client satisfaction and intervention effectiveness regularly find that the psychosocial qualities of the worker-client relationship are the major components in the success or otherwise of the service offered. The argument is that the psychological persona of both practitioners and users acquires many of their characteristics, including self-esteem, self-confidence and emotional intelligence, through the relationship experiences, throughout their life span. The level of understanding of social realities around them and the competence to deal with these, that people develop depends on the quality of their relationship history, as experts of personality development emphasize. If poor relationships are where psychosocial competences go awry, then good relationships are where they are likely to recover. This observation has major implications for the quality, character and skill of the relationship experiences offered to clients by social workers (Howe, 1998).

The importance of human relationships in targeting social development of individuals through social work practice is therefore obvious. Social workers identified the mission, as promoting individual well-being along with social change to promote values of human rights and social justice, since the middle of the twentieth century. The history of social work however reveals that social workers chose to work with victims of poverty influenced by Octavia Hill and Mary Richmond, while Beatrice Webb and Sydney Webb searching for causes of poverty lead to the development of sociology and other social sciences including economics and politics. One of the most important human needs is the caring and recognition, second in importance only to the survival needs, as Maslow discovered long ago, and hence humans can survive only in the company of fellow human beings. Subsequent researches on development of human personality, particularly in development of children, have proved beyond any reasonable doubt that human relationships play a crucial role in the development of a healthy personality and to live in harmony with their social environment. Therefore, it will be helpful for helping professions, including social work, to take note of the patterns of human relationships, and its linkages with human problems and sufferings, in families and communities, in the field of health, education and social welfare as a whole.

The pace of social change in human societies has increased during the last few decades impacting thought patterns and behaviours. The relationships throughout the globe including India, have undergone unprecedented changes. For example, the family relationships, have become more horizontal from the earlier hierarchical nature. The relationships are now contested, though the women empowerment and a true equality is a far dream, but the rules governing the rights and power, shaping the relationships are being questioned and changed. The new thrust in development is to give more importance to self than others, including the significant others such as parents, sibling and other kin relations. Now they are treated as a temporary phenomenon and the spousal relations have assumed the pivotal position till they last, thus spreading the term individual culture. The spousal relations and problems associated with it, form the bulk of social problems in the developed countries, as these relations could not sustain, leading to the break down of family.

The institution of family in India experienced a variety of changes, for example, the nature of family has changed from several generations living together to only one or possibly two generations sharing a household. The practice of sharing a household without sharing the kitchen, are some new ways of living together. The structure has become more horizontal from its earlier hierarchical nature. Its function has changed, role allocation is changing, communication patterns have changed and thus new patterns of relationships are emerging. The gap in the values of the different generation has widened, creating stress since it directly changes the expectation levels and outcomes. The marriage is still the general pattern of starting a new family, but premarital and extramarital relationships are taking serious roots in the society. Rural-urban differences in these matters are also fairly pronounced. The selection of mate has undergone a change in urban educated classes and has become more open and flexible, opening up in many directions, covering inter-class, inter-caste and inter-religious boundaries. The socialization of girls has experienced change on two counts, firstly the education and employment possibilities for girls have increased and secondly parental attitudes have changed as well. This has given them more self-esteem and self-confidence. This has impacted spousal relations to some extent with both positive and negative consequences. There is a growing respect for females along with resentment for loss of power and the total control exercised earlier. The communication patterns between the spouses have changed from earlier autocratic to more open and democratic in nature. The same is happening to relationships in schools, workplaces and communities.

Family is one of the crucial institutions providing training in social roles in terms of caregiving and a healthy attitude towards others. The success of a family in meeting the multifarious needs of its members is a collective endeavour, which serves as a strong learning experience of handling all future relationships. Now that the institution of family has changed it has brought about consequent changes elsewhere, some more functional, others creating stress. The authority and obedience pattern have changed significantly, creating stress all round as people take time to adjust and are not prepared for the new patterns of behaviour. Things are becoming more chaotic as the changes are neither uniform in nature, nor happening uniformly in different locations and classes. The relationships run smoothly, if the parties are clear about their respective positions in it, and the expected behaviour patterns. In the absence of clarity of boundaries and spaces, new behaviour patterns are creating stress which is seriously affecting the smooth functioning of relationships.

The cost of failing families, according to a non-government organization in UK, is rising and according to their estimates is likely to be around 45 billion British pounds. Families are failing, because the abilities to handle relationships are declining. The twentieth century was particularly bad for human relationships the world over. All this notwithstanding, is writing a text about human relationships worth the trouble, as most people think they know, all there is to know – about relationships. They also think they can cope with it as well. Every other person has a definite view about how to, for example, handle one's spousal or parental relationship. Yet, the cases of failure or problems, such as delinquency, alcoholism, even child and drug abuse are rising. The studies about state of human relationships, for example, domestic violence, child abuse, child labour, female infanticide, alcoholism and school dropouts, etc. are few, leaving a lot for people to guess and speculate. The main institutions hosting relationships are family, school, peer groups, workplace, communities, etc. There are relationships one is born with and thus there is little to choose, for example, an alcoholic and violent father, whereas other relationships are conscious choices, yet both can go wrong and significantly affect a lot of people. Why some people are more successful than others in handling relationships is not easy to explain. Bowlby (1969/82) has identified the caregiver's relationship with child making an important contribution. One of the facts, important in handling relationships, is what people bring with them into the relationship by way of expectations, beliefs, and personality traits (see Fletcher, 2007). Further, studies of parenting and families have suggested that family has definite influence on children's competence to handle all future relationships (see Parke et al., 1988). Besides attachment theory developed by Bowlby, and Mary Ainsworth (1982) and others, and a more recent study (Glick and Ross, 2013) found a child's relations with mother to be a significant factor in learning social skills and using them.

Not many persons have the ability or the inclination to think about their responses to others. Fewer still would consider any correlation with, why they succeed or fail in whatever they do in life, to have anything to do with, either their past or present human relationships. But it is by now well established that human relationships play a vital part in people's life. As one rightly remarked, antagonizing people when you don't have to, is like casting your garbage on the waters. One day it may come floating back, smelling worse. Social workers, psychologists in general, and other social scientists including caring professionals, believe that your relationships with others, make you not only socially competent and successful but physically and mentally strong. Positive relationships help you carry out many things in life far more efficiently than those who are unable to do so. Positive relationships open up new worlds to people. A common cause for individual and organizational failure has now been identified as poor human relationships by many studies. A. Maslow (1943), Fredrick Herzberg (1987), David McClelland (1987), and Victor Vroom (1964) were the early pioneers to point in that direction, followed by numerous others. The reason for relationships being so vital in human functioning is obvious and simple. Positive relationships mean low levels or a complete absence of stress, which increases the decision-making capacity of any person. The same logic could be extended to groups such as a family, a work team or a playgroup or even a community, which is made up of many groups both large and small. In small groups including families, healthy relationships lead to what is termed by sociologists as group cohesiveness, which in other words refers to bonding between members. A simple characteristic of a group where this happens to be the case is that no one wants to leave the group (see Siddiqui, 2008). The member's identification with the group is so strong that the group is able to structure their thinking and behaviour to a great extent (see Whitaker, 1995). The group goals are considered very important and individuals strive to achieve these without worrying about self, as they know that the group will take care of them. In the case of organizations, where a committed team undertakes a task, the success rate is very high (see Hoegel and George, 2001; Ezzamel and Willmott, 1998; Xyrichis and Ream, 2008). Members draw a lot of support and sharing from group members, thus reducing the stress in their lives. The development of social sciences in general and behavioural sciences in particular, has provided enough evidence that human relationships are not a chance occurrence. How people relate to others is determined by a number of factors including biological and the cultural context (see Duck, 2007). Sociological studies have discovered a link between nature and size of a society and its human relationships (see Cooley, 1902, 1909). For example, relationships in a village are different from the relationships in a small town, and these in turn are different from relationships in a metropolitan city. Cooley, thus, developed the concept of primary and secondary relationships indicating some very interesting features of these relationships. In human relationships the focus has generally been on family relationships, between partners and then between parent and children. Human relationships at work has received considerable attention since Elton Mayo (1933) conclusively indicated the close link between productivity and human relations. There are some research studies that indicate the existence of gender differences in the manner people view relationship but most of it has been carried out in developed countries. In long-term relationships, men tend to attach more importance to physical features or attractiveness and fun loving than do women, and women tend to give more weight to loyalty and warmth and to status and resources than do men (see Fletcher, 2007). In Indian subcontinent based on my experiences with my students and colleagues, the males preferred a more subservient partner than women, while the females preferred a more emotionally reliable and mature person with some status. The women thus are similar across the cultures in seeking a more stable and secure relationship, while men differ significantly in how they construct an ideal partner. Further, women are more motivated than men in intimate relationships (e.g. women talk and think about relationships more than men do and are more accurate at reading emotions and thoughts in their partners than men are). Second, men adopt a more patronizing (ownership) attitude toward woman's sexuality and reproductive behaviour. Third, men possess a stronger sex drive and a stronger orientation toward short-term sexual liaisons than do women, and finally, women are more focussed on the level of investment in intimate relationships than are men (see Fletcher, 2007). The professional expertise to understand and facilitate relationships can be put to use in almost all areas of human functioning. The helping professionals providing inputs to increase the well-being and development of human beings will immensely benefit from a theoretical understanding of human relationships. It will help them to analyse and use the facts more objectively to achieve greater success. Facilitating human relationships should emerge as a major area of social work practice at all levels, since helping the social functioning of individuals, groups and communities is the essence of social work practice.

Understanding Relationships

There are two important dimensions of human relations, firstly the actors and secondly, the behaviour they exhibit. The human development experts have, studied the actors and the behaviour they subsequently exhibit on a consistent basis. Most of these experts feel that the human relations experiences of the actors during their developmental process, is crucial to their development. The clinical practice authors place the same at centre stage in many areas of social work practice. They have furnished us with some evidence like the Bowlby experiments, and studies from groups, urging us that an understanding of human relationships and social development is essential for all those who work with people in distress and difficulty (Howe, 1998). Psychologically the individual cannot be understood independently of his or her social and cultural context. Children do not enter the world as a priori discrete psychological beings. The self and personality takes shape, as the developing mind engages with the world in which it finds itself. There is no hard boundary between the mental condition of individuals and the social relationships that they experience. Individuality, observes Burkitt (1991), is socially based. Personality forms as social understanding develops. All of this is the world of thc psychosocial – a conceptual domain that has long been familiar to social workers since the days of Gordon Hamilton in the 1940s.

Children enter the world, ready and able to interact. From day one, they show pro-social behaviours. But how things turn out depends so much on the quality of other people's response to those innate social proclivities. Therefore, the quality and character of children's close relationships matters greatly. It soon becomes apparent that many other factors will also affect the quality of these early relationships, including children's inherited temperamental make-up, parents' own history of relationships, and the stresses experienced by both parents and children in their social and material environments. Clearly, the quality of relationships will vary widely from family to family. But of particular interest and importance to social workers is the recognition that adverse relationships upset children's ability to develop useful and effective social and emotional understanding. Social competence is achieved within the context of caring relationships. Children raised in environments where care is less secure, less predictable and less responsive generally find interpersonal life stressful and frustrating. In turn, these frustrations may lead to a range of personal difficulties and problem behaviours. Indeed, as George and Solomon (1996) observes, phenomenon such as abuse, maltreatment and neglect always occur in the context of relationships. 'What has stood the test of time,' says Rutter (1993), '... has been the proposition that the qualities of parent-child relationships constitute a central aspect of parenting, that the development of social relationships occupies a crucial role in personality growth, and that abnormalities in relationships are important in many types of psychopathology'. The practitioners have to understand, the complex interplay between the past and the present, the link between psychological and the social, to make sense of going events and to intervene appropriately and effectively.

The process of interaction between two or more persons leading to building of relationship has been viewed from many perspectives (see Wilmot, 1995; David Howe, 1995; Hatfield et al. (1979). The main issue is how self reacts to others, and in order to discover this mystery naturally the formation of self is questioned as also its capability to act independently. A simple contention is that it is the other who directs the response of the self. This argument suggests that children do not enter the world as a priori discrete psychological beings. However, this view is now subject to correction as the researches in genetics indicate a strong possibility of a child inheriting some traits that produces a given psychological condition. The origin of behaviour lies in the brain and genetic formations such as the quality of response to any stimuli is to some extent determined by the inherited structure. The emotional response such as aggression or lack of it, is also genetically controlled. The cultural context provides the rationale for focussing these responses in given directions. The fact that these traits are different in case of all individuals makes any theory building in these matters rather difficult. Any study of behaviour will reveal some common traits between parent/s and children and yet they are different individuals and display very different behavioural patterns.

The consistency of behaviour is an important indicator of human personality, therefore, to understand a person's behaviour an exploration of the behavioural pattern displayed over a period of time is helpful. The relationships and the behaviour pattern consistency are significant indicators in arriving at an understanding of both the persons and the quality of relationships. The analysis should include changes in the economic, social or the political environment. Economic here refers to the economic status of the individual and the family, social refers to the value base of the individual and the environment around, and the political refers to the freedom the person has in choosing between different options available. The overall scenario, therefore, becomes detailed and a guideline to understand and explain any relationship changes, therefore, becomes complex making it difficult to arrive at a one to one relationship between two factors, producing a certain behavioural outcome. In analysing behaviour of individual actors in a relationship, perception of stimuli has a central place, that is what a person observes is not important, what is important is how a person interprets it. So we come back to our central issue, how the self observes, a social reality and how it reacts to it.

The social reality here again needs defining. For example, is the person reacting to the economic, social or political aspect of the relationship. The self-interpretation of the relationship and its power to reward or punish, perhaps influences the behaviour of respective parties. Here the capacity to interpret a stimuli then assumes importance. For example, education and cultural norms influence this to a great extent.

Embedded Self-View of Relationships

This paradigm makes a fundamental shift in its conceptualization of Self. Within this paradigm, Self cannot be seen as a separate identity, but must always be examined within the context of a relationship. To some extent this may be true in the sense a person controls self-responses in different relationships to suit their self-interest. Thus, the Self is not independent, and we begin to see people forming and reforming their selves within each unique relational context. In this view, the relationship itself is treated as a separate entity: Relationship has identity (Hecht, 1993). These views focus on interconnections and interdependencies that have created the Self. The very perception of Self is cast within a broader framework of family, friends, lovers, work, and the broader culture, limiting the freedom of independent action. The dependence of Self is however questioned by those, who regard Self as structured, which then acts in a particular manner to give primacy to Self or other. In the collective cultures thus the responses of different parties in a close relationship are clearly defined and are generally predictable.

Elaine Hatfield, Mary Utne, and Jane Traupmann (1979) provide a different perspective based on their review of the research (most of the research was conducted in the United States) and conclude that equitable relations appear more stable than non-equitable relations. The equitable refers to where both parties are viewing each other as equal and are prepared to share any role and space. The inequitable refers to a greater self-orientation and therefore attempts to dominate, resulting in inequitable relations. This formulation also supports what we argued earlier, an equitable or inequitable Self which is independent of the relationship. To conclude if both persons are self-oriented, the relationship will become impossible. Whereas where one person is self-oriented and the other is the opposite that is totally others-oriented, the relationship becomes a perfect fit. In the collectivist cultures, women are generally others-oriented to make the relationship work, though it is not equitable. However, where both have an others-orientation, the relations are equitable. It, therefore, helps us to conclude that the psychological structure of the psyche and its position on self-other continuum, is preceding the relationship and is independent of it.

A professional can explore the psychological structure of persons on the self-other continuum, to understand the general behaviour pattern that will emerge in relationships. The chances of success of a correctional approach will depend upon how amenable it is to environmental factors.

Human Relations: Definition and Nature

A relationship is an association between two or more people, irrespective of its duration or quality. A normal human existence requires a number of human relations, and thus, the fact that humans are fond of and exist in the company of fellow human beings. A person trying to live in isolation and not wanting to have any contacts with others is considered abnormal. Humans need cooperation of others to survive or meet their economic, social and emotional needs. A person, therefore, inevitably interacts with other human beings. These interactions involve a give and take process between persons and involve feelings or emotions towards each other. A relationship develops as the interactions continue for a period of time and the two components, positive feelings and a process of give and take, remain in place (see Byrne, 1961; Berscheid and Peplau, 1983; Maniaci and Reis, 2010). The sociologists categorize the relationships based on the nature of interactions such as, face-to-face and more frequent interactions as primary relationships and less frequent and distant interactions as secondary relationships. Sociologists suggest that societies evolve social norms and laws to structure relationships in society for example, family laws of marriage and divorce, inheritance, etc. and labour laws to govern work relationships and so on. The social norms designed to structure relationships have both positive and negative points. The structuring helps in clarifying roles and expectations, yet no norms are absolute and the dynamic nature of society keeps everything fluid. The dynamic nature of society makes it inevitable that interpretation of norms and laws would not be homogenous, making conflicts inevitable. Social exchange theorists suggest that all relationships involve give and take, though it may not always conform to expectations, that is the deal does not satisfy the parties, leaving scope for a bitter contest and consequently generating tension and stress. Psychologists consider feelings or the emotions as the more important part of a relationship, along with the psychological needs they cater to such as love, recognition, security, and so on. Sociologists however, argue that relationships lay down the foundation of social structure and social control and that socialization process is designed to play a significant role in influencing relationships. Human relationships are, therefore, a reflection of mutual dependence of persons on each other and the need for structuring this dependence to create an orderly society. If we take a close look, some simple facts about human relationships become obvious. At any given point of time a person is involved in several relationships including with self (see Figure 1).

Figure 1

Human Relations

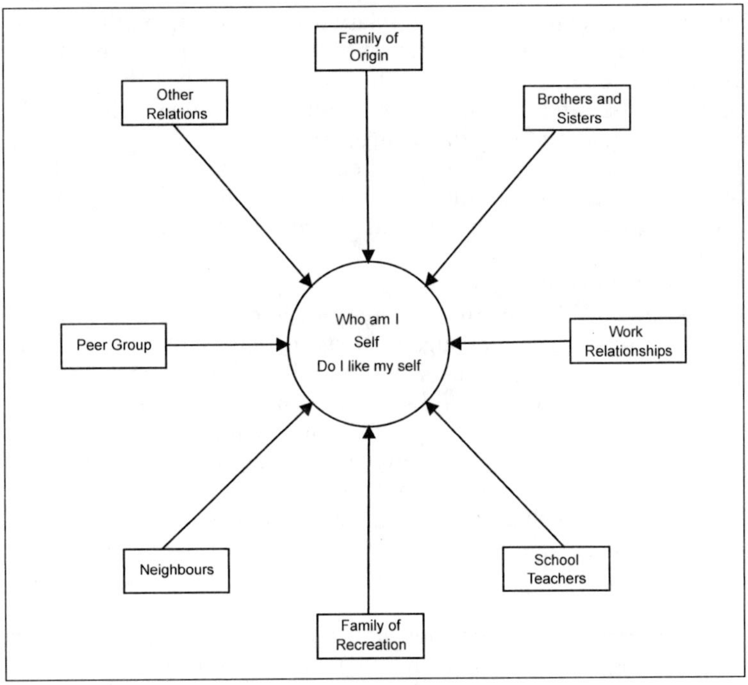

For example, some of these relationships are:

1. *Relationship with Self.*
2. *Family of Origin Relationships:* father, mother, brothers, sisters, uncles, aunts, etc.
3. *Family of Recreation:* relationship with partner, relationship with in-laws, relationship with children, etc.
4. *Relationships at School:* relationship with other children (Peer Group), relationship with teachers and other authorities, etc.
5. *Relationships at Work:* relationship with superiors, relationship with colleagues, relationship with junior colleagues, etc.

6. *Relationships in the Community:* neighbours, service providers, shopkeepers.
7. *Society:* relationship with other religions, castes, economic classes. (see Kelly, 1983).

These relationships have relative values for individuals. For example, a study of the importance of the above relationships would indicate, the value of these as relative rather than absolute. The socialization process and life experiences of people significantly influence, the perception about relationships. Therefore, the significance or importance of a relationship is dynamic in nature. This is expected to change with time. The change will affect the give and take process and feeling or emotions associated with it. In childhood, parents, in adolescence, friends and in adults, spouse and work relationships assume greater significance for people in general. Similarly the influence of these relationships on individual behaviour will also vary in accordance with its significance.

Laws of Relationships

1. A law of relationship is that an entry or exit in a network of relationships will change the existing nature of relationships. For example marriage, birth of a child, and death of a member, inevitably change the relationships in a family. A new entry in a group will change the group relations and so on.
2. Another law is, a person may or may not be conscious of the changes happening in the relationship/s. People who suddenly discover the change, are likely to be more emotionally affected by these changes, than those who are more aware of and anticipate the change. A good example is, parents who anticipate change in the relationship with children, once they grow up and particularly after they start a family of their own through marriage in India, and by entering a relationship with other sex, as it is called in the West. In India, there are families living under the same roof and having a common kitchen but even in these cases relationship with parent and children change, when parents grow old and become economically inactive or after the marriage of children.
3. All relationships involve mutual expectations (see Foa and Foa, 1974; Gergen and Gergen, 1981), or give and take (see Hatfield and Rapson, 2007). More the expectations and dependence, higher is the significance of relationship and its influence on a person's behaviour. For example, if person A expects person B to provide for all the needs, relationship with person B becomes the most important for person A, particularly if person

B is perceived as actually providing for all needs by person A. Expectations are socially constructed. For example, appropriate behaviour for a son towards parents, or the expected behaviour of a wife and so on is culturally determined. It may become part of the psyche in most cases, however, there are notable exceptions as well and a person may or may not fully incorporate these in actual behaviour, yet everyone is aware of the social norm. Despite the process of socialization, the process seldom accomplishes its goal fully. The process of psyche construction is a complex phenomenon, not given to social theorizing yet, as individuals in the same family may exhibit a wide variety of behaviours and yet values of different generations continue to reflect a continuing trend. The nature of relationship is significantly related to perception of individuals involved in a relationship. In other words, how different actors view and interpret each other. A significant factor is the gap between actual reality and how it is perceived. The theory of interpersonal cognition (see Baccus and Baldwin, 2007), refers to the thinking process which takes shape as people interact with each other. The key element is seen as the perception, interpretation and uses made of information or knowledge about others both concurrently and on a more continuous basis.

4. A relationship can be either positive or negative and it can be observed and recorded. Both primary and secondary data can be used for assessment of relationships. The self report and others opinions are sources for collecting the data about relationships. Definite indicators are there to assess the nature of relationships, such as the amount of time spent, nature of interactions, intensity of emotions, and nature of expectations and so on. The relationships of members within a group can be judged by level of harmony, its productivity or success level, and turnover rate, etc.
5. Relationships are interlinked and continue to influence each other throughout the life of an individual. For example, relationship with self will influence all other relationships, similarly relationship with parents, spouse, friends, work relationships, all influence each other. As we indicated earlier the significance of relationship is dynamic in nature. There may be one or several relationships, more significant than others in the life of an individual, at a given point of time, and exert greater impact on the individual relationships with others. It/these can be termed as the key relationship/s. It is

essential that there is no conflict between these intimate or more significant relationships for the individual to function effectively. Yet, a conflict between intimate relationships such as between mother and spouse, or even between father and son and/or spouse is possible, creating difficulties for an individuals' effective social functioning.

6. Conflicts are normal in human relationships. Two distinct forms of conflict may be identified: intrapersonal conflict and interpersonal conflict. Intrapersonal conflict denotes internal strife, signifying unresolved social, cognitive, or emotional issues. These may be a reflection of the process of maturation or development, generally very pronounced during teenage when a lot of significant changes are occurring, or it could also reflect a process of greater intellectual debate or an attempt to seek new answers to all questions. Interpersonal conflict signifies disagreement between individuals or groups which has the potential to disrupt relationships. The gap between the expected and actual behaviour of the other, constitute a serious disagreement also termed as betrayal (see Finkel, 2007). Like any human interaction when two or more persons are involved, the divergence of opinions or interests is a normal phenomenon. The differences can evoke a wide range of emotions among different persons, leading to short-term or long-term conflict. In a recent case, a conflict developed between two brothers of a well-known business family with enormous resources. Obviously, both the brothers must have had a great childhood, received best possible education, must have played together, shared so many moments together, both good and bad, loved and respected their parents particularly the father, who was a great businessman – in short, all the requirements of a harmonious relationship were there, yet a conflict developed. In sociology, it is known as sibling rivalry and the subject has been sufficiently researched but with no definite conclusions. It is difficult to explain why it develops, how long it will last and how it will affect the future relations between the members of a family. As Laursen (2006) indicated, chronic discord interferes with opportunities for social skills training in close relationships in early childhood. Children who adopt coercive conflict management strategies early in life, miss out on the crucial experience of negotiating resolutions and as a consequence, fail to learn the skill of empathy and role-taking. The theories explaining the etiology of chronic interpersonal discords highlight a number of factors such as

communication difficulties, self doubt and insecurity resulting in inability to trust others, value differences, either emanating from cultural or intellectual upbringing and so on.

It is difficult to view human relationships objectively. Perception of relationships is a subjective phenomenon. In other words, people are generally unable to perceive others objectively. For example, a person may term a spouse very caring and exciting but may actually find the same person as inconsiderate and boring. All relationships invoke emotions, such as love, respect, fear, anger, jealousy, hatred and so on and these exhibit a great deal of variation. A very significant indicator of a relationship is the intensity of emotions it generates and its consistency and sustainability.

A social psychological approach to close relationships focuses on the interaction between two individuals, paying close attention to both behaviour and what goes in people's minds (emotions and cognitions). Within social psychology, up to the late 1970s, research into relationships concentrated on interpersonal attraction; namely, what factors lead people to be attracted to one another at the initial stages of relationship development? This research tended to be theoretical and the results were drawn rather casually identifying variables that influence attraction, such as similarity, proximity, physical attractiveness, and so forth. In the 1980s the explanation shifted toward the study of the much greater complexity inherent in the development, maintenance, and dissolution phases of relationships. This shift was prompted by several key developments in the 1970s, such as Gottman (1994) and others began research to observe and carefully measure the interchanges of married couples in an attempt to predict who would divorce. Second, Zick Rubin (1970) and others became interested in love and devised reliable scales that could measure the concept. Third, Harold Kelley led a team of social psychologists in producing a seminal book published in 1983, *Close Relationships*, which provided a comprehensive explanation of close relationships from an interactional, social-psychological perspective.

Importance of Relationships

Research indicates that intimate relationships play a critical role in promoting health and well-being in adulthood, and that relationship disruption in adulthood is associated with a wide range of adverse health outcomes (see Uchino, Cacioppo, and Kiecolt-Glaser 1996). In her study of importance of relationships in children's emotional development Salisch (2001) described the importance of relationships to parents, peers, and friends particularly in how the children developed their skills of handling emotions. She argued that parents are important for their children's emotional development not only because they are attachment figures but also because of their cognitive and emotional expertise, which they use to instruct their offspring on the use of emotion labels, appraisals, expressions, and regulation strategies. In addition, it is well known that parents are an important source to introduce their children to cultural norms on emotions. For example, in many cultures display of any emotion, particularly grief, is considered undesirable for males in particular. Converging evidence suggests that display rules among peers promote the dampening of many emotions in many situations, especially those of vulnerability and anger. School-age children's increasing use of distancing strategies may help them achieve this "cool" public self-presentation. Intimate friendships which permit (and may even require) the disclosure of private emotional experiences, challenge pre-adolescents to learn how to be supportive, to a friend in need and how to manage anger and contempt in these close relationships.

In the past, most research studies have conceptualized these and other advances in emotional development, as rather solitary or intra-psychic processes. Few studies have taken a transactional or interpersonal perspective on emotional development, although all human beings are born as social beings who cannot survive or develop normally without significant relationships (Stern, 1986). Disregarding the social context is particularly limiting for the study of emotional development, because emotions are frequently generated in the context of social relationships (see Scherer, Wallbott and Summer 1986) and are often managed with the help of other people (Cassidy, 1994; Denton and Zarbatany, 1996). In addition, basic parameters, such as the frequency, duration, and intensity of emotional expressions, are shaped in the face-to-face interactions between children and their significant others (Malatesta and Haviland, 1982; Stern, 1986). The consequences of what could happen to members of family if the relationship is not warm and positive is brought out in a vivid manner needing no further explanations, by some of the occurrences in families. These incidences also bring out the structured ways of controlling the relationships in families. A conference of social scientists was held a few years ago to discuss how we might apply the knowledge of all social sciences to the problem of human survival. Anthropologists, present in the conference, however, felt that the topic of survival was outside their field. They perhaps did not realize the importance of tribal societies and that tribal cultures needed so little to survive and survived simply on the strengths of their human relationships. The modern life seems to be striving to destroy all human relationships under the pretext of making the individual free. Relationships are as important for the survival of individual human beings as they are for the survival of small groups, communities and for a society as a whole. The well-being of individuals and social organizations depends on the smooth functioning of all human relations. The relationships can be categorized on the basis of how important they are for individuals. It is obvious that survival of a human child depends to a great extent on the relationship with parents, at least in the early childhood, though even later in life, the support provided by family members is considered vital for the growth of the individual. The family relationships, therefore, are considered as significant in contributing to overall happiness of an individual. All individuals experience different kinds of emotions in their interactions with significant others around them. These experiences help them to develop what Bowlby (1969/1982) described as attachment styles. The individuals either learn to trust others and feel secure or they may become very scared of others. Based on these experiences they develop a concept of who they are and how far they can trust and depend on others. The psychologists consider the relationship with self, as an important indicator of relationship with others. In other words, the self-concept and self-esteem of an individual and his/her relationships have a significant correlation. The relationship with self therefore, is also considered significant although it does not fall within the definition of relationship which calls for two or more people for a relationship to take effect. We have, however, included it in our discussion to highlight its importance in human relationships. The mental health of an individual to a great extent depends on the smooth functioning of one's relationships. The mental stress has a significant relationship with a person's decision-making capacity. A wrong decision can disrupt a person's life for good.

Similarly the smooth functioning of a group of people, in any setting, depends to a great extent on the relationship between the individuals on the one hand and the relationship of members of the team with the leader of the group on the other. Similarly their relationship with other groups also impacts upon their success and happiness in general. The example when expanded further can explain many of the conflicts or problems in a community or society at large. Therefore, human relationships in any form contribute

Human Relations and Mental Health

1. A couple having three children, one female two males, was married for more than a decade. They often argued about things at home, in particular about children's behaviour. The wife wanted their eldest child, the daughter, to continue in school. The husband disagreed as he often did, as they had very different ideas about almost everything in life. They had very poor understanding of each other, consequently resulting in very strained relationship. One day the things went from bad to worse as the couple argued. The husband stabbed the children and the wife, was later arrested and sent to jail.
2. A very prominent political figure was killed by his brother, in his own house, as the family relations deteriorated.
3. A very successful business executive became alcoholic as he was unhappy with his spousal relationship but was unable to leave his wife as he had two grown up children.
4. My mother was a nurse. She thought nursing was too hard and wanted me to go into a different profession. But once I decided to become a nurse, she supported me. She was a quiet person and always believed that all responsible persons made their choices and were prepared to accept the consequences. I think she made me appreciate my privacy and the importance of friends. My dad died when I was eleven months old, so my grandparents looked after me. My grandfather was my biggest supporter and friend. My family taught me how to love and the importance of love and to respect others.

significantly to the overall functioning of various groups, organizations and systems in society. The central thesis of this book is that human relationships anywhere are a reflection of how self-oriented or others-oriented humans are, and the more self-oriented people are, the higher are the chances of their experiencing problems in their relationships and social functioning as such.

Case Studies

Case I

A woman loved her first born son and was very happy. She was an educated person and despite encouragement from everyone in the family including her husband, she never accepted a job as she wanted to devote herself to her child. The financial burden coupled with other problems, led to a deterioration of marital relationship. As the child grew up, he developed a poor relationship with the father. The child failed his school leaving examination, and started smoking at an early age. The mother became a diabetic and developed several other health problems. The husband developed a variety of phobias indicative of an increasing anxiety level.

It is a typical example of poor relations between husband and wife leading to; (a) behavioural problems among children, (b) poor parent-child relationship, emergence of health problems both among parents and children.

Case 2

I met Lata when she joined the department as a student. She was an ordinary looking girl, wearing a simple dress, which was a little different from the dresses of the girls brought up in urban educated middle class families. She would be quiet most of the time and even after six months in the class, had no friends. She never took part in any extracurricular activities, never participated in any discussions in the class. One of the female colleagues in the department noticed her behaviour and invited her to meet her after the class. She soon discovered that Lata came from a rural lower-middle class background, and was not well versed with English. Her language, dress and mannerism, always evoked rather poor responses from her fellow students, who came from elite families from urban areas and were fluent in English. Obviously Lata felt inadequate in comparison to her classmates, simply because she was different in some respect from others and thus concluded that others were superior to her. The comments and responses of others confirmed her conclusion. The realization of difference is however not the cause of her problem, it is the rating by others which results in her perceiving herself as inadequate and thus inferior, resulting in her response of escape.

This is a typical example of how one may develop a poor self-image and consequently, face problems in relationships. A poor self-image, meaning a low assessment of physical self, mental abilities or social skills is a sure symptom of a negative relationship with self. The usual feelings that go with this are, 'I am worth less' (emotional self) and 'I cannot do anything well' (low self-confidence) that 'others around me are superior and powerful' and 'I feel inadequate to relate with them'. Life generally is going to be rather difficult and miserable (social self-perception). The situation is known as intra personal tension or conflict. However, the situation can both be real and imaginary. In the case of Lata, the self doubt comes partly from her comparison of self with others and partly from her own poor self-assessment. In both cases, part of the reality may be factual such as her lack of knowledge of English or in general being weak in studies, but part of it is not based on facts. It is possible that some persons around her may look down upon her but yet all persons may not possess the same attitude towards her, and may even help her if she approaches them in a positive manner. At the same time Lata may have enough intelligence and she may be hard working and can do well, if she has more self-confidence. This negative relationship with self will influence all other relationships, creating a chain of reactions, harmful to the person's mental and physical health. A person in a situation of self doubt is generally miserable and may blame others, particularly the significant others, in the family, school or work place, as an explanation of personal failure or misery. A child or an adolescent doing badly in school and blaming both her parents and teachers for the situation is a good example. An employee fired from the job or demoted for being inefficient blaming colleagues or supervisor, for the situation is a similar example. Persons with negative relationship with self continually experience failure and unhappiness and pollute the social environment they belong to. Similarly, a person with negative self relations will be confused about role allocation and social status and is likely to face problems in social functioning. On the contrary, a person with a positive self-image would be more confident, understanding and warm towards others. He would be more objective in viewing the situations and people around and arrive at a more logical explanation of both. A child with a positive self-concept will view failure, as inadequate self-efforts rather than blaming others. Such behaviour is likely to receive more positive support and cooperation, in overcoming difficulties and in general any goal achievement. The general outcome is positive relations with others, no anxiety, and a sound mental health. Poor self-perception often generates, inferiority complex or a sense of insecurity, which is generally considered a major source of anxiety and a major factor of distortion of social perception. A distorted self-perception can lead to restricted ability to appreciate a situation from different perspectives or to act with social responsibility. In adolescents, such distortions can result in, instances of deviance from social norms. Early childhood difficulties usually continue to affect the entire personality growth and functioning of a person.

Intervention Strategies

Social work profession has emerged over the years as one of the professions, helping its members master the art of facilitating human relations in different settings. Social work strategies for reducing conflict and mitigating its adverse consequences have targeted individuals, groups and communities. Intervention approaches aimed at an individual have met with some success. Some are designed to reduce stress, whereas others aim to improve conflict management skills. Interventions, devoted to anger and anxiety management, have demonstrated promising results but more studies are needed to streamline these approaches. Studies of reduction of interpersonal conflict, categorizes the strategies that identify characteristics which may predispose people to anger or violent disagreement and those that limit impulsivity and aggression (Laursen, 2006). Social work with children's groups to develop social competence and problem solving skills have generally helped them but since little documented evidence is available it is difficult to suggest anything about how long these changes survive. Social problem-solving experiences being provided to children in some schools through socially useful projects also help children in the management of interpersonal difficulties as well. Social skills training programmes, if implemented in schools, can also help children in reducing behavioural problems. The divorce rate is not alarming in India but the rate seems to be on the increase (Singh, 2004), a testament to the fact that family conflict resolutions remain elusive or families are not seeking professional help. Peer conflict has also received considerable attention. There is evidence that the peer mediation programmes adopted by many schools to address rising levels of violence are successful in teaching children constructive strategies for conflict resolution and in training peacemakers to intervene in disputes. Experimental studies revealed that animosity could be manipulated through competitive and cooperative activities (Laursen, 2006).

Working with individuals can lead to better self-concept, an improvement in confidence level and a change of attitude to become more objective and positive in viewing others. Social group work with children, women and youth can develop skills such as communication, leadership, tolerance and adaptability to different situations which can help in avoiding and also managing conflicts. Greater face-to-face interaction and exchange of information with a facilitating worker has improved conflict resolution and facilitating community relationships.

Finally, though possibilities exist to deal with macro-realities at the societal level, to modify these in actual practice is a complex task. It is easier to deal with face-to-face relationships in a family, group or community. Secondary relationships, as Cooley (1902) termed these, are rather based on hearsay and are not generally based on facts. The number of people involved is very large and communication usually gets distorted and is not effective in bringing about an effective outcome. Mass communication is seldom able to bring about a uniform pattern of change in values or perceptions about others. The interventions at macro level, to bring about change in relationship between religious communities or caste groups, have generally not been very effective. We shall, therefore, deal with facilitating relationships at different levels in subsequent chapters to provide professionals a better understanding and how to deal with these more effectively.

2

Social Work and Human Relations

Problem of Definition

It seems rather ironical that after almost a whole century later, when social work emerged as a helping activity, if not as a profession, there is an uneasy feeling, about its nature and scope. Be it a student who is struggling to master the subject, to assume his/her rightful status in society or those who are trying to help these future practitioners, the simple question, what is social work creates a mirage. I was teaching a class of freshmen, (using American terminology, simply to denote, students who have no knowledge of what it means), about the concept and scope of social work, when I referred to the famous text by Morales and Sheafor (1995), *Social Work: A Profession with Many Faces*. I was quite confused to read and I quote, 'It is difficult to define what social work is.' Then it dawned on me when I started browsing through various definitions of social work, given by different authors, that the variety of explanations you come across is really baffling. In the early 20th century, the main role assigned to social workers was providing assistance to the needy (see Cheyne, 1926; Witmer, 1942), which forever tilted the natural thrust of social work to deal with poverty, and deprivation of all kind. Later the definitions started calling it a professional service to satisfy 'individual needs along with removing barriers' (Clarke, 1947; Friedlander, 1955), based on scientific knowledge. The concept of providing help in social functioning came later. The review of the literature during the period and the current makes it inevitable to concur with what Morales and Sheafor said. However, even before Sheafor has reached that conclusion, Khinduka has faced the same difficulty and in 1965, has observed in his edited volume *Social Work in India*, that the principal difficulty in defining social work is that of finding a suitable differentia, one that is brief, inclusive and conceptually flawless. Simply calling it a helping profession or activity does not serve the purpose, as almost all professions, help people to solve their problems, such as nurses, doctors, lawyers and so on. Further, helping in the Indian subcontinent in particular and elsewhere too is seen as a social and religious obligation, and hence poses difficulty in its acceptance as a professional domain, as almost all politicians and many others, take pride in claiming themselves as social workers. Any professional expected to help the needy without specifying a need area, given the task of poverty alleviation, or removing barriers in the path of success of the individuals, is asking for trouble, a sentiment Gore expressed along with many others in 1980s (see Nair, 1981). The definition has to be inclusive yet brief, which conceptually define each activity or role carried out by social workers. To be precise, what is the thread that binds you from helping an individual to bringing about social change. Further, professional expertise consisting of a body of knowledge, both about the problem area and possible solutions, discovered through a scientific process, is a necessary requirement as well.

It shows that an academic and descriptive approach was used to define social work rather than professional. A variety of social work academics individually, and collectively as professional bodies of social workers, struggled to define the nature and scope of 'professional' social work, the most recent being an attempt by International Federation and Social Workers (IFSW) and International Association and Schools of Social Work (IASSW) (2013). The difficulty is the variety of tasks being currently pursued by social workers and a lack of consensus about the core expertise needed to accomplish these tasks. I dealt with the subject way back (Siddiqui, 1987) when I was trying to work out a course curriculum for social work students. The dilemma I faced was, do I design it for students dealing with problems of adjustment/service delivery/need fulfilment/welfare (chose the term you like) or bringing about social change. I had then argued that a social worker would need a different theoretical knowledge base for accomplishing these tasks. Further, the time available for doing that and the academic background of students, coupled with faculty expertise, made it very difficult. It is not mandatory for students to have studied social work or even social sciences at the bachelor level to pursue a course in social work. However, I must admit that I had no clarity about the basic expertise then. Social work was all about, values and philosophy, methods and fields, where you can practice those methods theoretically. The body of knowledge and skills, that a social worker needs, and which is common to all social workers, no matter what they are doing, to qualify for professional practice, remains unidentified even now.

Just to pick up the debate in UK in 2009, Sheldon and Macdonald wrote;

> Social work's disciplinary territory is the poor, troubled, abused or discriminated against, neglected, frail and elderly, mentally ill, learning disabled, addicted, delinquent, or otherwise socially marginalized … . This is a dauntingly broad remit … . The sheer range of social and personal problems for which we acquired some responsibility has lead to the development of a discipline which has always been forced to borrow … from adjacent fields.

The problem is they are only worried about borrowing from adjacent fields, which I think is referring to psychology, sociology and psychiatry and may be other social science disciplines, but they are not worried about the vast range of tasks or how well these disciplines provide the practice wisdom. As Specht (1986) noted, a profession with a weak knowledge base is vulnerable to 'de-professionalization', and the practitioners will be vulnerable to identify with anything more popular such as change agent or development workers or consultant.

It is quite tempting to quote a few definitions to stress the point, but instead let us refer to the main themes running through these, to describe the confusion prevailing in defining social work. Let us begin by referring to the definition adopted by IFSW and IASSW in 2002. It refers to social work as providing help to sort out problems of human relations, bring about social change, ensure human rights and social rights, etc. Of course, the scientific knowledge, professional nature of interventions, and emphasizing the skills needed, are routine as well.

It is a common theme running through many definitions. The definition given by National Association of Social Workers, U.S. (NASW) is referring to what social workers do, which is basically providing services to their clients. It goes on to elaborate these by noting that they (social workers) help people increase their capacities for problem solving and coping, obtain needed resources, facilitate interaction between people and their environment, make organizations responsible to people and influence social policies, etc. The definition describes the tasks as is obvious, but not how these are linked by a central conceptual framework, thus making it part of social work. The problem these definitions create in the mind of a practitioner or a student is what exactly their job is as a professional? Further, if they are not able to provide a solution to the problem, but help the person to reach the professional person, since left on their own they will not be able to access that, will it dilute their professional status? Are they supposed to be proficient in all the tasks or only in some, which they prefer? Is there a shared understanding or theory of carrying out all the tasks, if all these are social work tasks and require an expertise?

For example, what is common between an expertise to increase individual capacities for problem solving and coping on the one hand and to influence the structural change in a society on the other. In other words what is the common thread running across these tasks. Let us take the example of law as a profession. The common expertise with lawyers which make them a professional is their knowledge of law. So where ever they work, the main expertise is law whether in civil matters or criminal or corporate matters or whether they help an individual, a group or an organization. Further, the task of reform of existing laws or enactment of new laws, to reform the justice system in the country, is a collective responsibility, as part of ethical and social considerations rather than considered as a professional task. Although it can be argued that the two has some linkages.

Mary Richmond, one of the founders of social work profession, in 1917 has raised similar issues.

With other practitioners – with physicians and lawyers, for example – there was always a basis of knowledge held in common. If a neurologist had occasion to confer with a surgeon, each could assume in the other a mastery of the elements of a whole group of basic sciences and of the formulated and transmitted experience of his own guild besides. But what common knowledge could social workers assume in like case? (Richmond, 1917: 5)

Sheldon and Macdonald (2009) are not questioning the ability to acquire the range of expertise, may be because they thought different social workers will acquire different expertise through different courses, but that is not the trend reflected by a review of social work education, which remained confined to BSW and MSW courses with marginal variation in the content. Specific courses such as Family Therapy, Child Welfare, Woman Welfare, Drug Addiction or Development Practice, etc. for at least one year duration dealing with these issues in depth are not very easily found, in schools of social work. Further, Mary Richmond's query, what is common knowledge among all these workers is still not answered with any degree of clarity.

The most recent attempt to arrive at a definition is the draft of a global definition put on the website of International Federation of Social Workers (IFSW) recently, which is to be finalized by July 2013, and they expect you to participate in deciding the future of social work. I produce the definition below for us to take our own stand:

Global Definition of Social Work

> Social work facilitates social development and social cohesion. Core to social work is supporting people to influence their social environments to achieve sustainable well-being. The profession is underpinned by theories of social work, social sciences, and indigenous knowledge. Principles of human rights, collective responsibility and social justice are fundamental to practice. (IFSW, 2013)

The definition uses the word core at least to centralize all social work efforts towards supporting persons to influence their social environments. The argument in this paper is, it is identifying an objective, which is vague and not defined or discussed by any discipline or theory, hence the expertise remains vague, thus it makes the professional knowledge-base weak. It thus makes it difficult, for the society to accept social workers as a professional.

The clarity of professional task a social worker is expected to perform based on his knowledge and skills; at all levels is the first requisite for defining social work. Friedlander (1955), Khinduka (1965) and many others used two clear terms; social adjustment and/or social functioning and human relationships. Let us describe in detail these terms and how these explain human problems or issues, with which social work, as a profession, has to deal with.

Boehm (1958) first proposed social functioning as a central focus of social work practice. Bartlett (1970) defined it as normative behaviour in social situations, and added that it has an overarching concern in all social work fields and methods including service delivery roles. Blackely and Dziadosz (2009) in a recent article have endorsed this view by giving example from a mental health setting. The term, however, is not found in the dictionary of sociology edited by Abercrombie, Nicholas, Stephen Hill and Bryan S. Turner (1994). According to functionalists, it refers to the roles society evolves to guide members of a society. G.H. Mead (1934) was the first to use the concept in a very creative way to suggest how children learn about society and develop their own social being (the self) by role-taking that is imaginatively taking the role of others such as fathers, mothers, etc. The purpose of doing so is to help the members understand the manner in which they will interact with each other, to fulfill their multifarious needs in society. An online medical dictionary refers to the term as ability of the individual to interact in the normal or usual way in society.

Skidmore, Thackeray and Farley, (1988) noted that social functioning includes the activities that are essential to satisfying relationships in the variety of social experiences, of daily living. They draw a triangle to describe the social functioning (see Figure 1).

Figure 1

Social Functioning

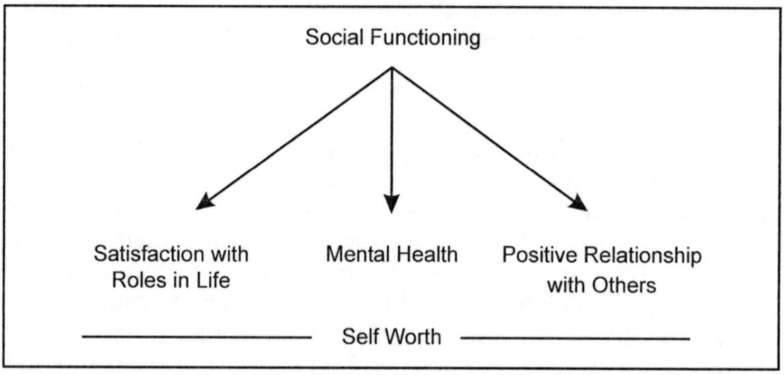

The base of the triangle is self worth, the right side of the triangle is positive relationship with others, and the left side of the triangle reads satisfaction with roles in life, and the end outcome is noted in the centre as mental health. They then go on to emphasise enhancement of social functioning as the key area of social work, which differentiates it from other professions. Sociology simply provides a description of social roles and social change, but no practice wisdom to fill the generation gap, or explain the gap within a generation.

Human responses to social roles constitute the other end of the problem of social functioning, and hence we cross the disciplinary boundary to enter the domain of psychology. The problem is immensely complex, as social science discovered, that each individual is a unique entity, hence it is difficult both to generalize and/or theorize, human needs and perception and response to the environment.

The beginnings of social work in the United States, usually dealing with poverty and deviance in Columbia University in New York, saw the problem originating in the development of human beings. The Columbia School as it came to be known, thus invented the first method of social work, now known as working with individuals, but then termed as case work by Mary Richmond. She searched for the causes of poverty and social exclusion in the interaction between an individual and his/her environment, but she argued that care has to be taken to focus on the person within his/her situation, which she termed as social diagnosis. Yet soon after, the Chicago University in Chicago, again dealing with poverty and deprivation, came up with a different notion of human maladjustment, focussing on the environment of the individual, thus giving rise to settlement house movement and retaining children in school and training of youth to help them find work and better values. In a way the focus is again on interaction between individuals and their environment, the service is helping them to get better results, which are expected to provide individual need fulfilment and better social functioning.

The expertise needed for a professional in dealing with these problems, is knowledge of social sciences, primarily sociology and psychology, to understand individual and his/her environment. The environment refers to the persons with whom an individual is interacting in a face-to-face situation, such as family, school, at work, etc.

The environment referred to by early scholars, can be constructed to be in fact generally referring to human relations. The elements of individual social functioning can be seen as in Figure 2.

Figure 2

Individual and Social Functioning

Self Concept	→	Relationship with Self and Others
Self Confidence	→	Need Fulfilment
Relationship with Self and Others	→	Parents, Peer Group, Siblings, Teachers, Spouse, Boss, Colleagues, Subordinates, Children
Group Relation	→	Family
Community Relations	→	Neighbourhood
Social Relations within a Nation	→	Religious Groups, Caste Groups Linguistic Groups, Gender
International Relations	→	Between Nations

Now it is obvious that the ambit of human relations cover a wide range, beginning from the relationship a person has with self, to human relations within a nation or even between nations. The purpose of doing this exercise is to highlight the scope of practice on one hand and the need for developing relevant theoretical material, to guide the practice. Given the recent developments in social sciences, we can find enough literature dealing with human relations at all these levels. Scholars have developed a number of perspectives to explain, self-concept, group relations in general including family, peer groups, gangs, communities and so on, to provide some understanding of human relations, but to what extent such knowledge can guide practice of social work, has been a subject of debate in social sciences since long (see Pathak, 1989; Gellner, 1986; Davies, 1981).

Figure 3

Social Work and Human Relations

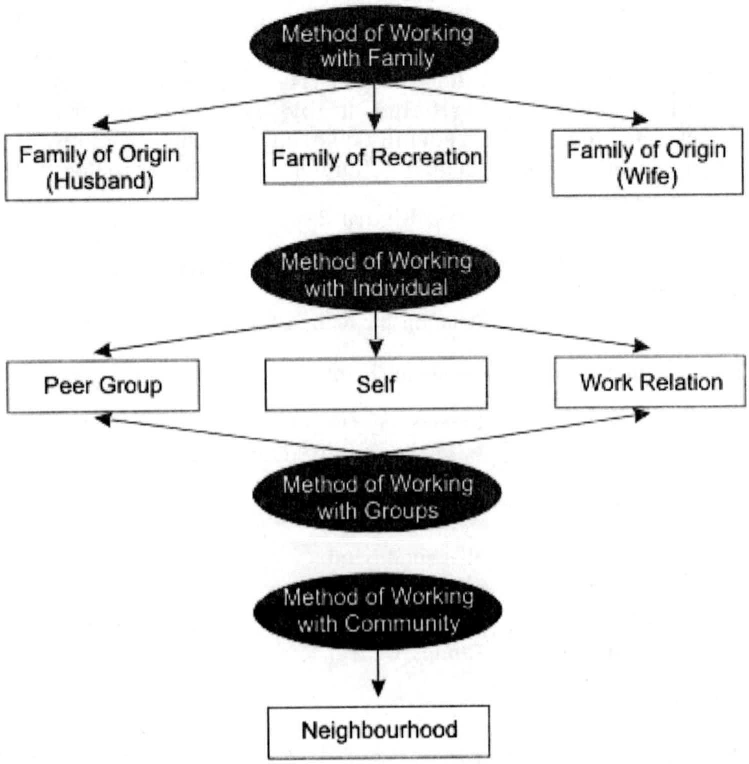

Applicability has never fascinated sociologists the way it has economists. Van Nieuwenhuis (1982) noted, and went on to explain that sociologists hardly ever bother to develop a theory into a planning model, hence the link between sociological theory and community development or between sociology and social work remains weak (Pathak, 1989). Pathak quoted Martin Davies to emphasize that the contribution of sociology to social work has been primarily a negative one ... . He even went on to add that various change or control strategies are normally of only limited value and may be counter productive ... (Ibid., p. 5). And finally sociology may yet succeed in proving that social work is irrelevant and misguided in its assumed role (Ibid.).

What Timms (1970: 2) noted is equally significant,

> social workers do not usually enjoy a reputation for sustained critical thought about what they do. They are seen characteristically in feminine terms, high-souled, low-heeled women, somewhat anxious to intervene in the lives of others.

We must also take into account the cultural differences that shape human relations, in different countries and in different places and time periods to make it impossible for sociologists or social scientists to come up with knowledge which can really guide practice. Further, to attain a greater consistency in outputs of an intervention it is necessary to focus on specific relationships rather than covering all.

In US, the tendency has been to focus on intimate personal relations of an individual, which are more given to theorizing and also where the professional is dealing with a more concrete reality. We will however suggest covering group and community relations as well, since in developing countries these are equally relevant, as these cultures are collectivist in their orientation. Some authors have suggested different approaches in handling human relations based on the cultural influence (see, McGoldrik and Hardy, 2008).

Social work hence, can be defined as a profession providing help to person/s in dealing with the problems arising out of their 'Social Functioning', or 'Interaction with their Social Environment.' I see the core expertise needed by social workers to help people in their social functioning as their expertise and skills in human relationships. Social work, therefore, can be defined as a profession to facilitate human relations to promote social development of an individual on the one hand and of a society on the other. I am using the term social development, both as defined by psychologists and as defined by sociologists. The psychologists are referring to the capacity of individual to handle all relations around him or her, while the sociologists are using a macro-perspective of relations in the society, though there is no unanimity. The social workers will have to choose the level they will specialize in practice. It should be noted that a social worker will find it difficult if not impossible to deal with issues of human relations effectively at all levels. The expertise of social workers thus can be used by individuals, groups including families, communities and organizations to deal with their problems arising out of human relations. Social workers can and do take up the role of bringing about changes in societies to ensure better human rights compliance scenario, including social rights as a socially conscious member of society.

The theoretical framework social workers can use to analyse all the professional tasks is given below (Figure 4):

Figure 4

Diagnosis

	Problem	*Source/Cause/s*
1.	Behaviour Problems in Children	Relationship with self and relationships in family
2.	Learning Problems in Children	Relationship with self and relationships in school/family
3.	Alcoholism	Relationship with self and relationships with friends/family/work
4.	Unemployment/Poverty	Relationship with self/others
5.	Domestic Violence	Relationship with self/partner/spouse/children
6.	Group Problems	Relationships in a group
7.	Community Problems	Relationships in community
8.	Organizational Problems	Relationships in an organization
9.	Social Problems	Relationships in society

Social work practice therefore, has to be a relationship-based practice in the sense that relationships are the most important influence on both our socio-emotional development and psychosocial behaviour. Persons facing difficulties in social life or exhibiting unacceptable behaviour or feeling personally distressed are highly likely to approach social work agencies as failing parents or problem children, depressed people or antisocial adults (Howe, 1996). Interpersonal relationships involve processes of incredible complexity at a number of different levels (Hinde, 1995). This being the case, any practice in this field is bound to be both complex and intellectually demanding, and can hardly be left to the rigidities of documents, devices and drilled people (Law, 1986).

So, to summarize so far, as the self and many of its major attributes including personality, esteem, efficacy, beliefs, affective states and behaviour from within relationships, any service that attempts to deal with people's behaviours and feelings as they arise in social environments – the person-in-interaction-with-their-situation as Hollis (1964) called it – would be at best foolish and at worst seriously negligent, if it did not build-in a deep understanding of the part that relationship-based thinking and practice must play in major aspects of our professional lives (Howe, 1996).

The social work profession thus can claim human relationships as their main area of knowledge and skills. A social worker thus would know very specifically what the role s/he is expected to carry out and what is the professional nature of her/his obligation. We already know that we use our relationship with our client/s as our core skill to interact with them, to gain their trust and acceptance of our professional expertise and also boundaries.

Dealing with relationships at the macro level is a very complex task, beyond the scope of an individual or even a whole organization, but it is possible to include it as a practice area, so long as we are clear about the theoretical expertise needed. We are including it as a practice area to take care of the often cited argument that social justice can only be ensured by raising social awareness and promoting social action. Since a number of social work definitions feel uncomfortable, in diluting the social justice and human rights concerns, and perhaps rightly so, we should retain these as our core values. However, studying development and human relationships, for example, tribal-rural-urban continuum, should be an important agenda for our practitioners at the community level. They are coming face-to-face with the grass roots realities in their community practice, the often are faced with questions they are not able to find convincing answers. In such situations if they are aware of a professional obligation to share, these questions and grass roots data with other practitioners, and other stake holders such as state, media, other professionals and organizations dealing with similar issues, they would have done justice to their social commitment. In other words, economic development, social structure and the ideal society are the complex realities a micro practitioner is seldom able to handle even at a conceptual level, but still s/he would have initiated a process to find academic knowledge and practice political/social strategies for dealing with them.

Radical left wing movements emerged in sixties and reached their peak in seventies, and then became non-functional, since they were not able to demonstrate any specific successes. Post nineties the world has become much more closed to structural changes in the Marxian framework. A training programme for professional training of social workers, as part of an university structure will find it difficult to do justice with radical ideas, which are political in nature. I have earlier dealt with these (see Siddiqui, 1984, 2005). It also did not help the student to find any opportunity for professional practice as Sheldon and Macdonald (2009: 30) commented, and I quote;

> Salaried revolutionaries saw their own employers as the main targets of change and they naturally stopped employing them.

Understanding poverty in a society and its impact on human relationships, is a very valid area of social work research. Thus increasing livelihood opportunities, working conditions or conditions of work, through better human relationships, can be attempted, as has already been demonstrated in community practice. The advocacy practice, can handle most issues aiming to restructure social relations as suggested earlier, with the help of grass-roots practice data.

Some case studies are provided here to highlight, the direct practice issues, to help the clients, and the advocacy practice issues to be taken up for suggesting policy level inputs, for social development.

Case Studies

Preventing Dropout in a School

The school social worker, who was placed in a school, as part of the field work placement, was conducting a routine check of student's attendance, to identify cases irregular in attending classes. One of the assignments, the school headmaster had given to the social worker was, to identify potential dropout cases, and to prevent it. The social worker made a list of students, whose attendance was below 40 per cent, during the last three months. The social worker then sent out a request to school teachers, to provide him a list of students not doing well in their class tests.

It was not difficult to see that a lot of names were common in both the lists. He decided to meet some of the students, to find out the reasons for both, their absence and poor performance.

Diagnostic Issues: A simple framework is to ascertain the cause, and to collect facts to determine the root cause or causes, and their nature, home based or school based or both. Is the problem rooted in the development of children? even if that is the case, for example their IQ is low, or they have cognitive problems, the relationships come into play straight away. The family relationships or a care giver associated with the child and the quality of that relationship will have to be screened. Subsequently relationship with siblings, peer groups, teachers are to be explored to arrive at the diagnosis of the child's problem. The need of working with other professionals is obvious. Referral can be made to educational psychologists or speech social workers or any other relevant professional for assessment of the child's need or problem areas. The social workers can provide help and support to child, to develop a positive self-concept, to parents to provide due love and care to the child, to teachers and school administrators to deal with the child with a positive and understanding perspective, rather than looking at the child as problem, to ensure that child stays in school and achieve his/her personal goal.

The social worker can use any of the methods s/he considers appropriate, depending upon her own understanding of the case, and her load of work, but what will best meet the child's needs. In third world countries, a large number of children need help and support to stay in school. Therefore, the group is a better medium for helping both children and parents as also others including teachers. Supplementing group efforts with individual inputs, is a much better approach as suggested by Trecker (1948), a long time ago, and supported by others (see Corey and Corey, 2006).

However, there is a possibility that there are systemic problems, for example number of teachers are not adequate, they are not properly trained, the resources in the school are insufficient, the children come from very poor background and the parents want them to leave school early and start working, or they want the girls to get married at an early age. As far as dealing with the concerned parents is concerned, the worker can and will include it in her/his professional agenda, but to change the poverty situation or the social norms regarding early marriages, will require advocacy practice, which a school social worker can make a note of and refer it to other stake holders, fellow practitioners and relevant organizations as suggested earlier.

An Elderly Drug Addict

Ms. Olin currently lives illegally in an apartment in a public housing. She is not named on the lease, but sleeps on a couch in the living room of a 'friend,' a person she knew tangentially in the drug world, who is the official tenant. She pays him a modest rent, but can only stay in the apartment, when she is there, as she will not give her a key. As a result she spends a lot of time on the streets. When she is in the apartment, life is also difficult because, she is trying to recover from a serious drug addiction, and her friend is currently abusing drugs. She felt depressed about her living situation, because of the fact that she has neither a home, nor any financial resources of her own to support her.

Ms. Olin talked about an intergenerational family history of substance abuse. She is the sole survivor of three siblings. Her father passed away many years ago. Her mother is still living but 'won't talk to her.' Both parents, she implied, had also 'had problems,' with alcohol and substance abuse. Ms. Olin then talked about having had two children of her own. 'I had one daughter who died of an overdose of drugs four years ago, at the age of 21.' She then went on to say, that she herself began abusing drugs at the age of 21, and that this is when she began to have serious problems. In an emotionless voice, she talked about the fact, that her other adult daughter is doing very well, 'has a wonderful job' right in the city, but that they have not spoken to each other, since a very long time. Nevertheless, Ms. Olin said that the fact that her daughter has cut her out of her life, is something that she does not dwell on or think about very often, because she does not want to become emotionally upset.*

The role of social worker suggested, has both service delivery and change perspectives as the worker is expected to provide different kinds of services, bring about change in policies, and monitor the impact of economic and social policies on the elderly persons. The worker is expected to review organizational policies for elderly as well, such as their working condition, benefits and so on. The duality of his/her role is academically understandable, but unless the worker is specifically trained in the process of doing that within his/her limited resources and work load, it would dilute his/her efficiency on all counts. It is, therefore, suggested to focus on his/her main role dealing with clients and pass on the data to other concerned professionals dealing with policy issues.

Failed relationships causing loneliness and resulting in isolation from social and community supports.

The problem was seen as caused by the lack of economic support system for the elderly, in particular for drug addicts.

---

* Teaching Workbook for Social Policy Analysis, Advocacy and Practice, Fordham University, Graduate School of Social Service.

Persons from alcoholic families are predisposed – or at risk to develop alcoholism.

Social and ethnic factors interface with early family experiences surrounding alcohol use.

Social Work in Medical Setting

A person was brought to the clinic of a doctor forcibly. The relatives of the person accompanying him, requested the doctor to give him a sedative, as he was becoming violent and short tempered, and has already beaten up her wife. The doctor asked the person accompanying the patient to leave him in his chamber and wait outside. He then asked the person to calm down and narrate his problem. The person said at the outset that he is not sick, but he is feeling a bit frustrated with his family members, who are maltreating him. The doctor encouraged the person to go on to narrate the full facts.

The person narrated, that he was working outside the country, as an unskilled worker for the past several years. He has been sending money regularly to his family members, in particular his wife and his mother. Now he has lost his job and he came back home only recently. He thought the family would have saved some money, but he soon discovered that they have not done so. More over while he was working, his wife and mother were treating him nicely. Now that he has lost his job they are not caring for him.

At this point the doctor referred the person to the hospital's social worker.

Diagnostic Issues: Cause of depression was identified as loss of job, coupled with failure of relationship, lack of awareness about use of economic resources, low level of education, etc.

The worker has to facilitate the family relationships. The systemic problems will be lack of education, no support system either for the migrant workers or their families, to advise them about their resource management and other issues.

We argued earlier, for a practitioner to undertake both, will create problems in his/her professional role, therefore, referring the policy issues to organizations handling advocacy practice, may be better. The second point to note is, this is merely a service delivery organization, the hospital. The competency guidelines are leaving the use of strategies to the worker either for changing the policies or to address service gaps, for assuring appropriate access to resources, etc. Leaving both to the worker, will lead to a lot of diversity in approaches. It is therefore suggested to sort out the professional and organizational priorities.

Looking at these cases, identifying the competence a worker should possess and how to develop it among future professionals, needs serious curriculum planning, including field experiences. While we are doing so, it would help, if we go back to the concern raised by Mary Richmond. What is the common thread between a school social worker, a social worker working with elderly, and a medical social worker. The point is, a profession follows a unified approach, to handle all its clients in all situations and therefore, delivers a certain expertise to diagnose, deal and follow up issues identified to the satisfaction of all stake holders involved.

Thompson (2010), giving examples of use of theory in social work, suggests that work with families, takes into account the family dynamics, using a traditional family perspective (Burnham, 1986) or narrative based approaches, (Vetere and Dowling, 2005), perhaps to explain any or all issues in the family. I think this is a good example of being vague, when social workers are trying to emphasize the use of a body of knowledge, to explain any issue or problem. Coming up with a scientific solution is another matter (Thompson, 2010). If we identify facilitating relationships as our basic expertise, then we can answer the use of theory, in a more precise manner.

3

Human Relations

Theories and Concepts

It is amazing to see Nirmal, a single illiterate mother, poor because of an alcoholic and abusive husband, living alone with three children, not a very well off young lady by any stretch of imagination, is so much at ease in holding a very cordial conversation with all and sundry and is generally quite at peace with herself. On the other hand Mrs Kalavati, a well-educated lady, married, her children settled abroad, is generally at loggerhead with all vendors, who dare to call on her, or for that matter her close neighbours as well. It is not difficult to guess then that wealth and education is not enough to make one good at having good relations with others. It then raises a simple question, why some people are good at forming and managing relationships while others find it very difficult. Further, while some individuals enjoy their relationships, others find these very taxing and irritating. The capacity to enter into and manage relationships is considered an important part of a successful human being. In other words, according to the argument around which the text has been developed, the other-orientation is more helpful in both managing relationships and maintaining relative stability of mental health, as compared to a greater self-orientation in general. Pursuing this line of argument, with the help of research findings, it is argued that the collectivist cultures are more successful in socializing children to develop others-orientation, with a view to maintaining institutions such as marriage and family. Further, studies have indicated that modern education increases the capacity of individuals to become more rational in their decision-making. The collective decisions are not always rational, at times in order to retain relationships they put pressure on individuals to opt for alternative solutions rather than accepting the most rational view. The divorce rate for example, in rural areas has been lower as compared to urban areas even in developed nations. The centrality of relationships and less stressful lifestyles still are preferred in many developing nations, which at times create problems for the economic development. The point is theory building in the realm of social development remains problematic. The practitioners therefore will do better, to study it from all possible perspectives to understand it in its uniqueness, rather than trying to generalize. Further, skill of managing relations is not a sufficient condition for a lasting relationship, as relations undergo a change along with the changes experienced by both parties necessitating a change in their priorities.

The concepts and theories relating to personality development help us to understand human nature, and provide an explanation for differences in human beings. Professionals dealing with human relations should take into consideration the concepts and theories for knowing their clients and their problems in a proper perspective. There is evidence that wisdom, emotional intelligence and social skills are linked to a series of day-to-day tasks leading to better results but less is known about cognitive structure and what factors influence its formation and subsequent maintenance. Interventions aimed at making persons learn new behaviour and attempts to change long held beliefs and values do offer hope of affecting a change in human behaviour and capacities to modify human relations. Emotional intelligence is not considered simply an inherited trait and it can be developed to improve capacities for handling human relationships.

A central concern in behavioural studies has been to study the biological and the environmental equation, what the individual inherits from parents and what are social correlates which influence a persons' behaviour, impacting the interpersonal relationships. There are no conclusive theories or studies yet, but the general conclusion seems to be favouring a mix of both to account for human behaviour, but some studies have argued the centrality of personal relationships read in other words social correlates in impacting mental health (see, Pilgrim et al., 2009).

It is well known that the physical structure of an organism is to a large extent determined by its genes. To put it more technically, morphological phenotype is a function of genotype where by morphological we refer to shape or patterning, by phenotype we mean all the observable features of an organism at a given point in time, and by genotype we mean that total set of genes which is present in every cell. Individual differences, Wright argued (see

Mayr, E, 1970) in morphological phenotype, both between species and within species, can be attributed primarily to differences in genotype, yet the environmental variation, such as a grossly uncongenial environment, prolonged malnutrition or disease, may also be associated with structural differences. They further pointed out that an organism functions in a context and as a result of stimulation from this context, to some extent this functioning is shaped by the context. Behaviour is an adaptive transaction between a living organism and its environment.

THEORIES

Personality Tests

Cattell's studies discovered a definitive list of source traits, which make up the fundamental structure of the total personality. Cattell (1967, 1971) has isolated a number of source traits also known as primary or group factors. However, the best known are the sixteen traits listed below, which are relatively independent and uncorrelated. The sixteen factors identified, are warmth, reasoning, emotional stability, dominance, liveliness, consciousness, social boldness, sensitivity, vigilance, abstractedness, privateness, apprehension, openness to change, self-reliance, perfectionism and tension. When people score high on any trait s/he is expected to show a particular type of behaviour and possess a certain attitude towards others, and when s/he scores low, the behaviour is generally the opposite. We can see some overlap in some traits and perhaps that is why others reduced the significant traits to assess how a person is likely to behave towards others or in general, giving the professional some facts to rely on during their analysis of a person (see Conn and Rieke, 1994).

Cattell was not directly studying human relationships as such but his attempt to study personality characteristics directly influencing behaviour is very helpful in studying the relationship patterns. For example, an outgoing person described as warmhearted or easygoing, willing to participate in interactions with others, will be far more at ease, in forming relationships, than a person who exhibits a tendency to remain detached. Similarly, a person who is termed as being emotionally stable, will have more stable relationships, as compared to the person easily aroused by different emotional stimulus. The personality traits or types are also helpful in predicting the relationships between two persons such as spouses or managers and employees.

We are discussing the personality to indicate how people will possess certain traits or specific characteristics to form relationships or have different kinds of cognitive structures to influence their expectations from others. The very process of how they view themselves and others, is also reflected by personality characteristics, and will significantly influence the nature of their relationships. Social workers and other professionals involved with helping people with relationship problems, have to understand their clients, strengths and weaknesses, including emotional intelligence, to change or relate with others, but not all social workers may possess, the expertise needed to assess and analyse the personality of an individual or the behaviour patterns. It is advisable to work with other professionals to get a good understanding of the personality traits of clients or their behavioural patterns.

MMPI Personality Test

The Minnesota Multiphasic Personality Inventory developed by Minnesota University known as MMPI, is a tool which is widely used by many professionals for assessing individual and family relationships. The latest version of MMPI known as MMPI-2 RA, is expected to provide information about 'Hypochondriasis' or in other words concern with body symptoms, depression, hysteria, psychopathic deviates meaning presence of internal conflict or struggle, anger and respect for social norms, stereotypical masculine or feminine interest or behaviour, paranoia or the sensitivity of a person to trust or suspiciousness, psychasthenia or level of worry, anxiety, tension, doubt, schizophrenia or social alienation, hypomania or level of excitability and also social introversion or in other words the most important skill in handling relationships, people orientation.

Some of the factors that generally affect expectation levels of different actors in a relationship are highly class and culture specific, but education and their spatial location, play a significant part as well. In many cultures, for example the female is expected to play a subservient role vis-à-vis, males in all relationships. Similarly some regions such as tribal and rural areas prohibit individualism to promote greater collective orientation. This is one particular reason for not educating them, as they fear that education will act as a deterrent. Further urban populations provide enough examples of individuals, not conforming to the social or cultural norms, as compared to rural and tribal populations.

Some scholars view relationships as an exchange. The basic elements of exchange view of relationships are;

Theory of Social Exchange

Human action is motivated primarily by the desire to gain pleasure and avoid pain. The actions of other persons are sources of pleasure and pain.

Actions of others are found pleasurable when in the final analysis they are giving more than the inputs (howsoever defined and calculated) by the receiving person (Gergen and Gergen, 1981). Hence the theory, people try to achieve maximum pleasure at minimum cost.

Foa and Foa (1974), on the basis of studies of social exchange in a variety of cultures, argue that all the resources that people use to benefit one another, fall in six categories; love, services, goods, money, information and status. Equity theory posits that when it comes to relationships, two concerns stand out: (1) How rewarding are their societal, family, and work relationships? (2) How fair and equitable are those relationships? According to equity theory, people feel most comfortable when they are getting exactly what they deserve from their relationships.

Equity theory: Equity theory consists of four propositions;

Proposition I: Men and women try to maximize pleasure and minimize pain.

Proposition II: Society, has a vested interest in persuading people to behave fairly and equitably. Groups will generally reward members who treat others equitably and punish those who treat others inequitably.

Proposition III: Given societal pressures, people are most comfortable, when they perceive that they are getting, roughly what they deserve from life and love. If people feel over benefited, they may experience pity, guilt, and shame; if under benefited, they may experience anger, sadness, and resentment.

Proposition IV: People in inequitable relationships will attempt to reduce their distress via a variety of techniques: by restoring psychological equity, actual equity, or leaving the relationship (see Hatfield and Rapson, 2007).

Theory of Interdependence

Harold Kelley and John Thibaut (1978) developed interdependence theory. It was developed around the same time as the exchange theory. Most psychological theories focus on the individual, suggesting that people behave in a particular manner because of their unique cognitions or personalities. As we discussed earlier, however interdependence theory views the relationships between people as important and explains how the importance of each relationship is developed by each actor, in view of the dependence on the other. Thus, the theory represents a much-needed model of the nature and implications of interdependence which helps in understanding people's specific relationships. It helps us to understand how a relationship affects the behaviour of each party, in view of the capacity of each party to affect the satisfaction level of the other.

Some of the Important Components of Dependence Theory

Level of dependence: This refers to the degree to which an individual is dependent on other. Let us assume that Kiran and Ramesh are dependent on each other. The question is to what extent or who is more dependent? If Kiran's action cause loss of sleep for Ramesh but Kiran does not experience the same because of Ramesh, this indicate that Kiran is not dependent on Ramesh and hence is more powerful. Unilateral dependence involves vulnerability on the part of one person, in that the less dependent person may behave as he or she wishes without concern for the other's well-being.

Mutuality of dependence: It describes the degree to which people are equally dependent. Mutual dependence exists when Kiran is as dependent on Ramesh as he is on her. Mutuality constitutes a balance of dependence, providing less room for manipulation and exploitation and more equitable relationship.

Basis of dependence: The basis of dependence is a very significant point and refers to the causative factor of dependence such as financial dependence, reward or punishment, recognition or caring, or pleasure seeking including sexual dependence. The person possessing the power to reward or cause hurt is more in a position to manipulate the relationship.

Covariation of interests: As we discussed in the theory of relationship that the best relationship is an interaction where the expectations of each party are fully satisfied, the covariation measures the degree to which outcome satisfies the expectation of a person. An interaction is simple when interests conflict: One person must lose if the other is to gain. Mixed-motive situations are more complex, in that they involve a dilemma of what to do, or a blend of cooperative and competitive motives, combining desire to benefit the other with temptation to exploit.

Temporal structure: This reinforces the fact that all relationships are dynamic and evolve over time. A relationship must be analysed in terms of both the immediate outcomes, but also in terms of the future outcomes. Further the expectation levels and the satisfaction levels will also vary in due course of time.

Availability of information: This refers to how often the parties in a relationship are in possession of adequate knowledge about each other and the reasons for either the imagined or actual behaviour (Please also see the chapter on problems in human relationships).

Intelligence and Personality

The results of a study reveal the high specificity of the relationships among personality and brain activity. The data confirm that effective dimensions of personality are independent of intelligence, yet also suggest that they might be interrelated in subtle ways, because they modulate activity in overlapping brain regions that appear to be critical for task performance. A prior work suggests that, at a minimum, it may be important to assess and control for psychometric intelligence when investigating personality differences in neural-processing efficiency. A third dimension of personality, openness to experience, has been consistently related to intelligence and cognitive function, so much so that it is increasingly referred to as openness/intellect.

The Theory of Self and Others Orientation

The explanation of human relationships advanced in this book, is based on two simple facts, which have been thoroughly researched by many scholars. First, a person's relationship with self, known as self-concept, and second the social environment referring to other significant persons around. The argument is, a person's psychological framework determining behaviour is located on a continuum from self-orientation to others-orientation. Others-orientation is a person's concern for well-being of others particularly significant others rather than self, and the argument is that others-oriented persons are more successful in developing and maintaining relationships. Regardless of an individual's awareness of any theory of relationships, most people tend to treat their own view of relationships as reality. Because of this egocentric view of reality, how one views self and others in relational contexts is of fundamental importance (Wilmot, 1995).

The main factor influencing a person's self- and others-orientation is the self-concept. A person who has a positive self-concept will generally be more others-oriented. A positive self-concept as discussed earlier refers to an individual's acceptance of the realities around in a positive manner and a realistic self-image, that is what your strengths and weaknesses are, which is acceptable to you. In other words, adequate self-esteem or trust and faith in self, person has nothing to hide and can express whatever one has in a creative manner. The expectations or goals are based on a realistic assessment of strengths and weaknesses, to function effectively. The negative viewing of others begins with uncertain and vague notions of one's own-self and consequently one's expectations in any transaction, leading to a distorted view of others' inputs and a desire to monopolize. It is possible to bring about a change in a person's self-concept and there by in any relationship but the success will largely depend on the commitment of the individual, to bring about the change.

Total Surrender

The concept of total surrender refers to, a total absence of self-interest, referring to a person willing to comply with all demands. It is argued that in the context of human relationships, acceptance of such a person is greater than those with any degree of self-interest leading to any resistance in a relationship. Conversely, a person who questions all transactions is considered troublemaker and unfriendly by others. In a relationship where one actor totally surrenders, it becomes a one-sided relationship and it lasts till the dependence of the person on the other continues. A relationship where both persons surrender to each other completely and consciously is a perfect relationship, which lasts forever, and is most satisfying. There is complete absence of anxiety as both trust each other and are aware of the outcome of all of their transactions. In a situation where nobody is prepared to even partially surrender to the other, is a contested relationship, where conflict is endemic, creating maximum anxiety.

The location of a person on self-other continuum determines how others-oriented or self-centered one is likely to be in dealings with others. A person who by nature is self-centered is likely to have more problems in relationships everywhere. An others-oriented person is likely to have fewer expectations from others as one is more focussed on giving rather than receiving, and therefore is likely to find all relationships comparatively more satisfactory than a self-centered person who is expecting far more because of focus on receiving rather than giving. In other words, there is an inverse relationship between needs and satisfaction in relationships, that is as the needs increase the satisfaction decreases and vice versa. A person who is more others-oriented generally is willing to leave more space for others to move, is willing to discuss and carry the dialogue rather than interpreting things more narrowly and making it difficult to understand the other's viewpoint. All these lead to fewer expectations from others and increasing the possibility of any transaction to be viewed more positively, creating the possibility of continuing a healthy and positive relationship. A self-centered person has greater expectations from others, because of failure to interpret others' response objectively. One is reducing the possibility of continuing the relationship in a positive way simply because all transactions with others are subjectively viewed and rated negatively. In effect this is what gives rise to development of a whole negative framework by looking at a half full glass and judging it as half empty. The text therefore argues the centrality of understanding the self-concept in diagnosing and redressing relationships in all contexts.

Self-Other Relationship

Wilmot (1995) conceptualized three paradigmatic views of relationships.

Paradigm I: Individual Selves Loosely Connected view of relationships. Self and Other are viewed as separate units loosely coupled by a fragile relational thread. The concern for Self is greater than the concern for other. Individual achievement and initiative is rewarded and respected (Gudykunst and Kim 1997), and views the Self as an independent, self-contained, and causative force guiding events (Harre 1989). Gudykunst and Kim (1997) go a step further to note that individualistic cultures favour individual goals over group goals, and include family within individual goals. It contradicts their assumption that individualistic cultures favour individual goals over group goals, since family is a group. Wilmot (1995) notes that the Paradigm I view 'emphasizes the Self, de-emphasizes the other, and reduces the relationships to a fragile connecting mechanism' (p. 37). This view of relationships is consistent with *Social Exchange* (Roloff, 1981) models of relationships (e.g. equity theory) where individuals try to maximize their outcomes (Hatfield, Utne, and Traupmann, 1979).

Paradigm II: The Embedded Self view of relationships asserts that Self is not a separate unit, but must always be examined within the context of relationship and hence is not independent since people's behaviour change in response to each unique relational context. In this view, the relationship itself is treated as a separate entity. Gudykunst and Kim (1997) note that groups (i.e. relationships and families) take precedence over individual's goals in collectivistic cultures. In contrast to individualistic cultures, collectivistic cultures have fewer in-groups but these in-groups have a strong influence on individual behaviour across situations. 'Collectivistic cultures emphasize group goals, needs, and views of the in-group over those of the individual; the social norms of the in-group, rather than individual pleasure; shared in-group beliefs, rather than unique individual beliefs; and cooperation with in-group members, rather than maximizing of individual outcomes' (Gudykunst and Kim, 1997, p. 57).

Paradigm III: Nonseparable Self/Other/Relationship view of relationships. In this view, the individual is not taken as a separate, sacred entity, but rather it challenges the very notion of an identifiable Self. Proponents of this paradigm would view Self, Other, and Relationships as so inextricably tied that talking about one entity would necessitate talking about the other two. That is, any change in Self necessarily changes Other and Relationship. In other words, we are constructed in our transactions with others. A view of relationships from the Paradigm III perspective suggests we cannot separate Self, Other, and Relationships and that duality itself is an illusion.

The Theory of Interpersonal Cognition

The theory of interpersonal cognition (see Baccus and Baldwin, 2007), refers to the thinking processes which takes shape as people interact with each other. The key element is seen as the perception, interpretation and uses made of information or knowledge about others, both concurrently and later on. As a number of studies of development of personality have indicated, the relationship with people and expectations that they inculcate among children, is a major source for providing a framework for thinking, feeling and action. The sociologists have emphasized the impact of social norms particularly those grounded in religious belief of people, in providing the overall framework, for perceiving and interpreting actions of other people. For example, a female spouse in the Indian sub continent accepts domestic violence and child abuse – use of physical force to enforce discipline, as a normal occurrence, and may even interpret it socially useful, in maintaining order. Interpersonal cognition focuses on discovering the framework or in other words value base of an individual, based on interpersonal relationships, which is a restricted view of the social reality.

Many researchers trained in a different cultural milieu, are not able to understand the true impact of a culture since they have not experienced it. For example, the concept of relational self, referring to the idea that people do not have a unified self-concept but a series of self-concepts, linked to significant others, is another way of looking at social roles. The socialization process clearly demarcates the role of a wife and a daughter, as also the expectations and boundaries, in the Indian sub continent. This structuring alone, serves as a major framework for females in viewing others and their own self in a relationship context. But the self-concept is a different phenomenon, which differentiates the responses of each female, despite the socialization process. How else we can explain the difference between two sisters in a family, undergoing the same process yet one more confident than the other, in dealing with life situations. Researches of interpersonal cognition exploring the mental representation of the self in relation to others (e.g. romantic partner, friend), is not a useful way of understanding the cognition process. A more useful concept is that changes in self can take place through interaction with others. A person can learn many new ways of behaviour through significant relationships, particularly where a person is making effort to retain a relationship. A spouse learns to enjoy different kinds of food or events one has not done earlier, just to make oneself more acceptable to the other or receive a particular response from the other. Some authors has referred to it as self-expansion theory (see Konarth Sara, 2009).

Theory of Attachment

Attachment refers to the strong emotional bond that exists between an infant and his or her caretaker. The theory of attachment explains the development of a bond, and its implication for human relationships (see Bowlby, J and Mary Ainsworth, 1992). Although attachment theory has primarily been a theory of child development, since the 1980s, the theory has had a large impact on social psychological theories of close relationships, emotion regulation, and personality. Attachment theory was developed by John Bowlby, a British psychoanalyst, studying infant distress, when separated from their parents. Later, Ainsworth's studies for developing attachment theory noted individual differences in infant attachment patterns. According to her three patterns exist; (a) those who are secure in their relationship with their parents, (b) those who are anxious-resistant, (c) and those who are anxious-avoidant. That these individual differences were correlated with infant-parent interactions during the first year of life, and these styles are likely to impact the future development of an individual. The data may partly support a moderate degree of stability in attachment styles from infancy to adulthood, but that there could be other factors as well to shape their current security levels (see Fraley, 2007).

Attachment has four defining features:

1. *Proximity maintenance:* the attached individual wishes to be in close proximity to the attachment figure;
2. *Separation distress:* the attached individual experiences an increase in anxiety during unwanted or prolonged separation from the attachment figure;
3. *Safe haven:* the attachment figure serves as a source of comfort and security such that the attached individual experiences diminished anxiety when in the company of the attachment figure; and
4. *Secure base:* the attachment figure serves as a base of security from which the attached individual engages in explorations of the social and physical world.

John Bowlby (1969/1982, 1973, 1980, 1988) proposed that attachment bonds involve two behavioural systems – an attachment system and a care giving system. First, individuals come into the world equipped with an attachment behavioural system that is prone to activation when they are distressed and that serves a major evolutionary function of protection and survival (Bowlby, 1969; Bretherton, 1987). The attachment system is, thus, a safety-regulating system that solidifies enduring emotional bonds between individuals that contribute to reproductive success. Although there are normative developmental changes in the expression of the attachment system across the lifespan, the basic function of the attachment system remains constant (Hazan and Zeifman, 1999). Freud has explained this as a child's response system when s/he is faced with a need. The child first tries to increase his/her activity level to achieve it, which Freud termed as aggression. If the child does not succeed s/he may call for help, which Freud termed as pairing, and if this response also failed, the child may resort to giving up, which he termed as flight. Freud has also argued that depending upon the childhood experiences the response systems of individuals get stabilized.

Adults as well as children benefit from having someone looking out for them – someone who is deeply interested in their welfare, who monitors their whereabouts, and who is reliably available to help if needed. However, research also suggests that parents over doing it, that is meeting the child's demands when a child becomes aggressive or cries, can lead to dependence which may influence his future behavioural traits negatively.

Unlike parent-child relationships, which have clearly defined caregiving and care-seeking roles, adult intimate relationships are reciprocal and mutual. Therefore, in well-functioning bonds, adult partners should be able to comfortably rely on one another in times of need, sometimes as care-seekers and sometimes as caregivers (Collins and Feeney, B., 2000).

1. *Secure* adults are low in both attachment related anxiety and avoidance;
2. *Preoccupied* (anxious-ambivalent) adults are high in anxiety and low in avoidance; they have an exaggerated desire for closeness and dependence, coupled with a heightened concern about being rejected.
3. *Dismissing avoidant* adults are low in attachment-related anxiety but high in avoidance; they view close relationships as relatively unimportant, and they value independence and self-reliance.
4. Finally, *fearful avoidant* adults are high in both anxiety and avoidance; although they desire close relationships and the approval of others, they avoid intimacy because they fear being rejected.

Secure adults develop relationships that are happier and better functioning than their insecure counterparts. Secure adults are characterized by frequent positive emotion and high levels of interdependence, commitment, trust, and satisfaction. They have high self-esteem, are generally positive and self-assured in their interactions with others.

Anxious/preoccupied adults, tend to be characterized by jealousy, frequent negative attitude, low levels of trust and satisfaction. They exhibit a controlling (over-dominating) interpersonal style.

Avoidant adults tend to be characterized by low levels of interdependence, commitment, trust, and satisfaction. They have low levels of distress following relationship breakup. They exhibit negative emotions and less positive emotions which stems from discomfort with intimacy.

Although insecure adults tend to have less satisfying relationships, their relationships are not always less stable (see Lee Kirkpatrick and Cindy Hazan, 1994; Kirkpatrick and Davis, 1994).

An important question is how far the influence of early childhood last and is the insecure nature entirely a product of caregiving. Bowlby believed that the mental representations or working models (i.e. expectations, beliefs about rules, or scripts for behaving and thinking) that a child holds regarding relationships are a function of his or her caregiving experiences. According to Bowlby, these processes promote continuity in attachment patterns over the life course, although it is possible that a person's attachment pattern can change, if his or her relational experiences are inconsistent with his or her expectations. In short, if we assume that adult relationships are attachment relationships, it is possible that children who are secure as children will grow up to be secure in their romantic relationships.

Research shows that there is a modest degree of overlap between how secure people feel during childhood and during adulthood. Of secure adults, approximately 70 per cent of them were classified as secure when they were 12 months of age. Taken together, these data suggest that there is a moderate degree of stability in attachment styles from infancy to adulthood, but that there is also plenty of room for people's ongoing experiences to shape their security. Further, though the caregiving plays an important role, other factors particularly some genetic factors giving rise to anxiety and intelligence are also responsible for shaping behavioural responses (see Fraley, R. Chris, 2007).

CONCEPTS

Emotional Energy

The concept of emotional energy is helpful in screening the values of a person and how strongly one believes in them. A person having a 'guilt feeling', when one violates some values one believes in, is an important indicator, (a) that a person has a healthy, honest relationship with self, (b) that the person has a value base, (c) it can indicate the areas that need to be addressed for change. The degree of emotions associated with any violation of these values is an indicator of extent of attachment for a person to these values. For example, a person who believes in an egalitarian philosophy and commits an act which is individualistic, will feel guilty, the subsequent action or non-action, depending on associated emotional energy, will be an indicator of commitment to these values.

A related concept is emotional intelligence, which is helpful in understanding how a person is able to control the emotions or feelings arising out of his/her interactions with others and achieve much better results in the process.

Emotional Intelligence

Goleman (1995), has conceptualized emotional intelligence as consisting of five dimensions or core competencies described by self-awareness, self-regulation, self-motivation, social awareness (empathy), and social skills.

Suzy Fox and Paul Spector (2004), have conceptualized emotional intelligence as a set of competencies that could be utilized by individuals to effectively use emotions to attain desirable outcomes. They measured three components of emotional intelligence, described as empathy, self-regulation of mood, and self-presentation. Bar-On (2007), conceptualizes emotional intelligence as consisting of five main factors: intrapersonal, interpersonal, stress management, adaptability, and general mood. The intrapersonal component is based on an individual's self-awareness and expression. This requires individuals to be aware of their emotions and effectively express them towards others. The interpersonal component involves an individual's social awareness and adeptness at social relationships. A key aspect here is the ability to empathize with how others experience social situations and the feelings they experience, as well as the ability to build and maintain relationships. Stress management deals with a person's ability to manage and regulate his or her emotions or feelings in difficult situations. Adaptability revolves around a person's capacity to adjust his or her feelings in order to effectively deal with emotional situations, whether internal or external. The last dimension, general mood, is based on a person's degree of happiness or overall feeling of well-being. The authors are using different terms but in effect the basic components are same as described earlier by Goleman. It is good to note that researchers feel that emotional intelligence can be developed through interventions (unlike intelligence, which is considered more biologically determined).

Anxiety

Anxiety has been conceptualized as a stimulus, as a trait, as a motive, and as a drive and has been defined as an emotional state, with the subjectively experienced quality of fear as a closely related emotion (Lewis, 1971: 77). There are physiological, cognitive, and behavioural components to anxiety. State-anxiety is the momentary experience of anxiety. Trait-anxiety is a predisposition or proneness to be anxious. A person having anxiety as a trait will find it difficult to trust others, take decisions in time and objectively and therefore will find it difficult to maintain meaningful relationships.

Betrayal

Betrayal refers to situations in which individuals (victims) believe that a relationship partner (a perpetrator) has harmed them by knowingly violating a norm governing their relationship. In this context, norms refer to expectations about how the relationship partners should treat one another. These, norms are usually ideals associated with cultural and social values. There are some values which cut across many cultures such as monogamy, respect for parents, truthful behaviour, politeness and caring for siblings and other close kins, etc. There are some values which are specific to cultures, for example, in the Indian sub continent, children are expected to marry with parents consent, no premarital sex or pregnancy, selection of spouse within caste or religion and so on. Typical betrayals involve any of these violated by a spouse or children or other close relations. In a recent case, for example, where a girl became pregnant before marriage and had selected a likely spouse from outside the caste, the parents felt the betrayal so hard that it leads to the death of the girl (see *Times of India,* 4 and 5 May 2010). Both parties can feel that they are the victim and view other as the perpetrator. For example, in this case the parents felt that they are the victim, but usually the children also feel that they have been victimized, in absence of freedom to take their own decisions, as an adult. This is also an indicator of self-orientation. Although betrayals are considered more serious in close relationships, but they can also be experienced in more casual relationships, for example, a subordinate, a student or a client not conforming to expectations. The possible reactions are forgiveness, retaliation or no action to simply ignore these. The reactions are indicators of self-orientation and self-confidence. Betrayal can create self-doubt eroding the self-confidence. A person having greater self-control will not retaliate. Similarly the chances of betrayals causing less damage increase, if the person committing the act accepts it and is willing to make amendments by accepting responsibility (see Finkel, 2007).

Frequent betrayals can cause real damage to any relationship. However betrayals can provide an excellent opportunity to evaluate the self and also one's position on self-other continuum, as forgiveness is a sign of others-orientation and retaliation, a sign of self-orientation.

Intrapersonal Conflict

Intrapersonal conflict encompasses four broad domains. At the emotional level, conflict reflects competing desires or impulses. Sigmund Freud (1962) attributed these base tendencies to aggressive and sexual proclivities with origins in the id (the unregulated physical self), which give rise to irreconcilable differences with constraints that are imposed by the superego (the social mores conveyed by family and culture). At the cognitive level, conflict reflects dissonance produced by incongruent facts, opinions, or modes of thought. Jean Piaget (1997) attributed these tendencies to equilibration, the innate human tension between a preference for stability and a drive to master the environment. Assimilation encourages stability by incorporating new information into existing mental schema. Should this prove insufficient for mastering the environment, accommodation is required to alter the mental scheme or, in extreme cases, the mental structure itself, in a manner consistent with the information available. At the level of the ego, conflict reflects developmental challenges. According to Erik Erikson, (1997, 1951) each life stage is defined by a distinct crisis that must be resolved. These crises represent choice points that collectively contribute to ego development and self-representations. At the motivational level, conflict reflects the need to choose between options perceived to be relatively equal in valence. Lewin Kurt (1997) identified three distinct forms of motivational discord. Two equally attractive options are described in contemporary terms as approach-approach conflicts. Two equally unattractive options are referred to as avoid-avoid conflicts. Options that contain both attractive and unattractive elements are considered approach-avoid conflicts.

Intrapersonal conflict is by definition a private experience. It cannot be observed, and it has no clear, reliable metric. Early scientific psychologists relied on introspection to glean insight into thoughts, a practice modified and popularized by psychodynamic psychologists to probe unconscious emotional states.

Interpersonal conflict may take place at the level of the dyad or the group. Dyadic conflict is a social episode marked by overt behavioural opposition. The function of a disagreement and the manner in which it unfolds varies according to characteristics of the participants and their relationship, the issue and context, the strategies employed, and their consequences. Group conflict refers to negative or incompatible attitudes and behaviours directed by members or representatives of one group towards those of another group. The nature and significance of intergroup conflict varies according to leadership styles and prevailing norms, member cohesion, resource availability, and the individual and collective talents and experiences of each group.

Conflict and Change

There is considerable support for the premise that the developmental significance of conflict depends on the relationship in which it arises. If a relationship provides power, closeness, and permanence it can produce conflict as well as change. All three are only found in spousal relationship and other significant kin relationships. Power describes the degree to which dominance shapes the relationship. Disagreements in horizontal relationships, social competence and social development are linked with interpersonal conflict. Disagreements in close relationships, are one of the primary means which forces individuals to redefine themselves and change their interactions with others. First, conflict may prompt changes in self-understanding and self-evaluation. Second, conflict helps to determine patterns of social interaction that may impact developmental outcomes. Ineffective communication once started, decreases the possibility of benefits that normally accrue from close relationships; in contrast, effective communication fosters a climate of warmth and problem solving that facilitates affective sharing. Third, conflict can help in redefining expectations about individuals and relationships, which is crucial in preventing future occurrence of conflicts. As has been argued earlier, a conflict occurs when the expectations are not met in successive interactions. In some cases, roles and responsibilities are therefore renegotiated to redefine expectations. It is more often the case that participants evaluate their own behaviour and that of their partner for clues as to whether current expectations are consistent with the capabilities of the relationship and the demands of the situation. Regardless of how it happens, successful conflict management is widely considered to be an important indicator of maturation of the participant.

Conflict management provides fertile ground for improved social skills because when power is shared, negotiation is necessary for a mutually satisfactory resolution; in vertical relationships, resolutions are more often the product of power differentials than negotiated settlements. Closeness describes the extent to which participants lives are interdependent. Disagreements in close relationships have the potential to profoundly affect other significant relationships. Permanence describes the stability of the relationship. Conflict management strategies, where coercion is gradually replaced across childhood and adolescence, with withdrawal and negotiation, have provided better outcomes (see, Laursen, 2006).

Control

The term control refers to influence over other people or over self as well. It simply means that a person can control others and control one's own emotions and actions to achieve desired results.

It could be psychological in nature such as love or fear or more physical in nature such as reward or punishment. Rotter (1950) was one of the first to realize the link between expectation and behaviour, therefore discovering perhaps one of the oldest technique in human history to control human behaviour, later worked out in terms of theory X and Y. Martin Seligman (1993) similarly, emphasized the importance of control over outcomes (either internal or external), in explaining helplessness and depression. Seligman felt that lack of control over outcomes, rooted in the environments, lead to learned helplessness. However, he did not specify whether this was based on facts or simply imagined. The term perceived control has been used in recent studies to refer to an internal locus of control or expecting to have control over outcomes. The point is that the notion of lack of control or having control can both be illusory (see Langer, 1997). Researchers have argued that human beings have a strong desire to perceive that they have control over outcomes. Langer termed it as the illusion of control. The concept of control over outcomes is also central to self-efficacy theory as outlined by Albert Bandura (2002) as he felt that being motivated required people to expect that they can obtain desired outcomes. For this to happen, one should believe that a particular behaviour will result in a desired outcome; and that one can do it. In the context of control, cognitively oriented social psychologists have drawn an important distinction between automatic and controlled mental processes. Automatic processes are characterized as operating without awareness, effort, or intention. In contrast, controlled responses require an effort and conscious awareness. In fact the job of a social worker lies in identifying the responses by auto processing which are creating a problem such as extreme agitation or anger, in a client and help to modify this. The auto processing begins with the cognitive mechanism perceiving and interpreting the stimuli leading to generation of emotion and action (see Moller and Deci, 2007).

Dependence Regulation

It is a relatively new concept that try to explain how partners behave if they are not able to trust each other. The central point is self-confidence and its impact on human responses in stressful situations. A central concern in a relationship is trust. Some people are not able to trust their partner. People with low self-esteem dramatically underestimate other's love and caring. Children with low self-esteem underestimate their parents. In such cases, illusion of unfulfilled needs for a partner's approval then create substantial difficulties within relationships. Feeling insecure, people look to specific events in their relationships to evaluate others, rather than being able to see the whole picture over a period of time. Since it is a prejudged activity to provide mythical support to their point of view, it generally is negative than positive in conclusion. For a low self-esteem person, a routine event, such as a minor conflict or an irritable comment, increases the fear. Low self-esteem people then protect themselves against such heightened anxieties by finding greater fault in their partner and by reducing closeness and if possible dependence. Not much research evidence.is available to support it, however. There is greater evidence to directly link high self-esteem with greater emotional control.

People with high self-esteem can trust their partners and are able to take even negative events in the relationships in their stride. A self-confident person is likely to react to a negative comment by saying, looks like you had a hard day and need some rest, a response which reflects caring and is likely to calm a person down. In situations of hurt or rejection people with high self-esteem are more in control and consequently resist the impulse to hurt the other in return. Consequently, people with high self-esteem are better able to cope with relationship ups and downs (see Murray, 2007).

Depression

Depression refers to a state of mind, involving feelings of worthlessness, diminished ability to concentrate, and recurrent thoughts of death. It is important to note that while many theories and hypotheses exist, the underlying mechanisms that cause depression remain to be established empirically. Psychologically, it is a condition created by loss of positive preoccupation, such as retirement from employment, loss of a partner in late stages of life, in general losing interest in future. A significant relationship gone bad can cause stress leading to depression over a period of time. Medically, the chemical imbalance in the mind in certain diseases may result in depression. On the contrary, healthy relationships can help people to come out of depression with some professional help.

Parenting Styles

Parenting style refers to the different kind of relationship one or both parents have with the child. For example, some parents have an anxiety to please the child and are very scared of child crying or contesting the parents directions for behaviour patterns. One proposition is that parenting styles affect child adjustment because they provide an emotional context which is not found in other settings, outside the home. For instance, Darling and Steinberg (1993) proposed that authoritative parenting may be effective because the warmth and involvement that characterizes this style may create an emotional climate in which the child is more receptive to parenting, which in turn influences its effectiveness. Also, parents' willingness to engage children in decision-making provides them with negotiation skills that may be useful in their social interactions with others outside the family, for instance, with peers. Therefore, these skills may facilitate children's competence in different settings. Finally, the combination of support and structure that characterizes authoritative parenting may be important to children's ability to regulate their behaviour (Steinberg, 2001). The same parenting practices, in the emotional climate of authoritarian or indulgent parenting, may have different meanings and therefore have different consequences for adjustment.

THERAPIES

Behavioural Couples Therapy

Behavioural couples therapy (BCT) is the most widely researched and well-validated model of couple therapy (Christensen and Heavey, 1990). Like individual behavioural therapy, BCT is derived from social learning and social exchange theories, which emphasize the influence of the environment and its behavioural and emotional rewards and costs. Behavioural couples therapy is built upon the idea that couple satisfaction is determined, in large part, by the positive and negative nature of spouses' interactions with each other.

Many distressed couples report feeling unable to communicate with each other or solve problems when they arise, which leads them to feel unhappy and frustrated with each other. According to behavioural theory, these negative interactions decrease the rewards couples gain from their relationship. In response to this reward reduction, BCT focuses on increasing the ratio of positive to negative behaviours for couples in distress and teaching them effective communication behaviours so that they may handle difficulties when they arise.

Couples seek counselling for many reasons, ranging from difficulty in communicating with each other to disagreements on parenting, emotional outpouring, sexual incompatibility, feeling neglected, etc. There are other reasons including individual problems, such as mental illness, or family difficulties, such as a child's problems in school. The role of the social worker is to help them cope with these difficulties together, solve them when possible, and, as discussed above, accept them when no solution can be found.

Cognitive Behavioural Couples Therapy

Cognition refers to mental mechanism providing meaning to different social realities or in brief, the belief system in place about different issues. Therefore it becomes imperative to screen the interpretations a client provides to several events and persons including expectations regarding partner's behaviour, and selective attention to some aspects of partner behaviour and not others (Epstein, Baucom, and Daiuta, 1977). Cognitive therapy interventions involves cognitive restructuring, a process of evaluating cognition strength, etc. The key is to help the person review these more objectively to be able to modify these, to generate alternative explanations that are more accurate and lead to greater positive feelings between partners.

Integrative Behavioural Couples Therapy

Integrative behavioural couples therapy (Jacobson and Christensen, 1996) gives emphasis on acceptance of problems that are difficult or impossible to change. In order to promote acceptance, social workers may help couples reformulate problems as differences, rather than deficiencies; help persons to reveal vulnerable feelings that often lie behind aggressive behaviour; encourage an objective analysis of the problematic patterns couples experience; or reenactment of behaviour in ways that promote increased tolerance. Not only are these strategies designed to promote acceptance, but they may indirectly foster change in the problematic behaviour and increase emotional closeness between the pair.

Emotionally Focused Therapy

Emotionally focused therapy, developed by Leslie Greenberg and Susan Johnson (1988), involves the identification of problematic interaction cycles between partners and the emotions underlying them. Relationship distress is believed to arise, when attachment bonds are disrupted or have not been fully formed, resulting in rigid interactional patterns that prevent emotional closeness (Christensen and Heavey, 1990). Emotionally focused therapy helps couples to restructure their interactions in order to create a more satisfying relationship. The social worker and couple work together to reprocess and redefine the relationship in such a way that it provides a more secure attachment base for both partners.

Family Systems Therapy

According to Fraenkel (1997) the foundation of systemic couple theory is that all problems, including couple problems, occur in a multilevel context, which ranges in specificity from the couple to their immediate environment (i.e. family, work, or school) to their larger society or culture.

For couples, intervention techniques vary widely, as a function of the specific type of systems theory from which they are derived (examples of different types include *structural, strategic,* and *experiential*). However, Fraenkel identifies some common goals of systems therapy, including focusing on strengths and resources, attending to the therapeutic environment as a 'system,' and identifying, stopping, and changing problematic interaction patterns. Family systems social workers may try to avoid dependence upon the social worker. The social worker may also model important concepts, including teaching how different family members may emotionally respond to each other and how partners may maintain their separate identities and perspectives while still working together as a couple.

A review of the therapies discussed above brings out some basic facts. The relationship between couple is considered important for the well-being of both the partners and the entire family (see Fraenkel, 1997). The cognition plays an important part in the occurrence and resolution of the problem. The communication pattern and its consequent impact on both partners, including all persons present during the occurrence, are other important aspects of the problem. Part of what the therapy is taking for granted, positive and negative communication may be just the symptom, and not the real problem. There is always a reason for the communication pattern found between spouses. It could be insecurity, different sexual orientation, inability to accept authority and so on. The ethnicity and cultural factors influence the cognition and communication patterns in a big way (see M. McGoldrick, Joe Giordano and Preto, 1996).

The argument here is that relationship should be the main focus. The actors should be assessed first in terms of their cognitive framework, pertaining to self and other. As we argued that despite these differences or deficiencies a relationship will remain functional or can be made functional if there is a possibility that a restructuring of the cognition about self is possible, the technique then is to increase the others-orientation or make them understand the significance of other in their life among both parties. Generally it is accomplished by developing a caring relationship with both the spouses and offering support in the initial stages of change. A further technique is to help them understand their original feelings and the source of these feelings towards each other. In the collectivist cultures there is an inbuilt mechanism to down play the importance of self and to learn to change and adjust once own preferences with that of others in all relationships. This greatly helps in stabilizing relationships and making the interaction process tension free. Therefore, the process of harmonizing relationships should begin with assessing their strengths and weaknesses to achieve change.

4

The Self-Concept

> Our Ignorance and Self-will and Vicious Pride Destroy the Harmony of Part and Whole.
>
> — Rumi

The most important psychological discovery of this century is the discovery of 'self-image'. This self-image is our own conception of the sort of person we are. Self-image is the key to human personality and human behaviour. Change the self-image and you change the personality and the behaviour (Malitz, 1960). While a number of philosophers and psychologists have addressed the idea, that behaviour is influenced by the way people see themselves, investigation into the importance of self-concept is, most closely associated with, the writings and therapeutic practices of Carl Rogers (1951).

Self-concept is an understanding which develops during the process of growing up. At some point of time during growing up, a person start noticing the individual characteristics such as physical, social, emotional and so on. As many researchers argued, these dimensions may be referred to by others: 'people think I have a great sense of humour'; and self-ideals (what or how one would like to be: 'I want to be like Sachin Tendulkar or as beautiful as Karina'). Carl Rogers emphasized the importance of self-concept, and how it influences our perception of persons and events. It there pore, plays an important role in maintaining healthy relationships. Self-concept according to Rogers, can be divided into categories, such as personal self-concept (facts or one's own opinions about oneself), social self-concept (one's perceptions about how others view him/her), or ideal self-concept (what one will like to be).

The self – its awareness is at the heart of Rogers' client-centered therapy and the philosophy behind it. According to Rogers, self-concept influences how a person regards both self and environment around. The self-concept of a mentally healthy person, is consistent with his or her thoughts, experiences, and behaviour. However, people may maintain a self-concept, that is at odds with their true feelings, to win the approval of others, and 'fit in,' either socially or professionally. This involves repressing their true feelings and impulses, which eventually causes them to become alienated from themselves, distorting their own experience of the world, and limiting their potential for self-actualization, or fulfillment. The gulf between a person's self-concept and his or her actual experiences (which Rogers called incongruence) is a chronic source of anxiety, and can even result in mental disorders. According to Rogers, a strong self-concept is flexible and allows a person to confront new experiences and ideas without feeling threatened.

Social psychologists believe that self-concept plays an important role in social perception – the process to form impressions of others, and attribution – the explanations of own and others behaviour. Rotter (1954) argued that the expected outcome of an action, and the value we place on that outcome, determine much of our behaviour. For example, people with positive self-concept believe they will succeed at a task, are likely to behave in a manner, that will lead to success, while those who expect failure, are much more likely to bring it about, through their own actions. In a general theory of personality, he developed subsequently with two colleagues, Rotter designated variables, based on the ways that individuals, habitually think about their experiences. One of the most important was I-E, which distinguished 'internals,' who think of themselves as controlling events, from 'externals,' who view events as largely outside their control. Internal-external orientation has been found to affect a variety of behaviours and attitudes.

It is inevitable for all professionals providing services to clients, with relationship problems, to understand the process of development of self-concept or notions that define their clients behaviour, in particular, the comparisons with others. However, unconscious factors influence the behaviour as well. A person may be unaware of strong feelings about some issues and not so strongly about others.

According to some authors, knowing self is primarily a matter of applying social labels, in other words how others describe us. Mead (1934) argued that one's concept of self is, a reflection of the

> He had grown up in an elite family with abundance of resources. He got good education and worked abroad. He tried to set up his own business and was nearly successful, when he felt betrayed by his romantic partner. He committed suicide at the age of 41 years after struggling to come to grip with the loss of a relationship. He loved his mother but did not know how to deal with his father. He often had difficulty talking to him. He told him in no uncertain words, that he would rather live his own life, but there were times when he felt uncertain about his attitude towards his father as well.

opinions expressed by significant others. Festinger (1954) suggests that social comparison plays a vital role in developing self-concept and self-esteem. What these findings suggests is, that persons generally have little objective knowledge of their own strengths and weaknesses and generally it is a second hand knowledge acquired, through others' assessment of what we are that generally shapes our self-image. The remarks of people close to us are more significant in influencing our self-concept.

As Malitz (1960) pointed out, 'To find life reasonably satisfying, you must have an adequate and realistic self-image that you can live with … . You must have a self that you can trust and believe in … . You must have a self that you can feel free to express creatively, rather than to hide or cover up. You must have a self that corresponds to reality … .'

It brings out the crucial importance of self-concept, the reasons for its distortions and the resulting consequences. For example, a person having no trust in self abilities, will be unsure of self efforts, thus leaving everything to chance. S/he may or may not succeed, but even if s/he does, will not see it as a direct result of self efforts, s/he will attribute it to chance. Further, a person who can't trust self, is likely to mistrust others. Malitz emphasizes the importance of not being ashamed of self. For example, a person does not chose the physical appearance, colour of skin or caste category, but s/he has a choice, how to feel about it. And lastly self-concept should be based on facts not on speculation.

Different Facets of Self-Concept

Physical Features

Physical aspect of self-concept is easier to form as the facts about height, colour of skin, facial features, weight and other physical features are concrete and can be observed and measured. The interpretation of physical features to form a positive or negative self-concept is crucial. The social context, plays a vital role in influencing the self-concept. Cultural preferences of physical features in males and females provide the framework for development of a positive or negative concept. In the Indian sub continent, a fair skin, a lean physical structure of medium height, with regular facial features is the preferred framework for females to be classified as beautiful. Many female children, not conforming to the prescription, face adverse comments from all sources, right from the childhood and develop a negative framework to look at self. These children are likely to develop an inferiority complex. This can lead to development of a negative self-image. A person with negative self-image, is likely to be shy in meeting new persons. The physical features of persons, thus influence the self-concept. It can override other qualities, such as mental abilities and social skills. The reasons for the powerful influence of physical features are, it has sexual undertones, is invariably noted and commented upon. During the childhood experiences in particular, the physical features play a very crucial role in leaving a very lasting impression on the mind of the child about self. The peer group is brutal in its assessment and makes each member aware of it.

Mental Abilities

Mental or intellectual aspects of a person are not easily discernable, as they take time to develop and manifest themselves in behavioural responses. The relationship between intelligence and personality is rather vague. A common person is guided by social labels, the others are unsure about intellectual abilities of others. The success at different stages of schooling is one indicator, to notice mental abilities. The general impression about a child's mental abilities is formed by assessing the child to grasp simple commands and the ability to communicate in a coherent manner. A quick witted child is evaluated higher and gets a positive feedback, strengthening the self-confidence. A child with communication difficulties, is considered shy and/or slow and is negatively valued and commented upon leaving a lasting impression on the child's mind. The cultural milieu, plays a significant part in giving rise to false impressions in evaluating mental abilities. In the Indian subcontinent, female children are presupposed to have lower mental abilities, compared to males, a notion not supported by facts. Female children as a rule have fared better at all levels, including professional education, but have been structurally excluded, earlier to establish male domination. However, not many female children know these facts and accept social evaluation and develop a low image about their mental abilities. Similar preconceived notions, about mental abilities have been applied to caste, rural and tribal groups. The social construction of self is culture specific and biased. The general assessment of mental abilities, does not however take primacy in forming self-concept of the individual, as is the case with physical features and other social factors.

Emotional Aspect

Emotional aspect of a person refers to, the ability to control emotions when faced with challenges, adverse and demanding situations. Every day traits are calm, anger, fear and anxiety in handling different situations in life. Freudian formulation of emotions is rooted in early child hood experiences, supported by Bowlby's attachment theory. The emotions have more to do with how the child was handled by the parents and other care givers. Yet, the social construction plays role. For example, social images of women are more emotional and caring than men and as such women may develop a similar notion about self. Men are supposed to be fearless and should refrain from showing emotions in public in particular. Male children, therefore, are expected to learn these lessons early, to avoid public criticism, develop a positive image, to control their emotions, particularly fear and anxiety. A person's self-concept is affected in an environment which evokes constant fear. It can become a phobia, e.g. fear of height, closed space, water, or darkness, etc. Fear of authority or strangers can similarly become a phobia, greatly affecting a person's self-concept and behaviour. This aspect is experienced by the person and also noted and commented by others, and affects the self-concept in a big way.

Social Aspect

The social aspect of self-concept refers to the ability to form relationships. Personality traits play a significant part in a person's ability to form and manage relationships, particularly with people outside the family. Prescott Lecky (1994), described personality as a system of ideas, all of which must seem to be consistent with each other. All new situations and relationships, become stressful for some while others enjoy these opportunities. A person becomes conscious of handling others as s/he grows. A number of factors contribute to the development of traits or ideas, giving a person overall rating of outgoing, meaning warm, open and flexible, or reserve which means rather evasive, cautious and rigid, in ones' approach to others. Early childhood experiences in the family, over-all socialization based on cultural prescriptions and exposure to particular social environment plays a crucial part in developing these traits. For example rural persons particularly females, brought up in a traditional family environment, develop a severe handicap in handling relations with others, particularly males. Similarly, language abilities and socialization about mannerism or graceful handling of self in public places, plays an important part in developing a positive self-concept. Education, caste and class backgrounds, play a vital part in the development of conceptual images, about social roles and status, there by significantly contributing to, self-construction in India. Caste hierarchies are fairly well defined and are still adhered to particularly in rural areas. The arrangements are very specific about inter-dining and intermarrying obligations, and other aspects of interaction with others. Similarly, class boundaries although not so well defined, yet are fairly well understood and influence interaction with others. The elite service class persons, professionals of different kinds and corporate executives, all consider themselves superior to layman and other class of people, and as such it influences their interaction pattern and expectations from others. Similarly political elites, landowning classes and big business families possess a higher self-image, and usually expect a more subservient attitude from others. Gender categories are also well defined and carry a system of hierarchy cutting across all caste and classes. A female is expected to accept a subservient attitude towards males both in her parent's family and later in the family of her husband. In Indian culture, also in other countries of the Indian subcontinent, husband have a total control over his wife, thereby significantly affecting the self-concept of the female, right from the childhood. For example, even a highly educated female, would seek permission from her husband to take up a career outside the family. As in other aspects of self-constructions, female self-construction is more rigidly and efficiently carried out, by social institutions including family and religion. Ironically, the social construction of a female self-concept is so successfully done, that even education including professional education is unable to alter it. Further, some sections believe it has resulted in maintaining the stability of family relationships, in the subcontinent. The argument is based on, that a clear understanding of status and role leads to its acceptance, irrespective of its adverse effects for the females. The public opinion plays a vital part in constructing self, in conformity with social norms. A person from a lower caste faces oppression, if s/he refuses to observe, a subservient attitude towards higher caste persons. The stress is far greater for a female and a person coming from a deprived social background.

Theories of Self-Concept

Self-concept is influenced by our sense of identity. Two things have powerful effects on our self-concept:

1. The opinions and judgments other people make of us, it is also known as Reflected Appraisal.
2. Social comparison – perceptions of the ways in which you are similar to and different from other people.

Reflected Appraisal

Reflected appraisal refers to, evaluation and appraisal of a person by others, particularly significant others. In other words, self-concept is formulated on the basis of social labels, provided by family members, teachers, friends and peer group members, etc. and later work colleagues and so on. People are so fond of praising and criticizing others, based on impressions or facts, and treating them accordingly. A positive person is treated with love and respect and is generally rewarded generously. On the other hand a negative person is rejected and punished. The reflection of positive or negative social reception, real or illusionary, helps in developing a similar self-concept and self-esteem in due course. The source of forming self-concept in this case is reflected appraisal.

Social Comparison

Social comparison influences the self-concept when others refer to, the group based on caste, language, place of birth and/or religion as a homogenous group possessing certain characteristics. For example, higher castes have a higher intellectual capacity and are superior to other human beings or people from Kerala or Bihar have such and such characteristics, or Muslims are generally very inflammable and violent. These views are comparing different groups of persons and therefore, generate stereotypes, or mental images of persons. The views thus provide the basis for forming notions about self as well as others.

Human beings are prone to holding firm opinions, not based on facts. For example, it is impossible to educate such and such category of persons, or only men can hold positions of power effectively. The degree of passion involved, separate a casual remark from a firmly held belief. These beliefs affect our interactions with others. An attitude may be defined as a readiness to respond in a favourable or unfavourable manner, to a particular object or class of object (Oskamp, 1977). The definition makes it clear, that the firmly held belief, both positive and negative, impacts the response of a person. The word attitude has been defined by Gordon Allport (1937) as 'a mental and neural state of readiness, organized through experience, exerting a directive or dynamic influence upon the individual's response, to all objects and situations, it comes across.' Bogardus (1925) defines an attitude as ' a tendency to act towards or against some environmental factor, which becomes thereby a positive or negative value', while Muzafer Sherif (1936) uses the word to refer to 'the main body of what is socialized in man'. In Sherif's definition, attitudes are the main constituents of the ego. Some authors have concluded that attitude and opinion are practically synonymous terms, but while opinions often reflect attitudes, it is evident that what a person says does not always corresponds with what he does (Brown, 1967). As quoted by Brown remarked, 'sometimes who you are sounds so loudly in my ears, that I cannot hear, what you say (Brown, 1967). The concept of attitude postulates a hypothetical mental structure, in order to explain what goes on between stimulus and response, what causes the stimulus to be experienced, the way it is experienced and acted upon. The behaviour is based on, what experience has taught the individual, to see the environment.

Gergen and Gergen, (1981) further elaborated the three aspects associated with any such action, the cognitive part implying the thinking involved, the feelings part and finally, the action part. The root cause of prejudices is, culturally held beliefs, made part of thinking through socialization; (a) to create a self-identity for a group different and superior or inferior to other groups, (b) to maintain a position of animosity or friendliness towards such groups or in other words favour or disfavour interaction with the group or a member. It is quite common to find such beliefs based on caste, religion, ethnicity and class. The other sources of such beliefs are; (a) experiences and conceptualizations (b) education, and (c) local environment such as, tribal, rural, small town or a metropolitan city.

Concepts

Self-Awareness

Self-awareness refers to the degree of consciousness about thinking, feelings and actions. Freudian theory argued that a person suppresses unpleasant thoughts, feelings and actions into the unconscious state, to avoid these. A person therefore is unable to explain self-behaviour causing stress and social rejection. Cambell et al. (1996) have developed a scale to measure self-concept clarity (scc) defined as the extent to which self-beliefs are clearly and confidently defined, internally consistent, and stable and examine its correlation with self-esteem.

Self-Esteem

Self-esteem refers to the evaluation of self, based on reflection or social comparison. For example, a person rated as intelligent, hard working, and stable, has a high self-esteem. Persons born in rich, high caste families, have high self-esteem, whereas poor and low caste females have a low self-esteem. As we said earlier, some part of this understanding comes from descriptions of significant others or people who one considers important and some part of this from, social comparison. The deprivations are powerful factors in influencing self-understanding and self-assessment. Physical deformities in particular, can have significant impact in lowering self-esteem. Similarly social deprivations, resulting from race, caste, religious and regional discriminations, play a vital role in negative self-assessment and low self-esteem.

Self-Respect

Self-respect is a concept closely related to self-esteem, it refers to a self-belief, to evaluate behaviours or actions, categorized out of bond, as these would lower, self-respect. For example, begging or revealing their poverty, economic weakness to strangers.

Self-Confidence

Self-confidence refers to the internally consistent feelings about self-beliefs. Self-esteem is positively correlated with self-confidence. M.W. Eysenck and Calvo (1992) elaborated the idea of cognitive-processing efficiency, to account for the effects of trait anxiety, on performance. M.W. Eysenck and Calvo drew a key distinction between performance effectiveness and processing efficiency. Effectiveness refers to an objectively measurable level of performance, such as the percentage of questions, answered correctly on a test. Efficiency refers to the ratio between effectiveness and the amount of effort needed, to attain the criterion level of performance. According to M.W. Eysenck and Calvo (1992), anxiety impairs processing efficiency more than it impairs performance effectiveness, thereby leaving open whether performance is actually impaired or not on a given occasion. Highly anxious individuals are hypothesized to be less efficient but can compensate by expending additional effort on the task. This understanding can help in reducing anxiety and improving the self-confidence levels but the fact remains that low or poor self-esteem can vitally affect self-confidence. Another correlate of low self-esteem and lack of self-confidence is, person with low self-confidence will perceive others, as superior, and it affects their interaction and expectations from others. On the other hand, people with higher self-confidence, perceive others more objectively. However, if their confidence is distorted, it can affect their interactions and expectations as well. A distorted notion may lead to an inferiority or superiority complex. Inferiority complex is a distorted feeling of inferiority to others. Such feelings may be real or imagined. It is often subconscious, and is thought to drive afflicted individuals to overcompensate, resulting either in spectacular achievement or extreme antisocial behaviour, or both. Unlike a normal feeling of inferiority, which can act as an incentive for achievement, an inferiority complex is an advanced state of discouragement, often resulting in a retreat from difficulties.

Classical Adlerian Psychology makes a distinction between primary and secondary inferiority feelings (see Makari, 2008). A primary inferiority feeling is rooted in the early childhood experiences of weakness, helplessness and dependency, developed through comparisons with older siblings. A secondary inferiority feeling relates to, an adult's experience of inability, to reach an unconscious, fictional final goal of subjective security and success.

The concept of personal power and positional power, is helpful in understanding the secondary inferiority feeling. Personal power refers to a person's current characteristics, such as intelligence, education, social skills, emotional quotient, etc. leading to self-confidence. Positional power refers to, the power that emanates from a position, a person occupies, administrative head of a unit, a political office. The secondary inferiority complex comes into play, when the personal power of the person is, lower than the positional power. In other words the person is not comfortable with the positional power assigned.

The complex is caused by parental attitudes and consequent upbringing of children, physical defects including speech problems, lower intelligence levels and social discriminations based on race, caste, religion, sex, or economic status, etc. It may lead to withdrawal from social contacts or excessive attention seeking behaviour, criticism of others, excessive obedience, and worry.

Superiority complex refers to a subconscious neurotic mechanism of compensation, developed by the individual, as a result of inferiority complex. Those exhibiting the superiority complex commonly project their feelings of inferiority onto others. Behaviours include, an exaggeration of self-worth, high expectations from self and others, the persistent attempt to correct others, vanity, extravagant style of dressing, excessive pride, sentimentalism and affected exaltation, snobbishness, a tendency to discredit other's opinions, forcefulness aimed at dominating and cruelty, etc.

Social aloofness, daydreaming and isolation could also be associated with the superiority complex, to evade the fear of failure related to the feelings of inadequacy to face the real world. Superiority and inferiority are often found together, as the different expressions of the same pathology and the two complexes can exist within the same individual.

Self and Others

The phenomenon of dealing with others is key to managing relationships. According to several studies, behaviour of a person reveals the motivation behind the action. A person who is taking care of self-needs in all interactions, is termed as self-centered, while a person who takes care of both self and others needs is considered a balanced person, and the person who gives primacy to others is called, others-oriented. A self-centered person, will be deficient in all human relationships. S/he would pay scant attention to expectations and feelings of others. People who are others-oriented, and make others happy at the cost of self, in all their relationships are liked by all. A balanced person is, neither self-centered nor totally others-oriented to the point of self-negation, will handle others more objectively. Though as pointed out earlier, early socialization particularly parental handling of the child, the experiences of sibling behaviour and other childhood experiences, make significant impact on behaviour. Yet, it is difficult to predict, strategies one would adopt as an adult, in dealing with others. How self-centered or others-oriented, a person would be and why, is still difficult to answer, with any degree of consistency, since human behaviour remains so unpredictable even now. Behaviour variations occur due to a number of factors.

Let us now consider indicators helpful in assessing a person, on self-others continuum. The first is the communication pattern of a person. A self-oriented person tries to dominate all communications. Over communication, tone of delivery and the content when analysed reflect self-orientation. Lack of awareness about needs and difficulties of others is another indicator of self-orientation. For example, a husband and wife come back home, from work place. The husband expects the wife to serve food promptly. Similarly many teenagers force their parents, to buy expensive clothes, etc. for them, despite knowing full well that their parents cannot afford it.

Going late in a meeting, not allowing others to speak, parking in such a way that you are blocking the road, playing loud music in the house or in your car, making people wait without a valid reason, not answering deliberately, when addressed, are some other day to day behaviours, indicating a self-orientation. A completely reverse behaviour in all these situations, is indicative of others-orientation. For example, a person would never go in for a long narration, would communicate briefly, make sure others get a chance to speak, would be very reluctant to spend any resources on meeting individual needs.

A perusal of written records such as letters, reports or diary entries can also reveal self-centered approach in the form of several references to self in different places rather than a more objective account of events and persons. For example overemphasis on self-achievement in a report, and exaggerating mention of problems relating to self rather than giving a fair space to knowing about others welfare. And finally the, concept of self actualization.

Concept of Self Actualization: Rogers believed that all human beings have a basic desire to achieve what they can, based on their potential. When this becomes a reality self actualization becomes a reality too. He also believed that every human being can do so. This is an idealistic notion, in reality creating a dilemma for many as they are neither aware of their actual potential nor the goals relevant to their happiness or needs. Further, self actualization or a strong motivation to achieve goals happen in the tune with the environment, as Rogers stated, which is where the dilemma becomes real, as the environment around is beyond the control of individual in most cases, if not as a universal rule. Herzberg therefore identified the factors as the essential requirement in his two factor theory of hygiene and environment (see Herzberg, 1987). And as Maslow (1943) suggested that self actualization is a human need but its importance is varied among individuals. He emphasized the importance of basic needs and its fulfillment for any motivation to become possible. The clarity that Rogers provide about environment is significant in understanding relationships. According to Rogers for self actualization to happen the environment around a person should provide the three basics, openness, acceptance or unconditional regard and empathy that is being understood by others. Social workers are able to provide these in their dealings with their clients to help them, but fail to modify their client's environments in their personal as also organizational settings.

To conclude therefore, help persons to become fully functional, the five characteristics according to Rogers will be required,

1. *Open to experience:* This refers to capacity to accept both positive and negative emotional experiences, and the need to understand the dynamics of negative experiences rather than escaping from these or to resort to ego defence mechanisms.
2. *Existential living:* This refers to living in present with different experiences as they occur in life, avoiding referring to past or worrying about future.
3. *Trust feeling:* This refers to capacity to trust and be trusted by others.
4. *Creativity:* To be able to develop alternative thinking and go beyond the comfort zone, not play safe all the time. This requires the ability to adjust and change to seek new experiences.
5. *Fulfilled life:* The most crucial part is to be happy and satisfied with present life, and yet seeking to change it, if and only if needed, not as a hobby (see Mcleod, 2007).

In India the self actualization/achievement of a person is valued more highly if s/he has contributed to the achievement of the group meaning family, team or organization, along with his/her own. In Western culture self achievement is more individual oriented. The importance of cultural context in influencing self-concept is obvious. A balanced conceptual clarity and a tendency to remain open and positive, is more effective in managing relationships, and at the same time achieving personal freedom and goals.

5

Family Relations

Family is a universal institution and plays a vital part in the socialization of children, and in meeting a number of other needs. The family and its relationships are considered sacred in many societies. Change in the nature of family relationship, throw up a lot of controversies and debate. As Oberoi (1993) in her study *Family, Kinship and Marriage in India* pointed out, a critical interrogation of family may be considered a violation of personal freedom, where most cherished cultural values are nurtured and reproduced. It is important to remember here that group's influence on members has also been researched by a number of studies (see Cooley, 1909; Mead, 1934; Sherif, 1966; Newcomb, 1943; Bales, 1950; Cartwright and Zander, 1968). There are several types of relationships commonly found in a family. Three sets of these relationships are considered here as primary;

1. The spousal relationship,
2. The parent-child relationship, and
3. The sibling relationships.

The Spousal Relationship

The spousal relations can be defined, as the relationship between two adults living together for meeting their sexual needs. It is the core relationship, which gives birth to family. Earlier it was common belief, that among the spouses one would be a male and the other a female or that all families would be heterosexual. Now in some countries a small number of families are composed of spouses of the same sex. In all countries relationships, between spouses is governed by both custom and law. Such matters, as age at marriage, the procedure, the grounds for terminating the relationship, etc. is generally determined by law and/or customs. In the case of India and other countries in the subcontinent, it is still governed more by custom than law. As Maine (1972) in his famous study *Ancient Law* pointed out 'the movement of the progressive societies has hitherto been a movement from status to contract.' Yet, in developing world, the tradition continues to dominate. In order to understand the nature of the spousal relationship, its structure, stability or fragility, common problems and issues it faces, and how it resolves these, and more importantly its impact on other relationships in the family, all dimensions of this relationship needs to be explored. Culture plays an important role in determining, the self-concept and consequently, plays an important part, in determining the spousal and all other relationships in the family.

Marriage is the basis of spousal relationship in many societies even now, though in some societies, laws governing spousal relations, marriage is no longer considered necessary for starting such relations. It is called a live-in relationship and is similar to marital relationship. Though some sections of the society may still frown upon such relationships, but many countries have accepted it, including India, for granting legitimacy to children, inheritance, and compensation for divorce. Social norms have for centuries laid down guidelines to govern the spousal relationship in the subcontinent. There are significant differences, among different cultures, in structuring spousal relationship. The survival rates of the relationship differ significantly, yet in some respects, there are significant similarities among different societies. Nature and functions of family significantly influences the spousal relationship. In collectivist societies stability of family is accorded preference over individual well-being. Marriage is therefore seen as an alliance between two families rather than two individuals. The continuance of spousal relationship becomes a social obligation and is socially considered a matter beyond individual preferences. Elaborate social rules and customs are, therefore, evolved to structure the spousal relationship.

Though modern societies are striving to make it a relationship between two partners with equal rights or in other words, make it horizontal in nature, but so far it has remained male dominated, in almost all societies. It is a vertical relationship, where one person has a higher position compared to the other. In majority of cases the male spouse is placed higher in the spousal relationship.

According to Maine (1972), the earliest form of family was a patriarchal family, which was like a corporation existing in perpetuity. The patriarchal family, according to Maine 'was a group of men and women, children and slaves … . All connected together by common subjection, to the Paternal power of the chief of the household. The senior most male has absolute power, including that of life and death, over all family members (Oberoi, 1993). In India as also in many countries of the Indian subcontinent it continues to be so, particularly in the rural and tribal areas.

Another similarity found in spousal relationship in many societies, is that the female spouse is younger than the male spouse. The age difference is usually 3–5 years, but it may go as high as 8–10 years or more, in some cases. It is also an unstated rule to make sure, that the bride has a lower height and weight than the groom. It is also customary in many societies, to maintain male superiority in education and occupation. In other words female spouse is, usually less educated and if she is working, her professional status should be lower than that of the male. These arrangements provide internal consistency to self-concept of spouses.

Cultural and Social Norms

The cultural influence on spousal relationship is considerable. In many cultures, the bride has to leave her parents home, to start the spousal relationship, residing either in the house of the groom's parents or in a separate household. In very few cases in some areas, it is the male who goes out to live with the family of the bride. The residence has a significant influence, on the spousal relationship in India, as Karve (1993) pointed out, the joint family in northern India, is a status group where husband, wife, parents-in-law, daughter-in-law have each a definite place assigned to them in relation to others. The work which each has to do, the pleasures each will enjoy, are more or less fixed by convention (Karve, 1993). Definite patterns are set up for female spouse behaviour with these relations. The female spouse has to contend with a whole new set of relationships, in an altogether different context, with which she is not familiar with. Coping with a new situation, exerts a lot of psychological pressure on a person. The pressure increases when the response is evaluated by a number of people, and the failure could bring humiliation. It can affect the self-confidence of the person. At times games are played in families, to just do that, to undermine the position of the new entrant, in the group. The family socialization process usually prepares the females, to accept these situations patiently.

The case is a good example of the new entrant put in her place, in this case rather brutally. This happened more, due to the self-centered nature of the male personality. However, the problem lies with the parental family, which seldom comes to the help of the girl.

The social norms play a vital role in shaping the expectations of the spouses. In the developing societies like India, Pakistan, Bangladesh, Nepal and Sri Lanka, etc. the spousal relationship is completely one-sided. The male spouse is given total control, over the female spouse. Expectations of a male spouse are limitless, creating a very difficult situation for the female spouse. For example a woman must stand up and cover her head and face, if she is in the same room as her parents-in-law, and the brothers and cousins of the parents-in-law. The mode of greetings for these relations for the women is to bow low to the ground and place her head on their feet (Karve, 1993, p. 61). The situation has changed somewhat in the urban educated families, but nevertheless the one-sided nature of spousal relationship is very much in place. In recent times exposure to mass media and other factors, like education has increased the scope of changes in the rural families as well.

Education

The nature of spousal relations is significantly influenced by education of both the spouses, and the significant others living with them, such as parents of either spouse. The enabling role of education, in making persons more prepared for accepting changes, has been documented by many studies. For example, education of spouses makes them amenable to changes, in their

> In a recent case, a traditional well-off business class family married their daughter in another rich business class family. The daughter aged 22 had received education up to school leaving stage. Within a year of the marriage the bride had to be hospitalized. She was so traumatized that she was unable to recognize anyone. She is still undergoing treatment and has now shifted to her parents' house.
> What caused the trauma?
> What can the girl in question do?
> Is she responsible for what happened?
> Will she go back to her husband's home?
> Will the girl's parent want to send her back?
> Is domestic violence accepted by girl's family?
> Is the domestic violence accepted by society?
> If so, WHY?

interactions within and outside the family. Gap between the education levels of the spouses, can create difficulties for both. As a general rule, greater the variations between the backgrounds of the two persons, the larger are the chances of relationship presenting difficulties. Education and resultant change in occupation and social status change, poses many challenges for the first generation learners. If both spouses are not prepared educationally to handle these challenges, it can have significant implication for spousal relations, parenting styles and parent-child relations. Education has impacted spousal relations significantly. Professional education of females in particular influences the spousal relations significantly. The spousal relationship in the urban areas, have undergone change, but its hierarchal nature is nevertheless in place. The rights of male, as head of the family, have been considerably changed by the educated younger generation. However, the male domination of spousal relationship cutting across all classes, castes and religion continues.

Work Status

Human relationships are a reflection of mutual dependence of persons on each other, as pointed out earlier. Social structure in India has placed the female spouse, historically in a dependent position in the family, by denying her a working status. It has only recently been realized, that female played and continue to play a significant role in the economic well-being of the family. Among educated families in India, a working wife is considered more helpful, as it enhances the family status considerably. An independent financial status of females, therefore, is helpful in creating the possibility of a more balanced spousal relation. The work status of women, therefore, can influence the spousal relation significantly, as it makes her much less dependent on the other party. In case of white collar educated women, it also provides them a network of support, in handling various crises, which is not accessible to full-time housewives. It also adds to her power of negotiating, a better deal with the other party. The self-concept of a female is bound to change, with her education and work status, which in itself is, a major factor in influencing any relationship. The attitude of the male partner towards work status of spouse is a significant factor in determining the spousal relations. The history of work status of spouse, i.e. she was employed, when relations commenced or took up employment after the commencement of relations began, and the male spouse reaction, should be analysed carefully to understand the current state of relations. The work status should be a major focus in analysing spousal relations and considering change strategies.

The Class Background

The class background of the spouses plays a significant role in shaping the behavioural responses of the parties entering the relationship, and other members in the family. For example, persons brought up in an upper class family, exhibit a certain degree of sophistication, in handling spousal relations. For example, exercising a higher degree of self-control in public places is considered important to avoid unpleasant situations. Showing due respect to others, avoiding public conflicts and keeping a reasonable distance in relations with others are few more behavioural patterns expected of upper classes. Intimate behaviour is considered a private matter, and is not meant for public display. Such sophistication and mannerism is generally not found in other classes. Women in the upper class families are more educated, more confident and are likely to have more skills of handling their relationships in all contexts. Similarly, persons from a middle class family background have rather conservative values, and find it difficult to accept new behavioural patterns, which are significantly different from their own. Different professional backgrounds, such as business class families, land-owning families having agriculture as the main source of income, and service class families, tend to have different traditions of family relationship. The relations between spouses are likely to be more hierarchal in the first two categories than in the last. The females may be more educated in the service class families and so on. There are significant differences in the manner of dressing, food preferences and other household matters as well. The spousal relations of persons coming from different class or professional background are therefore likely to be more problematic than where the spouses are from the same background.

Personality Factors

As is well known no two individuals are alike, for example, children born and brought up in the same family, think, feel and act in different situations. It is not uncommon to find, some children doing well in academic and professional growth, while others not. Children from the same family differ in their capacity to handle relationships within and outside the family. In spousal relations, the personality traits of spouses play a vital role. Some persons click well together and some don't. Clicking together when analysed, will reveal traits of personalities of both persons, complementing each other. While in case of conflict in spousal relations the personality traits are very diverse, making it difficult to live together. As the definition of traits suggests, a trait refers to consistent behaviour patterns. However, the difficulties arise in determining personality characteristics or traits and matching these, to predict better relations. For example, if we go by Cattell's personality traits, we cannot predict whether persons having high self-sufficiency will go well together or where one with a high and other with a low score and high group dependence, will relate better. To explain further, a person scoring high on self-sufficiency factor is likely to be resourceful and prefer taking his/her own decisions. On the contrary, a person scoring low on the factor likes to be group-oriented and prefers to follow rather than lead. Now an observer of human behaviour will predict that two persons, one having a high score on self-sufficiency and the other having a low score, will click together, as one will assert and the other will follow. Given the social and cultural background in the Indian subcontinent, probably one will prefer males to score high on self-sufficiency and woman to score low on the same factor to make the spousal relations go smoothly, in keeping with the traditional social norms. In fact that is how exactly the mate selection is done by parents, in India, to ensure that the spousal and in fact the entire range of family relations work smoothly, by ensuring an ever accommodating female. Well to be academically correct, it can work equally well if we pair a high scoring female with a low scoring male as far as their own relationship is concerned. The only problem is that invariably this is not rated socially high in the patriarchal societies of today.

This was just an example to suggest, how the personality factors can particularly be relevant in analysing relationships along with the social context. To strive to change one and leave the other unchanged create discontent. People with high anxiety levels, have a general tendency to get easily upset, are likely to face more problems in their relationships, than those who are considered more emotionally stable. Emotional intelligence is a key factor in smooth relationships.

Problems in Spousal Relationship

All persons face difficulties in negotiating new relationships, particularly in situations, where there is no role clarity. The spousal relations, for a majority of persons in India and other countries of the subcontinent, mark the beginning of a new chapter in their life. Many of them have no idea how to handle it and hence are likely to be a bit vague and confused in their early responses.

A good way to look at the problem areas in spousal relations is to look at significant factors influencing the spousal relations discussed earlier. For example, if the spouses are from different cultural backgrounds such as different religions, caste, linguistic regions, etc. they are likely to face greater difficulties in spousal relations. Different cultural and family background of spouses makes it difficult for them to anticipate, what others expect from them, hence leaving a wide gap in fulfilling expectations of all stakeholders. If the gaps continue to widen, the relations are likely to run into rough weather. For example, some cultures allow greater freedom of expression of love and intimacy whereas others don't. Similarly some cultures and classes are more respectful to each other in spousal relations, while others like to show the male superiority in more naked terms. The different backgrounds leading to different kind of socialization and role expectations, can therefore lead to a lot of misunderstandings between the spouses.

As mentioned earlier, spouses having a large gap in their education background are likely to face problems in spousal relations. The modern education in particular induces a number of expectations among the spouses, which are different from the traditional role expectations provided by the socialization process in the family. The key to any relations, is the expectations one brings to a relationship and the level and frequency of their fulfillment in the relationship. If these expectations are not met, the relations can deteriorate and become negative in due course. It is particularly problematic, when the spouses are not only highly educated but both are working full-time.

The status of families giving away the bride and the status of families receiving the wife is brought out by many studies (see Madan, T.N. 1993; Sharma, Ursula, 1993). The female self-concept in particular are structured to help them to have low expectation level or no expectations at all, in the spousal relationship to survive. The greater awareness brought about by education and work status, therefore, contradicts the earlier messages. The new generation of spouses is undergoing a period of relearning in the new situation, particularly in the urban areas. The male spouses have now to learn newer ways of sharing power with their spouses and children as well. In urban educated families the communication skills of partners, play a vital role in negotiating problems. Lack of communication skills or a complete break-down of communication between partners can produce more problems in spousal relation.

A survey of studies of factors causing problems in marital relations brings out the difference in problems faced by couples in western and Indian cultural situations. In USA and other developed countries the marriage is based upon the idea of romantic love. Affective individualism has become the major influence. Couples are expected to develop mutual affection, based on personal attraction and compatibility, as a basis for entering into marriage relationships. The emphasis, therefore, is on personal satisfaction, rather than any social obligation to get and remain married. The problems therefore, in marriage relations arise more on account of personal dissatisfaction of one or both parties, rather than social factors, where other actors such as in-laws, or inability to give birth to a male child, play or may play a role. But in educated families in the urban areas, the incompatibility of spouses is, now emerging as a major factor, in creating strains in spousal relations in the Indian sub continent. In middle and lower middle class families, the economic hardships are also responsible for creating stresses in spousal relationships, along with alcoholism and drug use.

However, the singlemost important factor creating problems in all relationships including spousal relations, is the severe differences in personality factors or where both the parties differ a great deal in their likes and dislike. Personality traits refer to a consistent tendency to behave or respond to a given environmental factor. A person reacts to a particular smell, food, a behaviour, or a crisis in a particular way, which could be similar or different from his or her spouse. The degree of similarity or difference in such traits is also a big factor in causing problems in spousal relationships. The wider the differences, the greater are the problems both in frequency and severity. The problem gets confounded, as it is difficult to change the personality traits for common persons. It is easier to match, for example, the age factor, the religion, caste and economic factor but very difficult to match the personality factors, in terms of how severe the likes and dislikes are and how far these are likely to change over the years. It is also equally well known that people are quite capable of hiding their true characteristics and to project a different kind of trait in a given situation, if they are deliberately trying to do so. At times a person can do it unconsciously as well, since the factors governing his/her response are hidden in the unconscious mind of the person. We have argued in our theoretical formulation of relationship that the position of a person, on self-other continuum is an important factor in relationships of all kinds, and that extreme self-orientation is likely to be a major handicap in building and maintaining relationships.

Parent-Child Relationship

Parent-child relations are important, as they leave a lasting impact on the personal well-being of the children (see Bowlby, 1969, 1973). Many studies have reported the significance of early childhood experiences, but as we pointed out earlier, it is still difficult to arrive at any conclusive understanding about these. For example, some studies suggest that young children may face difficulties in relationship, if spouses get divorced (see Peterson and Nicholas, 1986; Amato and Booth, 1996), yet others suggest that children brought up in institutional arrangements, other than family may not show any signs of development problems. Yet, the development inputs provided to the children by the parents/care givers, are considered significant for their future personality development. There is, for example, sufficient data from studies, documenting the link between parenting styles and children's capacity to handle relations. As a psychiatrist puts it rather succinctly, the problem generally lies with parental anxiety and not with children. It has only recently been realized in India, for example, the female children historically have been provided far less developmental inputs such as nutrition, health, education and recreation, than the male children, as part of parental anxiety to control them, resulting in a glaring gender gap (Government of India, 2007–2008). As Reimer (1971) pointed out, the age at which children dropout from school, largely determined whether they will work with their hands or with their minds, and what compensation and other benefits they will get. It is, therefore not surprising to find that it was parents themselves, who violated the basic rights of their own female children and censured the future of these children, without giving them a chance to have a say in the matter. The general understanding that parents are likely to safeguard the interest of their children may not be true in all cases and is subject to conditions. As we pointed out earlier, the male head of the family earlier enjoyed a total control over the children. The relationship, therefore, was very hierarchal in nature. In recent times, however, the hierarchal nature of parent-child relationship has considerably changed, particularly in developed countries. In India and other countries in the subcontinent, the parent-child relations have witnessed some change, more so in the urban areas particularly in higher classes. Education in particular has played a vital part in changing this relationship, since the younger generation is, generally more educated than their parents. The other factor that has influenced parent-child relationship in the family is, the number of children and the nature of economic resources of the family. If the number of children is large and the economic resources are poor, the relationship is likely to continue to be hierarchal, simply because the children are not likely to get better education and remain dependent on the parents. It could get worse in some cases where the children take to work, or otherwise the parents, in particular father becoming violent as they become delinquent. However, the working children are able to exercise more freedom in their relationship with parents. A decline in number of children followed by a rise in the economic resources of the family, is likely to make it more horizontal, though the parental expectation to dominate the relationship remains in place. The parent's education and profession or in general class background, plays an important part in shaping the parent-child relationship. In recent years, the declining number of children in urban educated families has played a significant part in shaping the parent-child relations.

The underlying assumption of much of the studies about parent-child relationship, is that ineffective discipline and monitoring practices are prime determinants for younger children's antisocial behaviour (Patterson and Capaldi, 1991). The authoritarian parents' attempts to shape, control and evaluate the behaviour and attitudes of the child, in accordance with a set standard of conduct, usually an absolute standard (could be theologically motivated and formulated), without considering the need for a dialogue with child, can have disastrous results (Cowen and Hetherington, 1991). The debate continues regarding the magnitude and importance of parenting effects, on the development of children's externalizing behaviour problems, in spite of the evidence that environments (as well as genes) contribute to individual differences in behaviour. Research, however has indicated an association, between harsh physical discipline and child aggression and conduct problems (Deckard and Dodge, 1997). Carr and Durand (1985) identified that behaviour problems occur, such as aggression, tantrums, and self-injury, due to low level of adult attention and high level of task difficulty.

The education of parents makes them aware of better parenting styles, along with the changes taking place in the larger society. The values regarding dominance and use of force in general, in handling their relationships with children, have undergone a change in urban educated families. The possibility of expression of dissent on the part of children, increases with their education and exposure to outside world, through mass media. As the child grows up, the socializing process is increasingly affected by the actions of the persons outside the family. The teachers as well as the members of peer group, play a very important role. The growing child and adolescent become a member of many groups, and is influenced by its members and their values and behaviour. The reference group a person uses to evaluate self exerts more influence on the person. Parent-child relations are therefore affected significantly by the reference groups of both parents and children. If the reference group is the same, the relations would be cordial. If they differ to a great extent, the relations are likely to create more difficulties, as the values will differ significantly. It is important to note, that parent-child relationship goes through several stages.

The first stage lasts till the child is around 12 years old and is dependent on the parents, except in cases where the children start working at an early age. The relationship during this stage is generally dominated by parents, trying to control their young children to behave, in a culturally desirable manner, by making use of the resources of reward and punishment at their command (Kuppuswamy, 1961). However, in present day urban educated families with only one or two children, this trend to dominate the relations, is replaced by an anxiety to please the child or children in many families and therefore reward power is more in evidence than the punishment. This may result in, what is generally termed as a pampered ego, leading to more power with the children in parent-child relations. This trend is also closely linked with changes in the educated families between spouses. In families where dilution of patriarchal male heads' authority is reflected in the decision-making process, more soft strategies of child management are likely to be used.

In the next stage as the child enters the teen age, an attempt at self-control and self-regulation commences and it may be the beginning of a more contested stage of relationship. The parent-child relationship at this stage, undergoes a significant change. As we pointed out earlier, if the child has become more powerful in the first stage, the second stage would become more one sided. Relations will be dominated by the child, as s/he becomes more conscious of the power and discovers new avenues for pleasure seeking behaviour outside the family. The desire to experiment with the unknown, is very pronounced at this stage of the child's growth, hence the greater possibility of behaviour deviating from cultural norms.

The third stage of parent-child relations starts when child becomes an adult. At this stage the relations are far more difficult to predict, as they will vary according to a number of factors. Most important of them all, whether they continue to live together or they separate, to start a new family, and secondly the economic relations between the two. But the original pattern, child dominated or parent dominated, is likely to continue. In the rural areas, where the father generally controls the economic resources, the father continues to be the decision-maker, till a formal division of property is affected. If a formal division takes place and new families come up, the relations become distant and secondary, the authority of father declines and generally children start living their own life. Economic decline of parents, for example if they have not retained any land, or are not healthy enough to work, and have no savings or recurring income of their own, can cause their position to erode. The economic dependence can cause difficulties in relationship with grown up children having their own families, at this stage. The marriage of the adult children has a significant impact on the parent-child relations, in the third stage. In the urban areas, in both business and service class families, the adult male

Table 1

Factors Affecting Parent-Child Relations

Type of Education	*Higher/ Professional*	*School Level*	*Religious*	*No Schooling*
Case I				
Parents' Education	x/–	Primary	x	05
Child's Education	x/–	Middle	x	08
Case II				
Parents' Education	x	Graduate	x	15 plus
Child's Education	x	Post graduate	x	17 plus
Case III				
Parents' Education	x/–	x	x	10
Child's Education	x	x		17 plus
Number of Children	3 or more	2	1	
Economic Status	High Income Group	Higher Middle	Middle	Poor
Profession of Parents	Industrialist/ Business	Professional	Service	Labourer
Gender Gap between Parents	No Gap	Some Gap	Large Gap	–
Parent-child	Generation gap in values between parent and children			
Relations in the	Nil	Low	High	
Family Structure	Vertical	—	Horizontal	–

children, if they take control over the economic resources, after the retirement of the father, or even if he remains nominally associated with the business, may become dominant, if they stay together. If they move out to some other place or move out within the same city to take up separate residence, the relations become distant and secondary. Many factors still shape these relations and make these either positive or negative in the final analysis. If parents and children had positive relations during the first two stages, are both others-oriented and have sufficient resources to survive independently, the relations would continue to be positive and healthy. The parent-child relationships in the deprived families, are becoming worse and a lot of violence and hardships are common occurrence in the family.

The above factors (Table 1) play an important role in determining the self-concept and the others-orientation of the parents and children, and subsequently parent-child relations.

These factors when analysed together can help to understand the parent-child relations. Taking into account these factors, religious education of both parents and children, large size of the family, middle or lower income group, business, agriculture or blue collar service status, and a large gender gap between parents, are likely to produce a hierarchical relations and English medium school education of both parents and children, small family size, higher middle or middle class income group, professional or white collar service status, and no gender gap between parents, is likely to result in a horizontal relationship between parent and children.

In the first case scenario, the self-concept of both the parents and child is likely to be shaped by their religious education. For example, the father would consider himself as the head of the family and having the power to control the destiny of the children. The children accept the power of the father, and would consider their role as obedience to parents. In the second case the self-concept of both parents and children are likely to be determined by their educational and professional status. The father retains the concept of head and his role as guide to the destiny of the children, but the role performance is determined by a number of other factors. The children may or may not accept his role as guide, depending on a number of other factors, in particular the spousal relations and the respective reference groups to which they belong. In the third case, where child receives a different kind of education than the parents, the chances of a value gap between parents and the child may increase, though it may or may not lead to conflicts between them. Many other factors also play a role in giving rise to a conflict situation between parent-child relations. In a situation where both parents and child, have no education the parent-child relations are generally likely to be vertical in nature, although other factors such as work status of child, peer group of child and interaction among them in general, play an important role. Poverty situation by itself have an impact on parent-child relations. Studies have shown that poor parents are likely to make greater use of physical punishment in trying to control the behaviour of the child, than middle class parents (Waters and Crandall, 1964).

It is interesting to note that there are less chances of conflict between parent and child in the first case scenario than in the second. For the simple reason that in the first case the children are not likely to consider dissent as an option, because of a number of reasons, but primarily because of their religious education, as Giddens (1991) pointed out the morality induced by religious codes is far more effective and lasting than that provided by man-made laws. The gender gap between parents plays a big role in shaping parent-child relations. A wide gender gap between parents leads to a vertical relationship between spouses, and it also provides the base for the father to assume, the sole responsibility of controlling the behaviour of the children, and controlling their future. In situations of no gender gap between spouses, there is a greater possibility of a more democratic relationship between spouses and parenting styles are participatory and warm.

Parent-child relations will also be influenced by the values held by both parents and children as we pointed out earlier, and the similarity of educational background of parents and children, is an important factor in reducing the gap between the values held by them. Several studies have indicated the impact of social changes over the years creating a big gap between the values held by children and parents, resulting in relationship difficulties. The phenomenon is also known as 'generation gap'. The parent and children find themselves following a different set of values, almost in every aspect of their life, beginning from food and dress styles to participation in decision-making. The value changes in particular, play a big role in parent-child relations at stage two and three. The generation gap can result in partial or total breakdown in communication between parents and children. The children are determined to make a statement that they are capable of taking their own decisions and parents are trying to avoid unpleasant situations. However, this is not the only factor in creating problems in the parent-child relations, the spousal relations, the sibling relations and the peer group, are other important factors, in determining the value base, and particularly the other-orientation in the child. There is not enough evidence to provide any definitive relationship, between marital discord and its impact on the children, or absence of a parent, on the personality of the child, but these situations are likely to have an impact, on the parent-child relations. Poor relations between spouses, particularly, use of violence and aggressive behaviour in general, can have negative impact on the child. Such behaviour pollutes the whole of the family environment and all members are affected by it. It can cause depression and severely undermine the self-concept and self-confidence of a child. To conclude, parents influence the children by what they say, what they do and what they don't do.

Magana et al. (2006) lists four different kinds of parent-child relationships based on how parents and children act with each other. The type of relationships are termed as secure, avoidant, ambivalent and disorganized.

1. *Secure Relationships:* A child feels secure in this relationship if confident that parent will be there to support when needed. S/he knows the kind of behaviour to expect from them. This relationship is built around the consistent loving and caring behaviour of parents. A secure child will generally have good relationship with others.
2. *Avoidant Relationships:* In this relationship a child does not feel secure. Avoidant children learn to take care of themselves, as they find that they cannot depend on the parents to provide for their needs. It may lead to difficulties with relationship with others. According to Magana et al., such behaviour is the result of somewhat uncaring behaviour of parents.
3. *Ambivalent Relationships:* Ambivalence usually refers to not being sure how to respond to their parents and others as the children learn that sometimes their needs are met, and sometimes they are not. They notice and remember behaviour that helped in the past and tend to repeat it. Such children can become over emotional and often resort to behaviour to seek others attention. This behaviour results from rather inconsistent response of the parent towards a child's needs.
4. *Disorganized Relationships:* Disorganized children do not know what to expect from their parents. Children in the other categories have all learned ways to get what they need, even if it is not the best way. This behaviour according to authors results from neglect and maltreatment by parents.

Individual Differences in Infants Relationships with Parents

Bowlby (1979) believed that his attachment theory captured the way children relate to parents. He recognized that there are individual differences. Some children, for example, may be more likely to view their parents as inaccessible or distant, perhaps because the parents have not been consistently available in the past. However, it was not until Bowlby's colleague, Mary Ainsworth (1989), began to study infant parent separations, that individual differences in attachment were incorporated formally, into attachment theory. Ainsworth and her students developed a technique called the strange situation in a laboratory paradigm for studying infant parent relations. In the strange situation, 12month-old infants and their parents are brought to the laboratory and are separated from one another and then reunited. In the strange situation, most children (i.e. about 60%) behave in the way implied by Bowlby's understanding of attachment. Specifically, they become upset when the parent leaves the room, but when he or she returns, they actively seek the parent and are easily comforted by him or her. Children who exhibit this pattern of behaviour are often called secure. Other children (about 20% or less) are ill-at-ease initially and, upon separation, become extremely distressed. Importantly, when reunited with their parents, these children have a difficult time being soothed and often exhibit conflicting behaviours, that suggest they want to be comforted but that they also want to punish the parent for leaving. These children are often called anxious-resistant. The third pattern of attachment that Ainsworth and her colleagues documented is called anxious-avoidant. These children (about 20%) don't appear too distressed by the separation and, upon reunion, actively avoid seeking contact with their parent, sometimes turning their attention to play objects on the laboratory floor.

Ainsworth demonstrated that these individual differences were correlated with infant parent interactions in the home, during the first year of life. Children who appear secure in the strange situation, for example, tend to have parents who are responsive to their needs. Children who appear insecure in the strange situation (i.e. anxious-resistant or anxious-avoidant), often have parents who are insensitive to their needs, or inconsistent in the care they provide.

Sibling Relations

Sibling relations refer to the relations between children of the same parents or brothers and sisters. The psychological explanations of development of the child refer to the birth of another child in the family and the reaction of the first child to this event. Some studies indicate, that the first child may resent the birth of another child, as it leads to sharing of the attention of the parent in general and mother in particular. They concluded that it leads to tension or hostility between the two. 'Sibling rivalry' is a term coined by David Levy (1941). He claims that for an older sibling, the aggressive response to the new baby is so typical, that it is safe to say it is a common feature in any family. A study of siblings pointed out, that while few adult siblings have severed their ties completely, approximately one third of them describe their relationship as rivalry or distant. They don't get along with their sibling or have little in common, spend limited time together, and use words like competitive, humiliating and hurtful to depict their childhoods (Leder, 1993). Sibling relations begin early and usually last long, the relationship patterns developed may be generalized to other relationships in adult life (Newman, 1994). Research suggests that the quality of the sibling relationship is more stable in middle childhood, than during adolescence (Dunn, 1996), so the emergence of the relationship pattern in early stages of life is important. The sibling relations are influenced by cultural factors as are other relationships.

The sibling rivalry in traditional societies where individualism is looked down upon is not as high profile as is brought out by studies in a developed society like USA. In India and other countries of the subcontinent a lot of emphasis is given to develop a sense of responsibility among children towards each other. An older female sibling is given the role of looking after all the younger siblings, similarly an older male sibling is expected to provide care and protection to the younger siblings. Older siblings may become a source of care and comfort was discovered by Whiting and Whiting (1975). The siblings up to the teenage play together and help each other in studies as well. They may prefer to spend time with their own friends as they grow older. The relations between the siblings are better, if the difference in age is greater, it may be more problematic if the age difference is one or two years only. In case of insignificant difference in ages the acceptance of respective roles of leader and follower becomes difficult. Female siblings get along better as compared to the male siblings with each other. An older female sibling is not generally jealous of her younger sibling/s, she may feel hurt, if a younger female sibling is allowed to marry earlier though. This happens as a clear system of a 'first come first to go', is socially put in place to create the seniority.

Violation of rule undermines her chances of marriage as it is interpreted as inferiority of the person ignored. Respect for seniority is well accepted but in recent years, it is getting somewhat eroded because of economic pressures. The number of siblings is a big factor in determining relations. In Indian subcontinent the normal size of the family is generally 5–7 including parents, particularly in middle and lower middle class families, which is coming down now in urban educated families. In large families, particularly in poor families, where both parents are busy in coping with the daily struggles of survival, sibling generally rely on each other, rather than on parents in dealing with the realities of life. They learn early to survive as a group, by helping each other and thus are not competing against each other. The sibling rivalry basically emerges to monopolize parent/s attention and/or trying to dominate the other, instead of helping each other out. Education and class background play an important part, in shaping sibling relations. As noted earlier, poor family siblings are forced to work together to survive, and hardly get an opportunity to think, in terms of self and their individual destinations in life. Their thinking process accord more priority to survival needs and the cooperation they can get from each other, rather than individual life goals. Modern education, which induces higher aspiration levels, is generally missing from their life. These children are likely to develop a higher others-orientation, as compared with children in upper middle and higher class families, with a much higher achievement orientation. The large numbers of poor siblings, therefore, are less likely to experience any sibling rivalry as such.

Here are some research findings about siblings relations in general as also in India:

> The siblings spend more time together during pre-school years than with parents, reflecting the growing influence of siblings (Dunn, 1996; Larson and Richards, 1994). They imitate each other. They provide each other opportunities for understanding each other's needs (Richman and Lansdown, 1988).
>
> Sibling relationships are similar to and yet different from peer relationships.
>
> Sibling relationships are not voluntary and are usually not symmetrical depending on the age-gap between siblings, the sex of the siblings, etc.
>
> There is a presumption that interactions with siblings provide practice, which is important for interacting with other children

(Brody, 1998). In a comparative study of children without siblings and children with siblings, Kitzmann, Cohen and Lockwood (2002) found, that children without siblings, compared to classmates with siblings, were less liked by their peer groups, but were similar to children with siblings, in number of close friendships and quality of mutual friendships.

Howe et al., (2000) hypothesized, that feelings of closeness and warmth in sibling relationships, would encourage siblings to share information and look towards siblings for emotional support. Howe found that sibling relationship warmth was associated with emotional understanding as well as self-disclosure between siblings.

Kitzmann et al. (2002) suggested, that children without siblings may be less able to manage conflict and could be more victimized and aggressive in peer groups. The study also suggests that social skills like conflict management in relationships, were more affected by the presence of siblings than by parents. Sibling conflict may provide practice with negotiation, compromise, and resolution of conflict. These experiences may help in developing better perspective taking abilities (Perner, Ruffman and Leekam, 1994). This may be transferred to other relationships like peer relationships.

The influence of other factors like sex of the sibling (especially in countries like India), temperament of the siblings, and other role models may influence relationship quality.

Seymour (1993) found that in South Asian cultures like India, the role played by siblings is more visibly outlined by the society, when compared to western cultures. For example, a set of brothers are expected to live together and cooperate, or brothers are expected to look out for the welfare of married sisters, who leave the maternal house at the time of marriage. Also, in Asian cultures, siblings are culturally obligated to be involved with each other throughout their lives, whereas in Euro-American culture, it is a personal choice in adulthood (Weisner, 1993).

Cousins may play the role of siblings, in the absence of siblings in a family, acting as playmates, when of a similar age or as caretakers, when of different age-groups. Moreover, children in India play in large groups, that require high levels of cooperation and sharing. Most of the children engage in play, that occurs in unison and involves physical contact like touching and holding, and this practice could continue beyond the preschool years (Roopnarine, Johnson, and Hooper, 1994).

6

Conflicts in Relationships

Conflicts are natural in interpersonal relationships, since individual differences is a well studied phenomenon. Values and perceptions bring people together or drive them apart. A relationship becomes possible with the acceptance of other. A give and take may follow. Conflict is a result of unsatisfactory outcome of interaction for one or both parties, irrespective of where it is located. The interpersonal relations become more prone to conflict on account of, differences in values, perception of issues and finally the tendency to demand more than one is willing to concede. A simple construction of interpersonal conflict is neither possible nor should be advanced. This is not to say that conflict in interpersonal relationships of individuals, in groups and communities cannot be understood and dealt with. An analysis of person's strengths and weaknesses, e.g. emotional outbursts, communication styles, decision-making, helps to understand the reasons of discord among human beings. The human behaviour is a function of both psychological and social influences. An analysis of personality characteristics of individuals and their social values thus provides, a useful starting point, for understanding the mismatch in human interactions. Analytical skills along with ability to obtain and retain trust, emotional support and a caring attitude helps in obtaining relevant facts to understand and deal with these at all levels.

Conflict

Conflict and development are bound together: Conflict both fosters maturation and is a product of it. Two distinct forms of conflict may be identified: intrapersonal conflict and interpersonal conflict. Each plays a different role in human development. Intrapersonal conflict denotes internal strife, the resolution of which may prompt social, cognitive, or emotional maturation. Interpersonal conflict signifies overt disagreement between individuals or groups that, depending on how it is managed, may either promote social skills and improve relationships or hinder social competence and disrupt relationships. Both forms of conflict appear to have a curvilinear relationship with developmental outcomes. Some conflict is necessary for optimal growth, but too much is counterproductive.

Intrapersonal conflict describes a state of emotional turmoil, intellectual dissent, or motivational equiponderance that occurs within an individual. Intrapersonal conflict encompasses four broad domains. At the emotional level, conflict reflects competing desires or impulses. Sigmund Freud attributed these base tendencies to aggressive and sexual proclivities with origins in the id (the unregulated physical self), which give rise to irreconcilable differences with constraints that are imposed by the superego (the social mores conveyed by family and culture). At the cognitive level, conflict reflects dissonance produced by incongruent facts, opinions, or modes of thought. Jean Piaget attributed these tendencies to equilibration, the innate human tension between a preference for stability and a drive to master the environment. Assimilation encourages stability by incorporating new information into existing mental schema. Should this prove insufficient for mastering the environment, accommodation is required to alter the mental scheme or, in extreme cases, the mental structure itself, in a manner consistent with the information available. At the level of the ego, conflict reflects developmental challenges. At the motivational level, conflict reflects the need to choose between options perceived to be relatively equal in valence. Kurt Lewin (1946) identified three distinct forms of motivational discord. Two equally attractive options are described in contemporary terms, as approach-approach conflicts. Two equally unattractive options are referred to, as avoid-avoid conflicts. Options that contain both attractive and unattractive elements, are considered approach-avoid conflicts.

Intrapersonal conflict is by definition a private experience. It cannot be observed, and it is difficult to measure as there is no reliable tool to measure it. Subjective experience as a topic of study was abandoned as the studies of behaviour became more popular.

However, studies have identified some factors which can precipitate conflicts in relationships.

Factors Causing Problems in Relationships

A lot of research now is available to highlight some common factors that are found correlated with problems associated with relationships. Some of these have been briefly referred to in the chapter on theories and explanations, relevant to relationships. A review of these factors in detail will be helpful for use in the facilitating process. The review can also help the self-help groups, to use these clues as topics for discussions, to address these during their own facilitation sessions.

- Strong Self-orientation
- Perceptual Distortion
- Communication Gap
- Betrayal
- Lack of Self-control
- Extreme Variations in Values
- Lack of Basic Minimum Returns

Strong Self-orientation

A website in United States offering advice to couples to sort out their relationship problems suggests setting up boundaries to protect the self. In another discourse, one originating in India, to tackle all worldly problems including that of relationships, one is advised to conquer the self or in other words, completely negate it. The two approaches to deal with the self are diametrically opposed but they do indicate the central position that self occupies. So it is important to know who you are, what you want and how far you are in control. The setting up of boundaries is a function of psychological caring a person receives in the childhood as Bowlby and a number of other studies pointed out. The ability to trust and respond opens up behavioural responses and the possibility of sharing. An introvert person on the other hand is handicapped because of inability to trust and share. The self-orientation refers to a condition, where a person is unable to look beyond and concede any space to other in an interaction. However, cultures to sustain family relationships, socialize the female to concede all space to their male counterparts, reducing the possibility of conflict. In other words, the gender is constructed to avoid conflict and ensure smooth functioning.

A belief in gender roles is different from a strong self-orientation, which means allowing little or no space to others. A strong self-orientation refers to inability to concede space to other, irrespective of context. A capacity to understand other, their needs and rights and respect it, is a prerequisite for harmonious human interactions leading to positive relationship. The conflict arises with total negation of space to other. For example, the wife lodged an FIR with the police of rape, after spending her honeymoon night with her husband. This is a classic example of a male, with a complete self-centered approach to relationship. Moderate or a balanced self-orientation can cause conflict, as people contest spaces in their interaction, but they can be resolved. A relationship survives with capacity of persons to negotiate.

The divorce rate in western societies, urban areas in developing countries particularly among the educated, is an indicator of development of a greater self-orientation, and a desire for protecting self. Strong self-orientation along with a weakening trend of total negation of self, makes the possibility for accommodation difficult, a basic input in stabilizing relationships.

Perceptual Distortion

Perceptual distortion refers to when individuals perceive a reality different from the actual reality, or in other words they perceive a reality, which only exist in their imagination. The phenomenon is common, further the studies suggested that, perception rather than reality influences behaviour. In relationships, the perception plays a crucial role as partners perceive each other, and react to each other based on their perception. The fear for survival is more real than the threat of survival. Emotional attachment is a factor causing negation of reality. Social workers often find parents having an image of their favourite child, unable to see any fact that does not conform to that image. The distortion at cognitive level refers to biases in the process of construction of a reality. The value framework, a person has acquired through cultural socialization play an important part in cognitive framework. For example, a person from a particular caste or religion perceives rights and duties of a male and female spouse, interacts accordingly. A lot of distortion and misinterpretation occurs also on account of different meanings that persons attach to a particular fact. The perception of an individual is largely a cultural product, including the psycho-social framework imbibed through both heredity and socialization. The relationships between persons brought up in different cultures can create many possibilities of distortions. Self-concept and self-confidence are also vital factors in helping persons to remain objective in perceiving and analysing social relationships.

Communication Gap

Studies reveal that communication gap can result in misunderstanding in relationship expectations. Misunderstanding arises from lack of clarity about respective roles, if not specifically negotiated and understood. For example, a social worker often is faced with a situation where he has to counsel a couple to renegotiate roles. This is a situation referred to as a communication gap. The communication gap can get worse, if there is no communication or parties are unable to see facts objectively. The cultural framework can lead to communication gap as the words, norms, and rituals are different and convey different meanings and expectations. In the traditional societies, cultural norms generally specify gender roles. Social changes can create grey areas in interpretation and constructing expectation. The traditional societies per se do not approve self-orientation, as groups such as family, clan, caste and community are accorded more importance viz-à-viz an individual. A person's self or social orientation is a different phenomenon than the social construction of gender roles and the consequent expectations. There are situations in many relationships, particularly spousal relations, where persons are not able to communicate or express themselves with any degree of clarity. It would, therefore, create a communication gap. The partners in many relationships are, neither aware of, nor feel the need to communicate expectations nor know how to communicate it. These persons can carry on with their relationship, without questioning it. All is well until questioned, or disputed.

Communication gap in case of work relationships in particular, cause a lot of bitterness and hardship for all. If the roles are not specified and communicated, it leads to non-fulfillment of expectations causing malfunctioning in the organization and strained work relationships.

Betrayal

Betrayal refers to conscious violation of basic norms of a relationship. The basic norms are social or legal expectations governing the behaviour of partners in relationship. It includes such matters as being faithful to each other including exclusive rights of different kind, sharing information, avoiding going public with private matters, avoiding criticism of people considered sacred or without their knowledge, etc. The betrayals among close relationships do more psychological damage than in general category, for example the betrayal by a spouse and betrayal by a colleague. The impact of betrayal has a direct relationship with the personality traits and the self-concept of individuals. For example, individuals with high anxiety trait are likely to be severely affected emotionally, compared to a person with greater emotional self-control. Individuals with a positive self-concept are less likely to be emotionally affected, compared to individuals with self doubts by incidents of betrayals, real or imaginary.

Responses in Betrayal

Persons feeling betrayed respond to the situation in a variety of ways, depending upon the actor and the emotion that is predominant. In case of spousal relationship, anger and revenge are common among the educated working class and higher class, whereas middle class spouses, particularly women, experience sadness and respond by withdrawing or becoming silent and cold towards the partner. Among siblings and work relationships, betrayal generally evokes anger and a strong urge to avenge including resort to violence. Parent and children feeling betrayed evoke sadness and withdrawal. Child response usually is anger and retaliation including violence and destruction.

Lack of Self-Control

Self-discipline refers to an ability to exercise control over emotions, and actions to avoid unpleasant outcomes. Self-control refers to control of instinctive spontaneous reactions irrespective of outcome. Uncontrolled reactions to exhibit extreme anger, anxiety, happiness and fear are symptoms of lack of self-control. Self-control helps a person to think, analyse and act in a disciplined manner, in any situation to remain calm. For example, words can hurt and once released it is impossible to take it back. The professionals therefore choose their words carefully. The manner of speech, its tone, body gestures can help or hurt. In relationships, one of the major problem areas, is uncontrolled and unplanned communication, including over communication. Not to know when to stop or what to say is a symptom of lack of control. Uncontrolled behaviour is a symptom of underlying tension in the human psyche, a person who is not at peace with self. Self-control requires attending to underlying tensions.

Emotions are a form of communication, consciousness of emotions determines behaviour. The emotional energy can work both ways, it can be relaxing or extremely agitating, depending on the kind of emotional energy is generated. Consciousness of emotional energy, its nature and consequences, helps in its control.

The explanations of emotional energy generation are dealt within the chapter on concepts and theories.

Extreme Variations in Values

In any relationship, difference in values beyond a point makes conflict inevitable. For example, differences about parenting style, use of resources, religious orientation, sexual preferences can evoke conflicts among spouses. In a group, differences in norms – democratic vs autocratic – can evoke conflicts. Ideological differences are bound to result in conflict.

Lack of Basic Minimum Returns

Relationship stability follow a simple norm of give and take. This may not be same and equitable in all cases, but so long as the respective parties find it satisfactory, it helps to avoid conflict. The change from satisfactory to dissatisfaction is the beginning of conflict. If not attended to or renegotiated it may escalate conflict.

Communication and Conflict in Family

A number of studies have explored the links between patterns of communication and conflicts in family. Most of these researches have been carried out in developed countries. Some of the findings are useful in India but generally the cultural context makes it a completely different reality. Montgomery (1988) thought communication is the relationship or its overt manifestation, however, communication in Indian context, is conspicuous by its absence or keeps a very low profile in many close relationships. The spouses in the typical Indian family hardly ever communicate or are visible doing so, same is true for parents and children. Even now a vast majority of children think, addressing their father directly is undesirable behaviour, listen and follow, more so in the case of girls. In case of girls, the father is later replaced by the husband, listen and follow. But what Montgomery suggested has relevance, Indian scenario is a reflection of lopsidedness of relationship.

Siblings relationships are more horizontal except where the age difference is greater. It may therefore be necessary to be a little cautious in using these insights in India, in practice particularly. Cultural locale of the participants is significant in understanding communication patterns. However, some segments of Indian population is beginning to resemble the conditions in the developed world, because of education and economic development, while another segment is free from traditional codes because of stark poverty.

Research on communication in family conflict is motivated by an interest in improving family relationships. Most of the studies try to isolate problematic aspects of communication, with the hope that this will help actors to become aware and take steps to suppress or change these. Controlling communication patterns is not easy, but they can be managed. For example, people control and change communication styles in different contexts, such as locations and power positions. Change in other factors that contribute to family conflict, such as personality traits; basic differences in individual values, goals, or expectations; social and economic conditions; and other structural factors are comparatively more difficult to deal with. However, a review of communication processes in marital and family conflict, can help in preventing family conflicts. Communication is a vital strategy of achieving quality relationships (see Montgomery, 1988). Further, the focus of studies is, on how families communicate about conflict and its implications for their relationship (see Gottman, 1994) and not the root cause of conflict, or what they do about it, or even how they are resolved. With some exceptions, researchers tend to treat the content of conflict as peripheral or unimportant, perhaps because underlying relationship issues are so often transparent (Wilmot and Hocker, 2001).

Accordingly, the studies of marital conflict are given primacy, followed by parent-child and sibling conflict. An analysis of conflict in family relationships relates to its location, the frequency and type, communication patterns, and subjective interpretations of communication. Conflict appears to be more common and intense, within families than other social contexts. Both adolescents and adults report greater conflict and negativity within family relationships by comparison to friend or co-worker relationships (see Adams and Laursen, 2001), however, studies suggest that overt conflict is not a daily or even weekly occurrence for most couples.

In case of parent-children interactions, Montemayor (1986) reported two conflicts per week, whereas Laursen (1993) reported high school students had 7.4 conflicts on an average per day, with parents included. This research trend, obviously is again referring to the developed world and from a culture which is highly individualistic in nature. In the Indian context, parent-child relationship conflicts are far more a case of demands being made by children, often conceded by parents and at times contested, it is not a conflict one associates with relationships. These are interactions between parents and children and are part of the process of growing up. There are, however, parent-child conflicts of serious nature, when the life goals or values are involved. In the Indian context these studies have not been done by either psychologists or other practicing professionals including social workers. It is also obvious that more parent-child conflicts occur after the children reach adolescent stage or start a new family of their own, or are about to do so. In rural areas in the subcontinent, land and property matters create more conflict, among parents and adult children, and among siblings.

Estimates of sibling conflict are more dramatic. One study found that conflict within two preschool-age siblings occurs on an average, seven times an hour (Perlman and Ross, 1997). Similarly, other studies and general observation of children during school age of most children, regardless of exact age, refers to more conflicts. Sibling relationships experience conflict, both children and adolescents, in developed countries (see Raffaelli, 1997), but the trend is unclear in Indian context, since no data is available. Further, Raffaelli, suggests sibling conflict tends to increase with increase in contact. The study found that spending time together, predicated the frequency of sibling conflict more than age, sex, family size, and other variables. In the Indian sub continent spending time is seen as a sign of closer bonding, as only sibling who trust each other more, spend more time together. Among siblings, the elder female and younger male combination work well at school age, while during adult stage, older males look after the younger females, reducing the chances of conflict, as there is an established social norm, recognizing the authority of the older siblings over the younger siblings.

However, these comparisons are tenuous, partly because they mark variations within specific relationship types and also because of the different methods used to quantify conflict. For one thing, observational studies (see Perlman and Ross, 1997) find much more frequent conflicts, than studies that utilize diaries or global self-reports (Kirchler et al., 2001). There is a general feeling that, over time, conflict increases in hostile families but decreases in supportive families. In other words, increased interaction with a sibling is positively associated with perceptions of warmth, whereas decreased contact is linked to perceptions of conflict (Stocker, Lanthier and Furman 1997). Presumably, once siblings are not forced to live together, their relationships become more like voluntary friendships.

Some authors have (see Sillars, et al., 2000) argued that how family members discuss or otherwise address conflicts, partly reflects the kind of pressure they are facing, and therefore, confrontational and emotional communication is expected during volatile and stressful periods. However, confrontational communication, is also seen as a reflection of the strength of both parties to a relationship. In developing countries this strength is not found, because it is not supported by social norms, which prohibit confrontation between spouses. Sillars (1995) also argues, that problem-solving communication probably has the greatest impact on relationship quality. It is difficult to say what a problem-solving communication is, but any communication, which helps in promoting mutual understanding, promotes respect for each other, will definitely promote the quality of relationship.

Context is important in understanding family conflict, type of family, nuclear, extended or joint, number of children, number of members, age and gender of members, the economic and educational status, etc.

Dickson (1995) identified a subgroup of long married couples, called 'dysfunctional separates,' whose joint story-telling interviews, revealed a cold and distant manner of speaking to one another, frequent contradictions, and sadness or anger when discussing the marriage. These couples maintained unhappy marriages for over 50 years, largely due to a sense, that divorce was never an option, especially among wives. This supports the general observation, about the relative significance of getting out, before it is too late, versus staying out of trouble, in a marital relationship. Gottman (1994) concluded that confrontation of disagreement, is important to marital satisfaction over time, whereas avoidance of conflict is generally dysfunctional. Specifically, Gottman identified one type of happily married couple, called 'conflict minimizers,' who minimized the importance of disagreements and engaged in little verbal give-and-take. The satisfied couples engaged in a great deal of avoidance during conflict discussions, including verbal denial of conflict and topic shifts, and they rarely use a negative tone of voice, maintaining instead, consistently neutral, nonverbal affect. Thus, satisfaction may be predicated either by engagement or avoidance, depending on how the pattern of communication fits, with the couple's preferred pattern of relating, i.e. interdependence achieved through discussion versus autonomy maintained through conversational restraint and strategic disengagement.

Communication Distortion

One of the most recorded features of intimate conflict is the tendency for individuals to construct profoundly different interpretations of the same incident or behaviour. Differences in perception are a basic, even defining feature of conflict (Wilmot and Hocker, 2001). Moreover, differences in perception seem to increase as conflicts intensify. Thus, a number of studies of marital conflict find, that unhappy spouses often hold sharply incongruent images of conflict (Fincham and Bradbury, 1991) and provide different interpretations for communication, including the emotional meaning assigned to messages (Guthrie and Noller, 1988), perceptions of self and partner, conflict behaviours (Sillars, et al., 2000), and thoughts, feelings, and intentions attributed to the partner during communication (Ickes and Simpson, 1997). There appears to be a reciprocal relationship between incongruent perception and conflict escalation/de-escalation. As conflicts escalate, perceptions and interpretations may become more selective, idiosyncratic and extreme. This, in turn, influences subsequent communication in such a way as to drive further escalation and entrenchment of conflict (Fincham and Bradbury, 1991).

Other authors emphasize the selective attention and interpretation of messages on mood state and the emotional climate in the relationship (see, Forgas, 2001). Fincham and Bradbury (1991) suggest that the observed negativity of distressed couples, is linked to selective attention to and recall of negative behaviour of spouses. Distressed spouses tend to see, their partner's negative behaviour as highly meaningful and relevant to self, thus they process it more fully, leading to elaborate, negative representations of the partner. In contrast, happy spouses are more likely to discount the partner's negative communication, because it does not evoke elaborate, well-rehearsed, negative memories. A common strategy for investigating family conflict is, to compare the communication patterns of couples or families who are experiencing an explicit form of family distress.

7

Working with Families

Family relationships and its problems are different from a group, since the family relationships are different from a group. The group relationships are voluntary and people can leave a group if they are not happy. Family roles and relationships are socially constructed but this is not the case with group relationships. Emotional content in family relationship is far greater than group relationships.

Family relationships problems are usually rooted in spousal relations and some time in parent-child relations. The hierarchal relationships in families create more problems than any other issues. It brings up gender issues and human rights violation issues. The social work intervention is needed to deal with these issues. A social worker is either approached by a family member or is deputed by an organization to provide help.

The stages of facilitating family relationships are same as discussed in the case of group, such as getting into an agreement with the family about the procedural details and getting their consent and commitment to work together for improving relationships in the family. Most families the social worker works with, are poor and illiterate. The agreement therefore is about assessing the desire on the part of family members particularly males who control others in the family. The general goals are:

- To help members to learn to trust others;
- To bring about change in hierarchal attitudes of males;
- To help members to express themselves;
- To help them learn how they feel about each other;
- To help members learn new coping strategies to deal with stress and so on.

The social workers generally work with an individual in cases where a member of the family approaches them. They are, in such cases, working with an individual and not a family. The process of working with individual has been discussed earlier, they can use family sessions to help the individuals in the family and facilitate family relationships, to achieve more sustainable results. Both the processes compliment each other. Some important issues relating to family a worker must take into account before starting working with the family are:

Family Structure

- Class and cultural moorings of the family are significant in moulding family relations.
- As a social worker, it is always important to understand the family structure and what the subsystems are, as well as the nature of the boundaries that is created among them. The power structure of family and type of family are important.
- Economic sustainability of the family is a crucial factor that affects the family relations. Very rich families create different set of problems in family relations, as it leads to highly self-centered personalities.
- Enmeshed families: parents always interfere in conflict among siblings that they never get to negotiate themselves.
- Disengaged families: parents don't get involved to an extent where they can't even show sympathy and support the children's feelings.

Communication

- Not many families have adequate communication skills or experience.
- It's unlikely that conflicts will get resolved before people start to listen to each other.
- Family members who learn to listen to each other with understanding, often discover that they don't need to change each other.

Domestic Violence

- The process of questioning if there is a suspicion of abuse could begin with the family present, but it is wise to meet with each member individually in order for them to feel free to talk openly.

- Social worker could jeopardize the relationship that he/she has been developing with the client, but at times, therapy needs to take second place, next to safety.

Extramarital Affairs or Betrayals

- Affairs and betrayals are crisis that can destroy a marriage. Couples normally go to third parties to deal with issues which can make therapy less effective.

Gender Roles

- One should look at: 'Do the gender roles established in a couple seem to work for them or there are unresolved differences, conflict, or confusion that appear to be sources of stress?' How does each partner experience the fairness of give and take in the relationship?
- Men typically value independence and try to avoid anything that will take that independence from them.
- Family dynamics influences gender socialization. Gender differences underline relationship problems.

Ethical Issues

- Therapy is for the client's benefit and not for the social worker to work on their own unresolved issues.
- Clients are entitled to confidentiality (can't tell parents, spouse, ...)
- Avoid dual relationship.
- Social worker should provide services in their area of expertise and based on their education and training.
- Social workers need to take drastic measures when personal problems interfere with professional duties.
- Need to be familiar with age, gender, race, ethnicity, culture, national origin, religion, sexual orientation, disability, language, socio-economic status and many other areas to provide appropriate help and if not, they need to refer the client to those familiar in those areas.

Process of Working with a Family

Each family will differ in its characteristics and resources. The worker will have to modify the role and addressing style in different sessions taking into account the capacity of the family as a whole and that of individual members.

Session I

- Introduce yourself.
- Ask parents to introduce their children.
- Introduce the initial goals and objectives for the meeting and ask each member's opinion.
- Create an alliance with the members by ensuring each member will get an opportunity to be heard.
- Ask the members how they felt about coming to the meeting.
- Become familiarized with each member's accomplishments and interests.
- Emphasize on family role and strengths.

Session II

- Identify important issues and highlight these in the family.
- Develop possible explanations in consultation with members.
- Analysing members feeling. Are people not happy with the process of decision-making, or the way the power is distributed among the group, i.e. structure, or is it the traditional family norms, or the relationship triangles, and limits imposed upon members freedom, etc.?
- During the session let members take on each problem and come to some understanding about priorities, let them focus more on interpersonal relations and how everything falls in place once people become more supportive rather than critical, keep an eye on constructive suggestions for changes in interaction.
- Provide every member to do some exercises in their free time and explain what they are expected to learn from these.

Session III

- Help the family members to see their respective roles in the problem and help them decide on their own how they wish to work for the change needed.
- At this point if you are uncertain about any issues do discuss it with your supervisor if there is one or other senior colleagues.
- There are times when the worker will have to use her/his commitments to the group to confront the family members, ingenuity to get around resistance, and empathy to get underneath their defensiveness.
- Do not, however, pressurize them into any action, let them take their time to come to terms with the reality.

- Foster individual responsibility and mutual understanding, as per the framework we are using to facilitate relationship. Explain the theoretical connotation of Self and other and help them to understand their respective positions on the scale of self *vs* other.
- Explain the current problem with the way a person with a certain position in the scale will view and react to the problem.

Session IV

- It is time to review the situation after the inputs made by the social worker. Look at the responses of all members. Are they showing any improvement? For example, has the flow of communication improved? Are members more attentive to and responding positively to each other and so on.
- Is the family satisfied with their achievement or would they like to continue with therapy?
- Is the family now clear about the core issue of mutual relationship and know how to deal with it in the future?
- Has the family's relationship improved outside of the context as well as within the family?

Lowenstein (2010) in their recent book have discussed some very innovative ways of using art, games and other creative techniques to involve the children in family therapy sessions. As Napier and Whitaker (1978) pointed out working directly with the totality of the forces that influence the individual, is such a logical idea, that it is hard to deny its validity. Taibbi (2007) pointed out that involving all the children in the family therapy, provides the social worker with a more accurate assessment of dynamics, interactional patterns, roles and rules. Children can contribute ideas to the family sessions. Including children rather than just the identified person needing help, helps to shift the focus away from the person and highlighting that it is an interactional or relationship problem. There are many other authors (see, Sori, 2006; Revell, 1997.) recommending the use of creative techniques in family and group therapy sessions. The use of creative techniques helps in breaking ice and making the commencement of communication easier. It allows for breaking of barriers, time to rethink persons' view of others and their own role in creating tensions as well as promoting harmony. The process is very simple and begins with information sharing with the parents about inclusion of children and the use of games and other techniques. This helps in preparing parents and dealing with their doubts about these techniques which can arouse a lot of laughter and feelings which they may not have associated with a therapy or helping session.

The first session as discussed earlier is given to getting information about the interactional patterns, family resources, perception of problems and persons responsible for or dealing with these and their priorities and strategies of dealing with these and so on. The inclusion of children helps in making the information more accurate as they are spontaneous, non-manipulative and therefore unbiased if not totally objective. Presence of children helps in controlling and keeping the environment non-aggressive to a great extent. People have to mind their language, tone and even body postures before the children.

The feedback session should focus upon giving everyone a chance to reflect on their learning about self and others. Here again for example, how a child generally perceive an adult in the family, can come as a surprise to many. Do they admit it? And if so with what feelings? Similarly any new facts relating to others, which either shock them or help them to understand them better will help.

The next session if welcome by the family, can focus on the interaction patterns, particularly during decision-making and while dealing with serious problems. The creative techniques help in making it more real and informal, such as asking the family to make plans for family, for the coming festival or holidays or marriage, etc. The technique compels them to make concrete plans giving full details, including expenses, preparing lists of actors and guests and so on.

The feedback session then seeks information about who played what role in the discussion and decision-making, their feelings about the same, level of agreement on the decisions made, any problems encountered and so on. This helps to assess the level of integration of the family, power structure, gender biases, etc. The integration here refers to capacity to accept individual roles and positions and the feelings associated with this acceptance. It could be fear or love or respect or a mixture of all these. This would help in relating the individual problems to the overall family crucible.

Termination

However, it is advisable to carefully assess individual changes along with group interactions before reducing the frequency of meetings or full termination. The assessment should focus on changes among members, for example, how they view each other now, the trust level, the communication patterns and so on. The clarity about group positions and openness among the group to handle all issues without any reservations, should be carefully assessed. A stress free discussion is a good indicator of progress in group relations, whereas frequent emotional outbursts reflect tension and unresolved issues. It is often seen that in Indian families, parents are very reluctant to discuss issues relating to friends and sexual matters with their children. Open and stress free group sharing of issues both private and public is a positive indicator of group relations.

8

Working with Individuals

The process of facilitating relationships is used by a number of professionals for example, psychiatrists, psychologists, social workers, human resources managers and lawyers as well. All of them follow their own disciplinary background to define the goals and strategies for achieving these. They also follow their own ethics for dealing with their clients. An attempt is made to look at all possible explanations, goals and strategies, with the sole objective of improving human relations per se. This may help practitioners to avoid making mistakes and be more positive about the outcome. However, as the first step itself underlines, changing human behaviour remains a rather complex phenomenon. The outcome is largely a function of determination of the client to identify areas needing modification and making consistent efforts in partnership with social worker or a self-help group to effect change. Various aspects of facilitating relations are discussed, but one is seldom able to anticipate all possibilities in dealing with humans, as each of them is a unique case. The manner of perception, interpretation, passion associated with issues exhibit a wide variety. So do not hesitate to think on your own to device new ways, to deal with the situations you come across in actual practice not dealt with here. It is important to remember that social worker as a professional can provide services to any person needing it, irrespective of their economic status. For example, an executive in an organization, a teacher in a school, a maid servant in a house or an unemployed poor youth, all are eligible to get help from a social worker.

The following stages are visualized for facilitating the process of intervention to help an individual to handle relationships in a manner, which is both socially desirable and personally satisfying. In many texts on working with individuals particularly developing a rapport with the client is emphasized. Establishing a meaningful relationship as it is termed, is a precondition at the start of a professional relationship, to encourage trust and confidence in the professional's capacity to help.

The social workers are trained to achieve this by using communication skills, warm attitude and empathy. The skills are discussed in detail in another chapter.

FIRST STAGE

Establishing a Contract

The first step is to clarify the role the social worker can play and what is expected of the client. Generally the clients approach a social worker with a positive attitude or a negative attitude, that there is nothing one can do. As argued earlier, the self-concept plays a vital role in relationships and therefore, the first thing a social worker has to clarify is the respective roles, client and social worker will have in working towards the resolution of change.

The social worker must ensure that:

- The person determined to bring about the change, is positive that it can be done and that it will have a positive impact.
- Make the person understand that it will be a long process and would require continuous efforts.
- Make the person understand that the quantum and quality of change, would be directly in proportion to the efforts made by the client.
- Make the client understand to trust the social worker, voluntarily share all the information including personal feelings.
- Assure the confidentiality of the information disclosed.
- All financial obligations should be clarified right in the beginning.
- Time schedules and the possible duration should be indicated and agreed upon.
- Make sure that there is no conflict of interest. A conflict of interest refers to where clients may be related to other clients. A professional cannot effectively protect the interest of clients who are related.

A Model Form of Contract

I hereby agree to abide by the following conditions:

1. I will come to attend the sessions regularly as per schedule worked out in consultation with me.
2. I agree to participate in the discussion on my own.
3. I agree to share whatever information is deemed necessary by the social worker.
4. I agree that the outcome of these sessions may be uncertain and in some cases unpleasant for me.
5. I agree to pay the sum agreed upon per session (if applicable).
6. In case I am not able to keep an appointment, I will inform at least a day in advance. If I fail to show up for the appointment, the charges for the session (if applicable) would be levied as usual.
7. I can terminate the contract anytime by filling up a form for the purpose.
   (a) Name:
   (b) Address:
   (c) Contact No.:
   (d) Email:

SECOND STAGE

Assessment

Once a contract has been signed or at least an agreement reached between the social worker and the client, the social worker tries to understand the client and the reason for seeking help, through the use of standard scales and techniques, the process is termed as assessment. It helps to develop an overall profile, providing details about the financial status, educational background, self-concept, confidence level, family background and perception of problem/issues for visiting the social worker.

In assessing a, client the background of the client such as education, occupation, income and willingness are important factors. Poor and uneducated males and females are different in responding to the questions. The assessment in such cases has to take into account the ability to respond and the willingness to do something about their situation. The language should be simple and format of questions should be more direct. The self report can be altogether discarded and observation and getting information from others may be more helpful.

A Suggestive Guideline for Assessment of an Individual (Questionnaire)

1. Name:
2. Age:
3. Education other training or skills:
4. Occupation:
5. Income:
6. Control over income:
7. Marital Status:
8. Age at marriage:
9. Any previous experience of receiving professional help including from a medical practitioner for mental health purposes:
10. Family History (Current family):

Note: Prepare a chart for filling information about people currently living with the client giving information about their relationship with client, age, educational status, occupation, income, marital status, etc.

Self-Assessment of Strengths and Weaknesses

This assessment form is meant for educated persons willing to bring about change in their relationships, Take your time in providing truthful answers. There is no right or wrong answer. Follow your instinctive honest reaction. All the information provided, will be kept confidential.

Which is a correct description of your usual self? (Tick whichever is appropriate)
(a) I like being with people
(b) I am afraid of meeting people
(c) I like being alone

My emotional being is usually quite (Tick whichever is appropriate)
(a) Stable: no mood swings
(b) Varied: some time I feel good on other days I feel low
(c) Unstable: I get irritated all the time

Which is true in your case (Tick whichever is appropriate)
(a) I am a carefree person
(b) I am an organized person
(c) I easily trust people
(d) I find it difficult to trust others

(e) I can take quick decisions
(f) I am indecisive

Can you handle any problem?

(a) Yes (b) No (c) Can't say

Can you handle any role assignment?

(a) Yes (b) No (c) Can't say

Can you handle any kind of people?

(a) Yes (b) No (c) Can't say

Are you happy with your physical self?

(a) Yes (b) No (c) Can't say

Are you happy with your social status?

(a) Yes (b) No (c) Can't say

Are you happy with your economic status?

(a) Yes (b) No (c) Can't say

What would be an accurate description of how you act (Tick whichever is appropriate)
Take too much time to think about options
(a) I judge people easily
(b) I try to be factual while judging people
(c) I worry about current problems
(d) I worry about future problems
(e) I am not the worrying type, I take things as they come

Would you agree that you are (Tick whichever is true. You can tick any number)
(a) Somewhat rigid in your thinking
(b) Impulsive in your behaviour
(c) Worrying type
(d) Indecisive in your approach to people
(e) Ambitious
(f) Lack patience
(g) Lack self-discipline
(h) Do not like criticism
(i) Cannot take orders
(j) Oversensitive
(k) Outspoken
(l) A complex person
(m) Reserved
(n) I don't think before I act

(o) Kind and caring
(p) Aware of others feeling
(q) I don't like hurting others
(r) I cannot control my emotions
(s) I am complaining about everything all the time
(t) I can take many things in stride as complaining does not help
(u) I am usually comparing myself with others and feel unhappy
(v) When I look at others I get depressed
(w) I am quite happy with what I am

Problems in my life happen on account of: (Tick whichever is appropriate)
(a) Others
(b) My own shortcomings
(c) Can't be sure

What reflects your general feelings? (Tick whichever is appropriate)
(a) My situation is hope less
(b) It can be redeemed
(c) I can do it my self
(d) I can do it with a little help
(e) I need to change my self
(f) I am a believer in traditional values
(g) I find many things in life unacceptable
(h) I like to assert my rights
(i) I try to please others

Comment on your relationships (Tick whichever is appropriate. You can tick any number)

With Spouse
(a) We are two very different people, yet we get along
(b) We have many things in common, yet we don't get along
(c) I want my partner to be more assertive
(d) I want my partner to be less demanding
(e) I want my partner to accept me as I am

Parents and others
(a) A I do not question my parents
(b) I have good relations with my siblings
(c) My parents are too demanding
(d) My siblings are jealous of me
(e) I love my children
(f) My children do not care about me
(g) I like spending money on my needs

(h) I would rather spend money for meeting my children's/ parents/spouse needs

General

(a) I want to dominate all my relationships
(b) I cannot accept any nonsense coming from anyone
(c) I think about others before I act
(d) I seldom think about how my behaviour would affect others
(e) I feel bad when people get hurt
(f) I think it is their problem if they get hurt

Interpersonal Conflict: Your Thoughts

In regard to the statements below, indicate whether you agree (A) or disagree (D) with the following:

1. Interpersonal conflict affects not only the persons directly concerned but also others in the family. ( )
2. A certain amount of interpersonal tension is natural, inevitable and can be productive. ( )
3. It is always a good idea to make the person at fault feel ashamed of himself/herself. ( )
4. Persons in conflict tend to see only the weaknesses of the other party. ( )
5. Interpersonal conflict can sometimes be reduced if each party expresses clearly what it wants. ( )
6. Blaming the other party is also a fruitful approach. ( )
7. Trust begets trust; distrust begets distrust. ( )
8. Many interpersonal conflicts are caused by poor listening. ( )
9. The expression of anger to the person occasioning it must necessarily impair the relationship. ( )
10. Conflict thrives on prejudice. ( )
11. Prejudices – and we all have them – distort out perception. ( )
12. In interpersonal conflict, both persons have the same definition of the problem. ( )

Space at the end (Feel free to mention any characteristic you wish to highlight about yourself)

- This process of assessment is meant to assess a poor illiterate woman in a poor community setting, where social workers face specific problems in helping these women. In many cases they are unable to initiate any action against an abuse either by husband or other relatives.

- The basic details about age education, income and family etc. are same as discussed above. The worker will have to fill in the details and the subsequent answers. The questions are suggestive, you can add or delete or modify as per your requirement.
- Assess the willingness to do something about the problem as suggested earlier.
- Assess the strength of the person to act.
- Assess the support network available such as parents/ friends/brother/grown up children/economic skills/ employer, etc.
- Assess the husband about drug use/alcoholism/income/ reasons for violence against wife/extra marital affair/age difference/other facts relevant in the context such as other family members and their attitude towards client, etc.

Note: Please also see assessment of individual in the chapter on techniques.

Social Worker's Assessment of the Client Based on Interpretation of Facts

Once the client has provided facts, the social worker would pursue the same areas, in the discussion during the sessions, to recheck the facts. In the answers provided by the client, one can look for contradictions, uncertainties or inconsistencies during the discussion, in the client responses, to arrive at a general picture. Check on how the client describes the people around and their contribution to the client's current problems. For example, a self-oriented person would generally blame others, would not own any responsibility for the problems. A social worker should explore all areas with patience to get to know the actual strengths and weaknesses or biases and values which shape a client's construction and interpretation of the persons around and their actions.

The focus of the assessment is to arrive at a tentative understanding of;

- Clients Social Orientation
- Self Orientation Level
- Superiority or Inferiority Complex
- Others Orientation Level
- Level of Leadership Qualities
- Personality Type

- Self Confidence Level
- Thought Pattern
- Values etc.

Other Sources of Getting Facts Helpful in Assessment of a Client

Records of communication with others: This refers to letters, notes or even records of meetings the person may have attended in a office, school or college, etc.

Audio or video records: Events showing the client in different settings, etc. can also provide useful details about the person.

Written communications: Letters, diaries or any creative writings or communications sent to any person or office by the person are also considered relevant sources of information.

Observations of the social worker: The social workers own records of observation of clients behaviour, in particular use of specific words, tone and show of feelings at different junctures of sessions are important sources to be used to assess the client.

Reflecting and Revising

The social worker in subsequent sessions with the client can keep exploring different aspects of the client's behaviour patterns, thought construction, feelings and values, with the dual objective of analysing these and to make the client aware of the areas where the client can bring about a change to impact the relationships. As we suggested the data provided by the client is the basis for exploration but subsequent explanations by the client also add to the existing facts and a process of reflection and review must be carried out all the time to help the client arrive at a self-understanding. The social worker never blames the client or level any criticism against the client, but simply raises issues for the client to ponder upon.

For example at one place the client says that s/he likes being with people and at another point s/he says s/he finds it difficult to trust people. During the facilitation sessions the client is asked to review both the statements to reconfirm which reflects the true picture. The social worker can provide an explanation by saying that usually people like being with other people if not only can they trust them, but also if they are able to accept criticism coming from others and do not get too emotional about these matters, in other words people with a certain degree of self-confidence are more at ease with others. There would be many other statements which would reflect how much self-confidence the client has. For example, a person who is more confident and knowledgeable about self would never or rarely answer cant say about any the statements. The social worker referring to many cant say statements can ask the client to think about why s/he is doing so, is s/he not sure and if so why? And as the review process goes on gradually leading to more explanations coming from the client which are subsequently explained or commented by the social worker, based on her/his expertise and experience. This process of reflection and revision to arrive at a better understanding of one's self with the help of an expert is the key to the facilitation process.

THIRD STAGE

Preparing a Client to Face and Accept the Reality

In the Indian sub continent not many persons ever realize that their relationships are not working out. Even when they do, as they feel unhappy about dealing with different persons in their lives, they still think that the problem lies with the other person. It could be spouse, children or the sub ordinates or colleagues. There are not many persons capable of self-analysis and review. Not many persons are willing to review their own behaviour with others. The few who may conclude that they need to review facts to deal with a situation like extreme anger or continuous tension, indecision, etc. may at best want to discuss it with friends or relatives. The idea of consulting a professional is not very popular. The very idea that you are not in control of your thinking process, hence experience difficulties, for which professional help is required, is not part of the general understanding. Consider these symptoms:

- you are not able to sleep,
- you are not able to focus on your work,
- you are losing temper every time you do not get what you want,
- there are times when you do not even know what you want,
- you are being told in no uncertain terms that you are not behaving,
- there is a general feeling of uneasiness.

Not even one per cent people think of seeking professional help. The general tendency is to think that it is a temporary phenomenon and things will sort themselves out. There is a general feeling that things are not working well because one is passing through a rough patch or bad luck and that things will pan out in due course. The social worker therefore has to drive home the following points;

(a) There is a problem.
(b) The part of the problem may lie with the person.
(c) The problem will not go away all by it self.
(d) It is far easier to change one's own behaviour than to change others.
(e) The professional helps in a scientific manner, like other professionals to address the problem.
(f) That it will usually be a long process to redress the situation fully, but one can start to feel the change, if one is consistent and determined.
(g) That the process may bring to the knowledge of the client certain facts, which may be unpleasant.

The person should be given sufficient time to think over these matters and can resume the process, after deliberating over the issues at leisure to make a determined start.

FOURTH STAGE

Listening to the Client Version of the Problem

The social worker as a professional understands, that the basic problem is rooted in either one or more relationships producing dissatisfactory outcomes causing stress, but the client should be given a chance to identify or explain the problem. The worker should patiently listen, encouraging the client to speak, and take note of specific terms used, the stress level and other feelings, body gestures, etc.

FIFTH STAGE

Developing an Explanation

The process of helping commences with the social worker helping the client to identify the source of the problem, by using the theory of self and others. The client is provided a balanced summary of self-concept and the position on self – to other continuum by providing specific examples, with the help of data collected earlier. The problem in relationship occur because of one-sided approach either too self-centered or to excessive others orientation.

For example, what relationship/s the client seems to be finding it difficult to cope with, is it spouse, child, or work relationship, or a combination of these. It could be that a person is confused about many issues and how to cope with these.

Helping the client to identify the specific causes creating the problem, for example, if it is a case of spouse relationship, does it relate to violent behaviour, lack of warmth, alcoholism, infidelity, etc.

Helping the client to explore what is causing the problem including how the client may have consciously or unconsciously contributed to it.

Once the worker is able to help the client agree on the nature of the problem, For example what is the nature of the problem, such as, is it concerning meeting of needs such as recognition, acceptance, respect, financial or sexual needs, etc. the next step is to arrive at an explanation of what can be done to resolve it.

SIXTH STAGE

Finding a Solution

In other words an explanation of why it occurred and what can the client do it. For example, in a spousal discord, is the client a victim or a cause of the problem or both. Once this point is negotiated, move on to what can be done or discussing the options. The client should review the options to accomplish desired results.

The following tasks are generally addressed at this stage to move towards the desired results.

Goal setting for example,

1. Changing self-concept, reviewing self-image and feelings,
2. Moving towards better emotional control,
3. Opening communication refers to give up acting cold towards the partner and resume normal conversation, etc.
4. Changing communication styles, the client is helped to bring about specific changes for example slowing the delivery, changing the tone, frequency, etc.
5. Moving towards a balance between self and other's orientation.
6. Confidence building, where the client is helped to look at the positive side of the picture, and reducing the anxiety level by acting out different scenarios, without the anxiety.
7. Script Change: The client is helped to bring about a script change, or the description of the same situation, to bring positive change in feelings. For example, viewing the partner as an adversary causing hurt deliberately, is changed to ignorant or impulsive, the behaviour becomes less hurting as there is no motive.

8. There are situations where the client is helped to change jobs, or residence or go out to a quiet place to charge energy levels.

Terminating/Referral

The process of facilitation is terminated after a review session to assess the client's clarity of the problem, client's confidence level, and clarity about goals, stress level and a shared decision that client can manage the problem independently. If there is a need for referral for sorting out other problems, the client is referred to specific specialists.

9

Working with Groups

The process of facilitating relationships in a group will commence after a contract has been made with all the members of the group. The terms of contract will be same as specified in the case of individual with suitable changes incorporated in view of the change of context from individual to group. All members will be part of the contract. A clause in the contract will be included to inform members that they will abide by the rules of the group agreed after discussion, specifying the conduct of the members during the group sessions. The group can be a family, a work group, a self-help group, a children's or youth play group, a sports team and so on. The size of group will therefore vary, but it is advisable to keep it small, where the worker can monitor every one closely. The ideal would be less than eight members, and upper limit not more than twelve. In the contract, the purpose would be facilitating relationships in the group, to achieve social development of all members. Other goals can be added with consent of all members.

Set the Routine

Once the contract has been dealt with, the group should decide about the frequency, place and time of meeting etc. Other matters regarding developing norms can be taken up at this time. The purpose is to set a routine pattern for group to follow. The most important task at this time is, to keep motivating the members, by clarifying their doubts about the feasibility of goals to be achieved and specific benefits that are likely for every member. The group routine will show some ups and down in the beginning, but is likely to become routine and stable, once the members become sure of each other and feel comfortable in the group. The rate of group development will depend on frequency of meetings and degree of similarity among members values and position on self-other continuum. It can slow down if members continue to be self-oriented and attendance is irregular. Some capacity building activities, such as communication exercises, can help in setting the momentum in the group.

In the next session the process of setting down the specific goals of the group would be discussed to make all members focus on these.

In case of serious relationship discord groups, the goals should be stated as:

- To help members to learn to trust others.
- To help members to express themselves.
- To help them learn how they feel about each other.
- To help members learn new coping strategies, to deal with stress, and so on.

In case of growth oriented groups of children/youths.

- To help members learn about their strong points.
- To help them learn about their weaknesses.
- To develop leadership among members.
- To help them learn various activities including sports and games, singing and story-telling to build up confidence levels.
- To help members learn to appreciate and help others.

Clarity about goals can motivate members and help them to assess their progress periodically. The goals should be explained to members along with the role they are expected to play. Members should be encouraged to clarify their doubts right in the beginning or any time during the process. Even arriving at this stage, during the discussions the worker will get a fairly good idea of who different members are and what strengths and problems they bring to the group.

Monitoring

Monitoring refers to a process of gathering information to keep track of all members, their interactions and activities. The process of gathering information requires working out specific indicators and guide lines and creating systems. It is therefore, necessary to be clear about, what information is needed and how it would be collected.

Prepare a Profile of Members

- Their educational status

- Their emotional intelligence level
- Their position in the group, in the case of work groups and teams, both formal and informal
- The bonding with group
- The self-confidence level
- The communication skills
- Interaction with others
- Leadership potential

This profile can serve as the bench mark to see what changes have occurred in individuals, as a result of their participation in group. The list is not exhaustive, the worker can add any other features depending upon the nature of the group.

Develop a system of monitoring the progress of individuals and groups by evolving indicators of change.

For Members

Attendance	Regular	Irregular	Absent
Contribution to group	Good	Average	Poor
Group tasks	Good	Average	Poor
Interaction	Very social	Average	Isolate
Relating to worker	Good	Average	Poor
Relations with members	Very social	Average	Isolate
Duplication others orientation	Good	Average	Poor
Trying to improve self	Good	Average	Poor
Helping others	Good	Average	Poor
Respecting group norms	Good	Average	Poor
Helping to enforce norms	Good	Average	Poor
Drawing out silent members	Good	Average	Poor
Communication skills	Good	Average	Poor
Duplication others orientation	Excessive	Moderate	Poor
Group consciousness	Strong	Moderate	Average
Emotional integration with group	Excellent	Good	Average
Leadership skills	Excellent	Good	Average

The data on most of these indicators can be collected easily as many indicators are self-explanatory. However, others-orientation and self-orientation or personality types, etc. require some skills in measuring these. Others-orientation refers to a tendency on the part of an individual to be conscious of other people's needs and rights. Self-orientation is a tendency to be preoccupied with self-interest even at the cost of others. Introversion refers to a person who likes to avoid interaction with others and extroversion refers to a person who loves interaction with others.

For Group

Meetings of Groups	Very frequent	Frequent	Infrequent
Attendance	Well attended	Average	Poor
Organization	Well organized	Average	Poor
Interaction	Warm	Average	Hostile
Leadership	Effective	Average	Unfocussed
Task Accomplishment	Good	Average	Poor
Programme and Activities	Interesting	Average	Boring
Programme and Activities	Interesting	Need based	Not focused catering to segmental needs

The data on all these indicators should be collected on a regular basis and analysed periodically to assess the change taking place or the progress of the group. The information on the indicators can be collected from different sources such as from members and leaders and from workers own observations. The sources can be decided, depending upon the nature of the group and the members. However, it is advisable to use different sources to maintain objectivity and to note, how different persons rate, the group interaction progress in goal achievement and each other.

Analysing the Relationship Patterns in Group

The relationships in groups, for example in a family, can become stressful because of a number of factors. A primary factor is the discord in values and an unsettled power structure, leading to lack of opportunities for discussion and sharing decisions. If the spouses are not in agreement about their own relationship, the children would become equally confused about their roles. In a similar situation, in a play group or sports team, leadership styles can create subgroups with poor relations leading to lack of team spirit, or group cohesion. A basic requirement for a normal functioning of the group is, a minimum level of compatibility among group members in terms of values, understanding and commitment to group norms, leadership and frequent discussions to sort out issues. The worker should initiate these to begin with.

This would help the worker to see the group functioning objectively, identify the short comings, share these with members and help them to discuss what they want to do about improving it. Barring some very difficult situations, for example where one or more conditions of normal functionality are weak, frequent focused group meetings helped by worker's expert caring interventions, to explain individual reactions and support to modify them, can bring about considerable change.

Indicators for Analysis

- Group power structure or decision-making processes and styles
- Degree of differences in values
- Frequency of emotional outbursts
- Communication patterns
- Degree of openness or sharing issues
- Financial position and sharing patterns
- Group bonding
- Growth oriented groups can continue for longer duration as experiences in the group will go a long way in increasing communication skills, confidence level, and others-orientation of members.

Group Conflict

When human beings come together to work, play or carry out any other activity, conflict is inevitable. To quote Rousseau, *'man becomes wicked in the company of fellow human beings.'* Differences among members in a group will occur in resolution of issues, such as to select the group goals, control over resources, strategies to pursue the goals, in creating a group structure and in distribution of power. In a self-help group of women, the concept of empowerment, financial contributions, loan disbursement and selection of office bearers are all issues likely to generate differences. Group conflict presents a wide variety, such as between individual members, between member/s and group, between a member and the leader/worker, between members and leader/worker and between sub groups. The reasons for conflict will differ, depending on the context. The nature of conflict in a treatment group, for example, will be different from that in a task group. Many authors agree that conflict will generally start in the middle, working or performing stage (see Toseland and Rivas, 2001). In a treatment group, conflict is generally between members. The reasons may be miscommunication, which results in lack of trust and defensive behaviour. Inadequacy to deal with diversity is a common cause of conflict, in all kind of groups. Similarly, exclusionary practices are a potential source of conflict, in groups beside ego clashes. Heated exchanges, silence, negative feedback, personal remarks directed against individuals, attacking the integrity of individuals, are all symptoms, indicative of conflict in a group.

Some potential sources of group conflict can be summarized as follows:

- Miscommunication
- Ideological differences
- Rigidity of group structure
- Cultural differences
- Inability to accept diversity
- Location of power
- Leadership styles
- Group goals not addressing individual needs of a sizeable section of group
- A plurality of options
- Outside environment
- Lack of clear group norms
- Paucity of resources
- Greater heterogeneity among members

The process of facilitating group relationships will have to address all or some of these problems as they present themselves in the group. For example, in case of miscommunication the worker will help the members to rethink and rephrase part of what they have understood, to set it right. In case of cultural differences playing politics in selecting goals or strategies to deal with them or selecting leadership, the worker's role is to bring it into open to show how this would spoil the group relationship and defeat the very purpose of group. Many of these problems in the group can be handled easily or may not arise if everyone is clear about the group norms and how they help in keeping relationships strong and objective. The group relationship or for that matter no relationship works when people get the impression that they are not being treated fairly.

10

Working with Communities

In social work, the term community work has several meanings. Community work literature tends to be prescriptive. It suggests what community workers should do and how. But it is difficult to define what they do (Checkoway, 1995; Butcher, 1992). The term therefore has evoked some confusion as to what the core task of a community worker is. For example, if a worker looks at the task as a development worker, the primary task becomes development of a particular area. Since development has a very wide scope and requires various inputs involving various professionals, it cannot solely belong to social work. It was included as a subject in social work curriculum in USA in 1940 (Government of India, 1987). It was not until the 1960s that schools of social work, were willing to regard it as a legitimate area of practice when student enrollment in the subject increased from 1.5 per cent in 1960 to 9 per cent in 1969 (Rivera and Erlich, 1995).

The community work began in UK to organize charity to help the poor: The settlement houses, started for the rural poor, who migrated to urban areas, led to the intellectuals taking up the cause of the poor, to highlight the poor conditions in which they lived, at the close of the nineteenth century in UK. Similar work was started by US to cater to the needs of poor migrants from Europe at the end of the nineteenth century. By the turn of the century community councils were formed, to attend to the physical and social aspects of slums. In India, the term is used to describe a method of social work to intervene in the life of a community. It has now become a widely used method of social work in India. This method became particularly popular since the rethinking in social work, to adopt a developmental approach to human problems. Despite the growing popularity of this method, in India and other developing countries, a theoretical perspective to guide its practice, remained elusive. To begin with, what exactly does the term 'community organization' refers to? It has different meanings for different groups. Professionals in the field of health education and social welfare understand the term somewhat differently, from issue-oriented community groups or ideologically committed groups (Chatterjee and Koleski, 1970; Burghardt, 1982; McMillan and Chavis, 1986; Bracht, 1990; Green and Ottoson, 1994; Dixon, 1995). Chatterjee made an attempt to develop a typology of community organization by examining the efforts of both professionals and other community groups, with a view to conceptualize different forms of community organization (Chatterjee, 1975; also see Patton and Chissell, 1990). But the debate is still on. Further, community work is eclectic, since it is culled from a wide spectrum of disciplines, practices and experiences. Before we proceed further, let us examine the term community, and then try to conceptualize, the need for working with it. Leonard (1977) identified four elements in a practice framework:

1. Community or neighbourhood;
2. Local organizational and political context;
3. Wider structural variables;
4. Process of community work.

We could include the organization/person undertaking community work, to complete the list and shall deal with theoretical concepts dealing with the process of working with a community later. At this stage, we will concentrate on definitions/concepts relating to community, its needs and the central concerns of working with communities.

Concepts Relating to Community

Of all the words in sociological discourse, community is the one that most obviously comes from wonderland, in that it can mean just anything. In 1995, Hillery listed 94 definitions and suggested that the only common thread was people (Smith, 1996). It is attractive to politicians of both Left and Right, judging by cross party interest in the communitarian ideas of Etzioni (1995).

However, the notion that 'community' is an intrinsic good has been challenged, for example by Edward Norman (1994), and Pahl (1995). They argue that traditional community was morally and culturally narrow minded, oppressive to women, outsiders and minorities, less harmonious than painted by nostalgia and inimical to individual rights.

David Lyon pointed out in (I984) that the halo of 'community' can be used by the Left to justify almost any local political action, and the attempt to build diverse types of alternative utopian collectives. Meanwhile, the Rightwing use 'community' ideologically, for example to disguise welfare budget reductions as care in the 'community', by unpaid female kin. The notion 'community' is often used to sanitize the most individualized and regressive taxes, it is also used to curb individual freedom and divide the larger society in smaller conflicting segments.

Definitions of community fall mainly into two categories. In one, the main concern is place or neighbourhood. The second approach focuses upon, the notion of solidarity or communion, which may go beyond a particular location. It is impossible to talk about community today without taking into account both aspects (see Davies and Herbert, 1993). The focus of analysis in social work is generally on locality (Cooke, 1989) and the restructuring of local economies (Smith, 1996). In developing countries, the communities social workers choose for their intervention are: urban slums; rural villages; and semi-urban communities, which are in fact villages close to urban areas and losing their rural characteristics in the process of urbanization.

The view of the small community as a basic unit in society was most explicitly developed by Robert Redfield (1947). For Redfield, the little community had four defining qualities: distinctiveness, small size, self-sufficiency and homogeneity of inhabitants. This conception, like many others similar to it, has been criticized on a variety of grounds (Worsley, 1970). Hence these defining qualities should not be taken for granted. It is more useful to acknowledge the fact of communities within communities, and the influence of outside factors such as, the State, the nature of economy, the dominant social values and the political process. Theoretical explanations of any issue in a community cannot be simple and straight forward, but the common thread that Hillery (1995) noted was people. The very notion of community emerges around the human actors in an area, for example who they are, how homogenous or diverse they are, the nature of their economic, social and political interactions, giving rise to patterns of mutual bonding. If we follow this paradigm, the success or otherwise of any intervention in a community will simply depend on, how the bonding patterns could be made more inclusive, in their orientation. In other words relationships between people in a community become extremely important. The social worker hence would have to study and analyse all major relationships in a community, such as; between different religions, caste, linguistic, regional, economic, occupational, and political groups. Further, social norms governing gender relations, between age groups, family members particularly spouses and parent and child, etc. assume significance in giving the community its unique nature and consequently its responses to its needs and issues to survive.

In communities, inhabitants interact with different people for various purposes, within a range of administrative and institutional boundaries. The abandonment of the simple view of community as a unitary whole leads us to consider overlapping and complex social ties as the reality a worker is called upon to handle. S/he cannot therefore take unity and harmony for granted, but should take into account divisions, specializations and conflicts among people. The central theme in community work practice therefore has to be to strengthen human relationships to the extent possible, to accomplish any change in one or several areas in the life of the target population in a community. The central concern of the community worker is to develop co-operative and collaborative attitudes and practices in the community and increase its resource base to reduce its dependence on outside resources. The task for social worker is to improve community dialogues and relations, while other professionals can help them in improving the community resource base.

Communities and its Environment

The current models of community work based on learning, action, or resource development giving rise to a multiplicity of tasks create confusion in understanding social work field practice (Sayer, 1986). An understanding of the diversity among personal and community issues will help in bridging the gap between individual and collective or personal and institutional change.

In facilitating relationships in a community the central concern of the worker are the community needs whether economic, social or physical infrastructure for example roads, water, electricity or communication, etc. Even safety needs of residents fall within the community needs. The idea of facilitating relationship is to evolve a consensus around these issues and strategies for tackling these, keeping in check the personal issues or preferences.

Gloria Levitas (1967) argues that there is evidence that people will put up with 'all manner of discomfort' to maintain the pattern of culture that gives meaning to their lives. She suggests to pay more attention to the organizational structure that underlies these cultures and consequently the living conditions and housing patterns that go with them. The marginalization of localities mirrors not only social and spatial inequalities but also cultural differences and the wish of the dominant culture to establish its 'superiority'. New social and spatial forms can be created when cultures as adaptive systems are allowed to play their part in the continuous interaction between technological, political, religious and other structures. The realities of ethnic and cultural groups cut right across concepts of locality and community as we define them. The struggle for cultural hegemony could, therefore, destroy the more organic social ties and making the superordinate legal and political systems weak and fragmented. Community work, thus, will not create radical change in itself, but is part of the mass of interrelating micro practices which create thinking about social life.

Aggregate-level analysis emphasizes the ways in which community environment influences the character of interpersonal interactions, exposure to local conditions, and the availability of societal resources to manage those conditions, but they offer little understanding of the proximal experiences that directly impinge on the lives of individuals. Communities define the context of children's development by shaping the likelihood that children will experience a variety of advantages and disadvantages. Thus, children's development cannot be fully understood without considering communities and their characteristics. The empirical validity of this claim has been established in analysis which finds strong neighbourhood effects on children's IQ and behaviour problems (Brooks-Gunn et al., 1993), teenage childbearing (Crane, 1991), and delinquency (Hagan, 1985). Children's mental health is influenced to some extent by economic experiences in their immediate families as well as by experiences common to persons who live in the same area. The environment of the neighbourhood as it is sometimes referred to, influences children's behavioural pattern such as school aspirations, career choices and so on, irrespective of children's economic status.

The unique disadvantages of urban environments have been debated, with some viewing them as more alienating, more fragmented, noisier, and more crowded than rural differences. However, in developing countries urban environments are more conducive to providing education to children particularly girls compared to rural communities. Urban communities provide more conducive environment for lower caste and women empowerment.

Although results are inconsistent, several studies indicate that rates of persons following collective norms are higher in rural than in urban areas for both adults and children. It is significant to note that there is a vast difference between rural and urban communities in developed and developing communities, consequently leading to very different conceptualizations of community and its impact on people. There are some studies who found greater cohesiveness in communities which are more homogenous in terms of religion, caste and occupations.

Frank Bonilla (see Worsley, 1970), in his study of Favelas (hill side slums) in Rio de Janeiro, found that in urban slums, despite the problems of illiteracy, malnutrition, alcoholism, crime and violence, some form of human co-existence and social cohesion existed. The attitude of people towards various institutional agents outside their 'social world' was revealing. Labour unions and students (two groups that have stood as champions of the poor in Latin America) were viewed as among the least helpful, and least interested in the life and welfare of the favelados (people living in slums); priests and school teachers were regarded as somewhat more sincere in their efforts to help (Worsley, 1970). Bryan Robert's study in Guatemala City (1973) also shows that the poor participate less than the better-off in voluntary associations.

Community can also be broadly defined as the compromises people make to coexist in an interdependent relationship. Community work then becomes a discourse to develop a sense of interdependence requiring efforts to coexist.

Community Activists/Leaders

Community activists are seen as persons investing time and resources in dealing with common problems of the persons living in the area. They may initiate a group to deal with a social problem, work with an existing group to deal with a social problem, are member in organizations concerned with public issues, contacting public officials about a social problem. In many ways community activists are similar to what political party activists do; they both follow a general activist pattern and they both have a high level of psychological involvement in community matters. The main difference is that community activists are much less concerned with politics than are party activists.

Major Community Concerns

Full literacy: In India full literacy is a distant goal and even in urban areas a lot of people are illiterate. Efforts in motivating them are not very successful, yet many non-governmental organizations getting funds to carry out that work undertake it as part of their efforts to work with communities.

Hundred percent school enrolment and retention: This is a more relevant task and both government and non-government funds are available to carry out this work in the communities. This work is needed both in the urban areas and rural areas.

Drug and alcohol free environment: Alcohol use in poor communities both in urban and rural communities is spreading very fast. It creates additional problems of domestic violence, thefts, health problems and poverty, as many alcohol addicts either become economically dysfunctional or waste their resources on alcohol and drug use.

Economic improvement: Economic betterment of poor families is important to achieve full enrolment and retention of children in schools and particularly helping in dealing with many gender related issues. Generating livelihood opportunities for both men and women particularly in poor communities is a major concern.

Conflict free communities; Conflicts in communities are common, some conflicts are short-term outbursts of anger and frustrations, but the divide peoples energies and resources. Tackling these are important in organising people for better community facilities. Major conflicts either among caste groups or religious groups can prove more harmful for the community.

Better health and sanitation facilities: The poor communities are neither planned nor possess any resources to undertake sanitation work. The drainage system, lack of toilet facilities and safe drinking water are some common problems of both rural and urban communities.

Recreation facilities are missing in many areas due to limitation of space and lack of resources to develop these. The importance of recreation is a very low priority in the life of poor people, hence the very concept of parks, sports and cultural activities for children and youth are no where to be seen in many communities. This gives rise to a lot of problems both for children and youth as they resort to unhealthy practices for channeling their normal needs and energies. Providing and maintaining proper recreation facilities in communities remains an important development concern.

Planned and effective community work requires, an analysis of both the general context within which practice takes place, and of the specific issues that are to be tackled. Therefore, there is a need to develop a local theoretical perspective and plan its application in a specific context, such as the population characteristics, the cultural and social norms, the economic resources and prevailing relationship pattern, etc. The analysis of the context within which practice takes place therefore requires an understanding of the social, political and economic structures, which determine the issues which influences the day to day lives of the people. We are, therefore, also concerned with the historical process of current realities in a particular area, for example the nature of religious and caste interactions, the current social relationships, economic resources and its distribution, and its linkages with local political power equation, etc.

As Fischer (1973) noted, the social work tradition views the community essentially as a social organism; it focuses on social issues such as building a sense of community, gathering together social service organizations or lobbying for and delivering social resources. It assumes that basically the community's problem is social disorganization. The organizer functions either as an 'enabler' to help the community gather itself together or as an advocate to secure additional services for the community. The strategy is gradualist and consensual, which means that organizers assume a unity of interest between the power elite of the neighbourhood and common man and assume a willingness of at least some in power to meet community needs. Mere willingness on the part of a few elites is not likely to be helpful in meeting the needs of the communities as experience even in developed countries has indicated (Rahman, 1990; Smith, 1996). What we need now is more willingness among the common people to work for and share the community resources in a more just and transparent manner with the elite. In other words, diverse segments living together and developing a better understanding of relationship with a more inclusive approach for sharing scarce opportunities and resources is likely to enhance the successful completion of any project in a community.

Political linkage in the Indian context is yet another important factor in community work in India. Any effort at working with people in India will inevitably have political implications. The professional approach to define 'community organization' often makes no reference to it. The social work process of community work tries to prescribe a value-free position for the worker, and advises the worker to keep away from political discussions and controversies and not to take sides. The community work practice has taken it seriously, consequently limiting the scope of effective community work practice. The Indian situation calls for a rethinking on this issue. Political education and not propaganda should form an essential part of community work in India. Therefore, a more viable definition of community work in India would be: a process through which a worker or an organization intervenes in the life of a group of people to initiate some projects for the development of the community. The scope of these projects may vary from organizing for ensuring human rights for the exploited and vulnerable segment to delivery of services, by facilitating better relationship among the diverse population of the community. Community work thus no longer remains confined to a single neighbourhood, and may have to forge wider networking to deal with local issues common to many neighbourhoods/communities. In doing so, it may well have to cope with existing political realities and to seek support from political networks.

In facilitating relationships in a community, the first stage of the process begins with defining the community itself. In some cases it may be a neighbourhood in an urban area, in another a village and in a different perspective a large group of persons with common needs and issues such as Female Sex Workers or Dalits, etc.

In facilitating relationships in a community, a contract is not needed in the form it is done in case of an individual and group/family. Instead a process of awareness and understanding and need for reviewing the existing relationship and redefining it is initiated.

Since the number of persons in a community, is generally large different strategies for communicating are generally used.

However the community worker must be clear about the purpose of working with the community, which in our case is facilitating relationships, since we believe if we can achieve this objective, subsequent issues will sort themselves out with some help from professionals.

The community worker, therefore, begins her work with an analysis of the community relationships or in other words what are the current boundaries which divide people in this community. The analysis will begin with identifying prominent groups and their relationships in the community. For example, screening relationships of different religious groups, castes groups, political groups, etc. will greatly help in identifying the existing tensions there and in dealing with these. Rank the nature or intensity of relationships in the community to concretize your understanding to assess the possibility of achieving a working relationship.

Identify Major Conflict Areas

- Identify major actors interested in promoting conflicts.
- Assess the possibility of promoting a dialogue between differing parties.
- Initiate communication between different interest groups to motivate them to agree to a code of conduct, and identify common goals.
- Develop a core group representing all sections in the community to accept joint leadership.
- Develop groups of young volunteers and train them to carry out different tasks in the community in collaboration with the core group.
- Train both the core group members and volunteers.
- Assess the stability and accountability of both over a period of time, say every six months or a year and so on.
- Identify all government schemes providing different benefits to the members of the community; assess the awareness and usage level.
- Communicate these to the core groups.
- Identify possible sponsors of welfare projects needed in the community.
- Help the core group to get in touch with these sponsors directly.
- Review the relationships in the community.
- Case study of gender relations in a community as reflected by non-participation of girls in education.

Getting to Know the Community

In developing countries, the type of communities social workers choose for their intervention are: urban slums; rural villages; and semi-urban communities, which are in fact villages close to urban areas and losing some of their rural characteristics in the process. Though the term 'community' is used for different purposes in sociology, in the description and analysis of society, in social work literature, it is used to denote a particular spatial or geographical unit.

The worker is expected to develop familiarity with the people in the community to begin his/her work. The worker can only get to know the community by spending some time in the community. There are two ways of doing this:

Seeking help to get an introduction: The first approach is to approach the community through some one living or working in the community. Generally, the worker approaches prominent people like leaders, schoolteachers, doctors, or any other person and explains the purpose of his or her visit. The worker may straightaway reveal his or her plan to open an adult education centre or a similar project or just express the objective as to work with the community to get to know them and their problems.

Informal approach: In the informal approach, the worker simply starts visiting the community and meets people at tea stalls or pan shops. S/he may chat with people sitting on the roadside outside their houses. S/he may tell people informally that he/she works for an organization which has been doing some work in a particular field, and explain his/her presence by simply stating that the organization is exploring the possibilities of doing similar work in this community.

In both approaches, what is obvious is that the worker clearly lacks a sense of direction. S/he has no idea of where to start and how to cover the entire community.

Professional Approach

A professional worker will have a definite plan of action. Therefore, in a programme of community work, identification of the area is the first step. Depending on the size of the area and population, the worker should make a tentative plan of households on a map. S/he should then try to divide them into pockets or wards.

Ideally each unit should consist of 15–20 houses, or all the houses in a small lane, and so on. This should be done on the worker's first visit to the community. The worker can then prepare a plan of talking to each household in one unit. He/she may then schedule his time for meeting people in different units for the purpose of getting to know them. In the process, he/she may make preparations for the second stage of work, by collecting useful information through listening and observation. He/she can begin to sense the relationship between people. During the preliminary visits in an Indian context, the easiest group to approach is children playing in the street or open spaces. The worker can spend some time playing and chatting with them. Children are a very good means of approaching their parents.

At this stage, the worker should not give false hopes, or make tall claims about what he/she or his/her organization can do for the people. One should also avoid developing relationships by invoking caste, religious or regional loyalties, since this will prove counter-productive in the long term. The use of such loyalties may convey the impression to people that the worker is prepared to accord preferential treatment to people of his/her own caste, religion or region. The worker must counter such expectations and tendencies, in order to prepare people to work together. The worker should not hide his caste or religious identity either.

Similarly, excessive reliance on any particular leader, individual or group to establish initial contact and a working base in the community, can create similar problems. The worker and agency themselves are a kind of resource for people. Hence, there is always an attempt by a section of the community to monopolize them by granting certain facilities. However, when they realize that the worker will treat them all equally and is unlikely to oblige them with favours, they might tend to become disenchanted with the worker and the programme.

Some people have a tendency to become personal at their first meeting. They want to share their personal troubles with the worker, and some may even be interested in finding all about the worker's own family. The worker should politely divert such queries towards a discussion on general issues. The worker should exercise a conscious control on his/her desire to lecture, win over, impress or push people to accept his/her viewpoint.

Beyond a certain point, to express his or her own preference for certain political parties or leaders, observance of any religious or other traditional practice must be avoided. The worker should convey an impression of being open, flexible and accommodating, rather than having a closed mind and a rigid attitude.

Other Methods of Entry into the Community

The approach discussed above will be helpful if the worker is approaching community work with an open agenda, which Baldock (1974) termed as the Ultra Non-Directive Approach. However, this is not generally the case. In India, the worker or agency has a definite goal in mind. In such cases, the worker follows what Baldock terms a 'selling model' approach. This requires sharing with a group of people in the community, what the worker/agency proposes to do. It is quite common for agencies interested in adult education or awareness-building to announce their programme in the community. The programme sharing is done by using various techniques, such as wall posters, film shows, informal discussions, or even door-to-door meetings with families. The worker will stand a better chance of enlisting community participation if he/she permits some flexibility in working out the details of how the programme should be made operational.

The method usually followed by community workers, particularly where they have already obtained funding for a project, is to establish a specific service like a non-formal education centre for children or women. The worker tries to develop links with the wider community by running the service in the area. He/she may try to take up other programmes later on as he/she gets to know the community in the course of time, and may also initiate a process of developing a community structure which can take over the programme and run it through indigenous resources. However, such an approach has been found to encourage people's passive dependence on the worker/agency, and it has generally created problems in running the programme through indigenous efforts. The main difference between the two approaches is that in the former, the idea is first shared by the people, and other details such as location and the nature of the programme are decided in consultation with them. In the latter approach, the involvement of the community begins after the establishment of the service in the area. This, however, must not lead one to conclude that service delivery is the main objective in both approaches, especially in the latter one.

There are numerous examples which indicate that workers have used service centres as the focal point of entry into the community to achieve much wider objectives, such as mobilizing women or landless labourers to get organized and fight for their rights. We have discussed these here as possible approaches to rapport building in the community. Community workers should realize the need for clarity and develop skills in communications which are extremely important in community work.

People consider community action as a viable option when they are convinced that some thing good can happen. They come together by the common recognition of a problem or a situation, striving to do something about it. The only difference is that, today, some organizations consciously initiate this process by making people aware of common problems which require collective action on their part. This collective action often covers more than one community and\or neighbourhood. Examples of this include organizations working with women, landless labourers, slum dwellers, tribal and other sections of the rural poor. Even purely service delivery programmes of education, health and child welfare may be simultaneously undertaken by an organization/group in more than one community.

Task-oriented community work has two models: One, which is identified by Rothman (1969) as the 'neighbourhood development model', aiming at service delivery to meet needs in one or more communities; and a second, the 'developmental model', which aims to bring about changes in the consciousness of the people with whom they work, to influence public opinion in general and public policies at local, district or state level. The boundaries of community action and social action may not always be easy to demarcate (Siddiqui, 1984).

Developing a Community Profile

A community profile is information about the community and its members. This information will help the worker to understand the members of the community and the existing discourses.

These are some guidelines on the kind of information the workers should know about the community. There is no need for developing a perfect understanding in the beginning itself. That would be counterproductive, since the perceptions may undergo change, or the realities may change with the time. It is necessary to have a variety, of information, to provide a good description of the community. The knowledge should be acquired in partnership with the local leaders and the community members. The purpose is to look at the facts with them, in their cultural context. The use of participatory rapid appraisal (PRA) is a well-known technique to collect information about the community (see Chambers, 1994) in both rural and urban areas. Information collection process, if applied with due care provides a forum for an unbiased dialogue with different stakeholders in the community. This may help the worker to understand the difficulties faced or visualized by participants in attempting any development or change in the community.

The guidelines provided are suggestive and the workers may use their imagination in different context in adding and subtracting whatever is necessary. The starting point however is to know the basic facts such as,

What are the boundaries of the community?

Population of the Community

What is the total number of people involved? It is helpful to know the number of families living in the community and the details such as; children both female and male, the number of young persons, and the number of older people.

Economic Profile

What do most of the people do for a living? What do most of the women do? How many children go to school? What do the other children do? What do the teenagers do? How much money do the people earn and how do they earn it? Identify the number of earning members in a family, the kind of assets they own, the difference in income and the patterns of consumption. Migration patterns, if any.

Social Profile

Social attitudes and relationships. Average years of schooling. Type of schools in the community. Importance accorded to education. Gender differences in access and levels etc.

What languages are usually spoken in the community? Which one is used most? What language (s) can the people read and write? How many people can read and write well enough to use simple instructional material? Gender differences.

Culture and Gender Relations

- Specific cultural rituals, festivals and events
- Role of women, freedom and mobility
- Factions and cultural groups

Religion and Caste

What religions and castes are present in the community? Do any of these have special rules that have to be considered, such as holy festivals and days, rules for women?

What groups are there, in the community? For example, women's groups, caste divisions, religious groups, regional groups, economic and occupational groups etc.

General Facilities

- Places of worship
- A meeting place and who can use it and when
- Health care facilities
- Co-operatives and market
- Physical facilities
- Types of housing, water supply, roads, electricity etc.
- Transportation and communication facilities in the community.
  (Also see assessment of a community in the chapter on techniques).

Determining Community Needs

The worker should make a list of the needs. These may be, basic needs such as better health, water supply and sanitation or better roads etc. Information' needs such as, to find out about a particular service or government policy. Economic needs such as, how to produce better crops, or find employment or becoming self-employed, getting a loan etc. Educational needs such as informal education, better education facilities, technical education etc., textbooks and supplementary coaching facilities such as computer training etc. or recreational needs such as sports facilities or organizing cultural and religious festivities etc. There may be people who want help in protection against eviction by the State or the land mafia.

The worker analyses the data to find answers to following queries:

- What are the main areas of concern in various groups?
- Are there differences in the concept of need?
- What is the level of willingness of the groups to work together?
- Is there a gap between expressed and actual need?
- What could be the different phases for developing the programme?
- What are the community resources?

Programme Planning

Programme planning means that by now the worker or the agency has enough information about people living in the community, and has some data about what may be termed as 'need' or community issues, as expressed by different groups. A decision regarding the plan of action that will help in meeting the needs identified or issues raised has to be prepared.

Mobilizing Peoples Participation

Many community workers find themselves frustrated after years of hard work since they discover that no one seems to be interested in what they are trying to do. Ambitious plans of community development in India fail partly due to the lack of peoples' participation. As the old saying goes, you can take a horse to the water but you can't make him drink. Human beings are even more difficult to handle. It is much more difficult to even take them to the water. For example, the efforts at adult literacy, social education, and even health education have failed miserably because people just did not respond. There is no magic formula to motivate people to participate. Yet, there are some insights, which years of experience of working with the people have brought to light. The concept of 'felt need' is the one which is generally mentioned by most authors. It suggests that the worker must always take up work in the areas, where there is a 'general acceptance' of its need. In practice however, this is not an easy task. First, one has to decide what the people think is needed and secondly whether it is a need of a section or the people in general. In response to preliminary inquiries by the worker, people may show great enthusiasm about a non-formal education programme for children or women. But as the worker soon discovers, not many people turn up when a programme is started.

Identify the system of administration and decision-making in the community. The actors involved, a local government officer, a community committee, a political worker, or a group of elders\elites. The way decisions are made, and who are the prime beneficiaries. The centres of dissents and how the, dissent is dealt with.

Factors Affecting People's Participation in a Community

- The extent of participation envisaged by the worker or agency and stage of the process of working with the community,
- The culture and spatial characteristics of the community,
- The gap between community needs and programmes the organization is expected to carry out.

Participation is too often conceived as an effort on the part of individuals to assist in the implementation of plans already made. This kind of involvement prescribes the passive acceptance of services and the provision of support in cash or in kind, in giving money for a pump, digging a well for water supply, or laying bricks for a health centre or a school. Other forms of participation that we envisaged are making use of services offered, like attending classes at the adult education centre, making use of health services, or sending children to school. In such a scheme, participation begins only after the programme has been put into place. In another approach, the community is expected to participate right from the beginning, as it is involved in thinking, planning, deciding, enacting and evaluating the whole programme, with the overall objective of socio-economic development. Theoretically, it might be obvious that an organization is more likely to emerge in the latter case, but considering reality in the developing countries, this may not be feasible in many cases.

The worker should critically examine the feasibility of any proposed project before s/he puts it to actual practice. For example, check the details of forming of a self-help group or generating livelihood opportunities and be clear about what they can deliver.

Secondly, even in a situation where the worker wishes to undertake a pre-determined programme, she\he must plan a strategy for involving people in its implementation. It is often found that in his\her anxiety to achieve concrete results or success, the worker rushes ahead at a faster pace than the people can follow. In order to enlist people's participation, the worker must continuously enable them to do things and take their own decisions. S/He can suggest what can be done, but refrain from pushing them to do something unless they are ready for it. It may be better to have small periods of inactivity rather than a short period of hectic activity followed by a total withdrawal from the programme. Too much must not be expected too soon. The feeling that problems can be solved in a short period is not necessarily based on the fact that traditional societies take time to change. The programme-spread can become too fast and hence get diffused.

Capacity Building

The worker should understand that in the context of the current socioeconomic milieu in rural areas and slums, the capacity of people to participate is severely restricted. The quality and pace of their participation will gradually improve if the worker is capable of analysing factors which impede their participation and takes timely steps to remove them. Helping people to participate at a level and in issues in accordance with their capacities, will be a better strategy rather than expecting them to participate in all issues. A process of capacity building is very helpful at this stage. Making a beginning through small groups and gradually selecting people and preparing them to participate at a larger level, may yield more positive results. Similarly, allowing for a period of apprehension and mistrust, which restricts their participation, should also be kept in mind. Finally, the worker must keep in mind that the people will participate if they are convinced of the merit of the programme, both individually and collectively.

Inter-group Dynamics

Theoretically, one can argue that a worker should identify important factions in a community and its leaders. He should then approach them all with a view to enlist their cooperation in his efforts to identify problems or needs of the community and to explore ways in which these needs can be met through collective efforts. The practice accounts of community workers, however, reveal that even where such an approach is used, not all leaders show a positive response towards the worker at least in the initial stages. Further, they start making demands on the worker, insist on reordering priorities to suit the needs of their own faction, rather than identify issues relevant to the whole community. Even such a small issue as to where the venue of the meeting should be, or where a non-formal education centre should be started, creates difficulties for the worker. Each faction wishes to monopolize opportunities. Generally, the worker in such a situation is governed by one or the other group and in the process, other groups may start feeling discriminated right from the beginning. The worker should avoid closely relating to any one particular group or faction in the community, or even giving an impression of doing so.

Community work therefore involves dealing with various groups in a community. One of the central concerns of the worker is to understand the dynamics of inter-group relations. There are two sets of explanations provided by social psychologists to understand the nature of such dynamics: the conflict-of-interest model and the social-identity model.

The conflict-of-interest model explains group conflict as the direct outcome of a competition between different groups to achieve the same goal, or when they have different and mutually incompatible objectives (Sherif, 1966, 1988). For example, when two groups based on caste, religion, linguistic affiliation or political ideology wants to capture power, conflict between such groups would be inevitable. Similarly, a group wanting to provide a better role for women in society, and another wanting to maintain the status quo, will come into conflict.

Sherif further points out that when different groups are faced with a situation where they both want to achieve a common goal, hostilities between them are likely to decline. For example, different caste groups may come together to prevent another group, belonging to a different caste, religion, region or linguistic affinity, from capturing power. Various groups in a community may sink their differences, if the existence of the whole community is threatened.

Tajfel (1970) suggested that social identity is the cause of inter-group conflict; the mere fact of the classification of people into different groups is sufficient to give rise to inter-group conflict. Each person acquires his\her social identity from his\her group affiliation. They would, thus, endeavour to deprecate the out-group, to establish the superiority of their own group, hence leading to a conflict.

Two models have been suggested for the resolution of inter-group conflicts. Sherif values the introduction of super-ordinate goals, which means the identification of goals which are equally important for the conflicting groups, and which forces them to come together. But this strategy will only last up to the point where the super-ordinate goal is achieved. Inter-group conflict is likely to recur once the goal is achieved.

The GRIT model (Graduated Reciprocation in Tension Reduction) for resolving inter-group conflict was mooted by Osgood (1962), and was basically designed to deal with conflicts between nations. This simply means that one group should unilaterally launch a peace offensive, which is likely to generate a reciprocal response from the other party. Such an approach is usually found to be more effective when the more powerful of the groups resorts first to a conciliatory approach.

The community-work approach to the resolution of inter-group conflicts should be based on an understanding of intra-group and inter-group dynamics, and shall apply both these models simultaneously. The creation of a super-ordinate goal in the form of a common community identity, coupled with persuasion of the more powerful of the contending groups to consider a conciliatory approach towards the others, could succeed in at least containing conflicts, if they cannot be altogether resolved.

The power of group norms and their influence on individuals is a natural phenomenon and therefore some glorification of the in-group and partial deprecation of the out-group is likely to remain, despite one's best efforts.

Importance of Cultural Orientation

In India, traditions and customs have a strong hold on common people. On the other hand, urban educated people have a different world view towards different issues. The community worker may or may not have the socio-economic background as the community s/he may work with. His\her world view on many issues may greatly vary from ideas and practices of people s/he works with. It is, therefore, important for the worker to be conscious of such differences. A worker, for example, may believe in free interaction among different sexes, whereas in a tradition-bound community, it is unthinkable. The worker should not impose her\his ideas on people. The worker should understand that each culture has its own logic, that he should respect people's right to follow their traditions and customs. Dress restrictions, language codes, greeting rituals or even food restrictions may exist, the worker would do well to get along with such local customs in order to gain acceptance and respect of the community.

However, this does not mean that the worker should support customs harmful to people. For example, there are a number of areas, superstitious belief for healing, negative attitude towards female education, family planning or early marriage, etc. which could actually be the intervention areas for worker thus should not be supported. Even in these cases, an attitude of respecting the cultural differences is usually helpful. One may try to change a community's attitude towards female education, without insisting on co-education facilities. Similarly, one may try to prevent early marriages, on health grounds.

Developing a Community Organization

Once the core group in the community has stabilized, it can be developed into a community organization and can be termed as resident welfare association. Rules regarding the organization, such as number of members to be elected/selected by the residents, other office bearers, their terms of office, duties and powers, etcetera can be worked out, to formalise its structure.

Capacity Building of Members

A programme of training, both for the members and office bearers and the residents in general, should be undertaken for making them capable of communal living and developing and strengthening a positive attitude towards each other for stabilizing collaborative attitudes. The training programmes of this kind are offered by a number of non-governmental organizations, whose help can easily be enlisted. In poorer localities literacy classes, human rights, family welfare and awareness generation programmes relating to health can easily be put in place. Income generation related skill training, both for men and women, has been found to be quite popular in poor neighbourhoods.

Evaluation

A periodic evaluation is necessary for monitoring the progress of the process of facilitating relationships in the community. It requires developing suitable indicators, such as incidents of minor and major conflicts between members, families and groups, manner of sharing common resources such as water, open spaces, community toilets/bathrooms, and like, increase or decline in community meeting, participation in capacity building programmes, school participation rates of both boys and girls, etc. Any major achievement in terms of starting new services, financial inputs, construction of new roads, lighting arrangement, etc.

through collaborative efforts, should be taken into account and given due place in the evaluation report.

Withdrawal

A withdrawal plan should also be prepared by the worker in collaboration with the core group/community organization. The stabilization and smooth functioning of the residents welfare association and functioning of capacity building programmes and its success are a good indication of the time for withdrawal of the worker, however withdrawal does not mean a total delinking of the worker/organization which has initiated the process of facilitation. It simply refers to gradual decrease in inputs by the social worker. Yearly progress reports, visits and periodic inputs if needed or requested by the community should go on to keep the effort going at building peaceful communities.

11

Social Action

Dealing with Macro Realities

The industrialized economies, going through the process of development in the late 19th century undertook efforts at social organization or rather reorganization of societal relationships. The democratic welfare ideology was to reduce the gap between economic classes, give equal opportunity to common man to participate in the development of the society. The religious and social categories were melting away gradually. The modern state's belief (Offe 1975, 1996) that the state could overhaul social relationships using education and technology, remained firmly in place in these industrialized societies throughout its attempt at social development. It is however, not the assumption that the state will be the only actor in the process of social development or social reform and change. A lot of the responsibility is generally transferred to the community and market forces to bring about the needed change however, there is no consensus on its extent, form and process.

To be precise, there are three important aspects of relationships in a society; first the economic, second the political and third the social relationships. The societal relationships are between different communities and classes on the one hand, between state and people and between people on the other. In India, the economic relations are posing a major challenge since its inception as a modern state. Despite several policy shifts, the gap between the rich and poor and the proportion of poor people, have not declined. A major problem is the vast rural population in India, which has not participated fully in the process of development. The wage rates in rural India are far below the minimum wages fixed by the state, as there is hardly any mechanism in place to monitor that.

The state has to launch a programme of generating employment, to provide a minimum number of days of employment for all, to ensure a minimum level of income. This is an indicator of the state of employment opportunities and poverty, in rural economy. The land owning patterns and subsequent problems, are dealt with more details later, but the point is that rural sector and its current economic vibrancy is far from adequate to support any development initiative. The economic status of minorities and other socially backward classes are creating tensions between these groups. These tensions result in major conflicts and a rising chart of violence and crime in both urban and rural areas.

The political relationships in the country suffer from social backwardness of people. The low representation of women, minorities and backward classes, has led to the political tension and exploitation of common man by elite classes. However, the economically poor segments are unable to find adequate representation in the political decision-making. The state and people relationships are tenuous and fluid. Despite its welfare ideology, state is unable to deliver social and welfare services efficiently. The rural urban divide in delivery of services is very wide and the state appears to be helpless in containing the trend.

India is on the brink of a demographic revolution with the proportion of working-age population between 15 and 59 years likely to increase from approximately 58 per cent in 2001 to more than 64 per cent by 2021, adding approximately 63.5 million new entrants to the working age group between 2011 and 2016, the bulk of whom will be in the relatively younger age group of 20–35 years. The number of million plus cities has more than doubled. The population of metropolitan cities has crossed 10 million in Delhi, Calcutta and Bombay. This tremendous increase in urban population is certainly going to aggravate the problem of already precarious living conditions of a large chunk of the population. The absolute magnitude of the growth of the urban population is so large that a close new look at the existing policies concerned with urban development is needed. However, in spite of best efforts to improve the condition of rural masses, large scale migration from rural to urban areas will continue to take place in the coming decades (Sivaramakrishnan et al., 1993). The pace of urbanization is likely to increase and in absence of adequate housing and infrastructure for meeting the needs of the growing population in the urban areas the cities would face the problem of expanding slums leading to the deterioration of life of all people in urban areas.

What can the social work profession do to deal with these macro issues? The usual models found in different texts for social development are usually based on economic development models of different shades. There is by and large an agreement in these models, that economic development is the key and subsequent efforts at provision of social services, will deliver the goods in the long run. Postmodernism proposes that social phenomena vary according to the social and historical context in which they operate. International social work, therefore, questions the global effectiveness of Western models of social work practice. Among the most important consequences of the development of postmodern thought is an understanding that there cannot be a universal idea, to deal with the socio political and economic inequality within and across societies. This is important, because inequalities create social strains between different groups and psychological stresses for individuals. Social processes that create inequality and injustice constantly change. Usually, social workers formulate their practice in terms of local issues and national policies. Increasingly though, international trends and pressures influence these. Some authors have argued to have a globalized version of social work practice, to be able to understand international relations and how these influence the social relations in a society. Although these are very well meaning thoughts, but the current practices and situations are rather more complex, than these simple notions and ideal beliefs. Most social work students, educators and practitioners do not cross national borders in their work. Daily practice may lead them to experience some local consequences of globalization: international migration, asylum seeking, and refugees. They may also experience concern about forced marriages, cultural conflicts and terrorism, that are a product of the social trends of globalization. The uncertainty about how to evaluate and respond to these emerges from lack of any coherent ideology or strategy.

A worldwide view of social work might be richer, if it included ideas and perceptions from non-Western countries. For example, Graham's (2002) work on African worldviews suggests alternative perspectives on family and community that might lead Western social workers to value shared experience and collective spiritual, family and community engagement in resolving social and personal problems. There is evidence that alternative forms of social work, are available for adoption or adaptation. However, dealing with small fragments of the reality will bring about some change in society, but it will not be able to change the society as such (Madan, 2009).

The major religions in the present day social constructions in the developing societies particularly influence the structure of social relationship. Generally all prescribe; rules for marriage and divorce, the nature of relations between spouses and other members. Some religions are more conservative and passionate about there formulations than others in the society. They prescribe very specific rules for who can marry whom and who can dine with whom and so on. The main thrust of this structuring is to retain old power structures. Reference to religion in structuring relationships is important to deal with the power that religion wields, in determining their relations in a developing society such as India. The modern states have been trying to restructure societies, to create a humane and just society. The world not so long ago, was divided in different ideological groups, to develop principles based on which the global social structuring should be carried out. The events in the last two decades have significantly changed ideas and as a result the very notion of social justice and structuring has changed. The point of interest now is only the principle or principles, which should guide the structuring, at least in theory, so that relevant social policies may at least be evolved, generally to determine the relations between state and people.

As far as social workers are concerned, the principles of self-determination coupled with democracy, ensuring universal human rights, social justice, etc. are adequate to guide them, in their process of facilitating relationships in a society. The problem pointed out by many and discussed later in this chapter is, first arriving at any consensus around basic goals or how radical a restructuring is required and secondly, finding suitable strategies to implement any of these theoretical formulations in practice. The historical difference between Gandhi and Nehru in the Indian context, is a case in point, one opting for a total rural orientation, the other opting for an industrial society. Other shades of differences, including division of the country based on religion and the later policies of socialism, with or without any control over the market, are still being debated. The more recent change over to an open capitalist approach is a decision on which there never was any consensus and there never will be any. And that is why it is much easier to take recourse to the democratic framework of the rule of so called majority. It is necessary to realize the difference between social and economic relationships as well. Although some scholars include economic and political within social relationships, but social relationships can be confined to gender and relations between major social groups based on religion, caste and linguistic or regional affiliations. We therefore run into the same difficulty of arriving at a consensus about the inter-dependence or linkages between three sets of relationships.

In social work practice, the process of facilitating relationships to bring about any change, for improving the overall living conditions of the community members, often forces the worker, to think of wider relationships between communities, castes, religious groups and even classes. For example, while trying to improve the participation of girls, children from lower caste groups or economically poorer sections, it soon becomes evident that the roots of the problem are far beyond the community boundaries. That is where it becomes necessary to explore the ways of possible interventions in reaching out or thinking beyond the community boundaries. Though the social worker can initiate some work in that direction but there are some serious limitations a worker faces, in taking up a restructuring process of societal relationships.

First of all, as some scholars have argued restructuring or dealing with macro issues and concerns requires a different set of skills and background knowledge than the skills of dealing with micro level, face to face practice in social work (see Pathak, 1989; Siddiqui, 1989).

Further, looking at relationships in a society one has to develop a framework for explaining these relationships to members, to help them see the need for change. For example, a most talked about relationship these days is, the gender relations, the relationship between spouses, brothers and sisters, mother and son or between a female officer and a male subordinate, or just any boy or girl and male and female. It is ironical that while the world opinion, particularly on a public platform, irrespective of any boundary, is unanimous in granting total equality between sexes, but no religion in the world believes in this equality between sexes and hence provides different roles for them, thereby creating gender roles different and unequal. This has made the task of social workers very difficult, since not disturbing cultural norms is a ethical principle in professional practice. A convenient understanding in public practice in this respect is, not to disturb cultural norms, therefore many a times closing options, while suffering continues. An unresolved dilemma for a professional worker is, the religion vs human rights issue and how far can s/he take it without being disowned by all, and hence becoming professionally dysfunctional as well. Education and empirical reality have not established a proper linkage through a system of feedback, leaving the student rather academic in their understanding of issues of wider concern in practice (see Pathak, 1989).

A seminar recently held on the topic of current social concern and social work response identified the following macro issues in India.

Globalization of Economy

Globalization is a fact not an option as Parikh and Shah (1999) noted while commenting on second generation reforms. "The communications revolution has turned the world into a 'global village' where everyone knows, what is going on and what is available", they noted. Nothing could be farther than the truth. The correct picture is that the elites in the world have become more integrated on account of the phenomenal achievements in the information technology on the one hand and the lifting of the trade barriers between nations on the other. The collapse of the communist has helped in this integration as well, since it made the economic development through the market mechanism, the only option. It has shrunk the role of the state in the economic sector but the state presence in the social sector is still vital. Though there is some criticism of its large social spending leading only to greater corruption. The two programmes Mahatama Gandhi National Rural Employment Guarantee Scheme and Food Security have generated major criticism on account of large funding allocated to the programmes and the states inability to monitor the funding to avoid leakages.

The globalization of economy, simply speaking, means that both the production and distribution of goods and services would not be restricted by the national boundaries. Direct implication of this change is, the ownership of means of production and the process of production would become global in character. Therefore, what would be produced and where, would be determined by multinational corporations rather than the State. The price controls and subsidies would become history. It is not possible to deal with the issue in greater detail here, because of paucity of space. But we are told by the World Bank that so far this process of globalization has generally resulted in accentuating inequality both between and within nations. The new rules of globalization – privatization, liberalization and tighter intellectual property rights – are shaping the path of technology, creating new risks of marginalization and vulnerability. Tighter control of innovation in the hands of multinational corporations ignores the need of millions. For poor people the technological progress remains out of reach (Human Development Report, 1999: 68). New patent laws pay scant attention to the knowledge of indigenous people, leaving it vulnerable to claim by others. These laws ignore cultural diversity in creating and sharing innovations .... The result is silent theft of centuries of knowledge from developing to developed countries (Ibid., 68).

The participation in a globalized economy requires more skills, which in countries with huge illiterate or semi literate population renders them out of bonds. The result is rise in incomes of many 1.5 billion people, (more than a quarter of the world's population), in the same period however, economic decline or stagnation reducing the incomes of 1.6 billion people, (again more than a quarter of the world's population). In many countries, average incomes are less than they were in 1980 – and in some countries less than they were in 1970. The world has become more polarized, with the gulf between the poor and rich of the world widening in recent years. In the past 30 years, the share of the poorest 20 per cent of the world's people in global income declined from 2.3 per cent to 1.4 per cent, while the share of the richest 20 per cent rose from 70 per cent to 85 per cent. The ratio of sharing of the richest and the poorest went up from 1:30 to 1:61. Economic growth in promoting human development, in identifiable instances has become the source of human misery and frustration. The instances are; jobless growth, ruthless growth, voiceless growth, rootless growth and futureless growth.

The Human Development Report (HDR) (1999) itself noted globalization, the most recent prescription for speeding up economic development, is creating new threats to human security in both rich and poor countries alike. The relentless pressures of global competition are squeezing out caring relationships, invisible heart of human development. Poor people and poor countries risk being pushed to the margin in this proprietary regime controlling the world's knowledge. After nearly five decades of efforts, about 840 million people are malnourished. A vast majority of them are to be found in India, Pakistan and Bangladesh. The overall consumption of the richest fifth of the world's people is 16 times that of poorest fifth. Nearly 1.3 billion people live on less than a dollar a day and close to 1 billion cannot meet their basic consumption requirements. The share in global income of the richest fifth of the world's people is 74 times that of the poorest fifth. As Sen (1999) noted, the complex reality about human development and deprivation remains a mystery even now. The world GDP increased from 3 trillion to 30 trillion in the last 50 years, but the share of poor countries fell from 20 per cent to 10 per cent (HDR, 1999: 25). Taking a look at the country specific data on income distribution points out that the share of the poorest 20 per cent remains less than 10 per cent of the total national income, while the share of the richest 20 per cent is around 40 per cent in three countries in Indian sub continent. The social workers should initiate a debate on such issues by highlighting the facts about these issues relating to society, but offering a professional solution to such issues require a much bigger movement consisting of all stakeholders in society. The Human Development Report (2013), while acknowledging the economic growth in developing countries, particularly in India and China, cautioned that economic growth alone does not automatically translate into human development progress.

It is worth deliberating the social work strategies in combatting this global process, which is creating more inequality in society and promoting the acceptance of only one global culture. Are there any alternative models of economic development or development per se of a different kind which the social workers should help the societies to consider?

Marginalization of State

The World Development Report (WDR) (1997) noted that around the globe, the state is in the spotlight. The globalization of economy has raised certain basic questions about the role of state; what it can do and cannot do. The last fifty years have shown clearly both the benefits and the limitations of state actions, especially in the promotion of social and economic aspects of development. The social services such as education, health, employment and housing have helped in widening the base of the middle class and reducing poverty to some extent. But state machinery has become a hurdle also in promoting speedy development due to incompetence, corruption and lethargy and above all, as the WDR (1997) pointed, out, in not having a clarity of what its role was. The globalization of the economy would pressure the state to cut down its spending and minimize its role viz-à-viz, economy, in particular, withdrawing from its role of controlling the key sectors of economy. In other words it should privatize the public sector enterprises. As often happens with such radical shifts in perspective, countries sometimes react in a manner which distort the very purpose for which the shift was effected. For example, in the pressure to reduce state expenditure, the state may squeeze critically important programmes of education, health and infrastructure development instead of cutting expenditure in maintaining inefficient bureaucracy or maintaining loss making enterprises. This would thus not only retard economic development but also accentuate inequalities and poor quality of social services generating frustration among the masses which get translated into conflicts and violence.

Growth of Social Iniquities

Despite the development efforts of past fifty years, there are wide disparities between the rich and the poor, urban and rural sectors, male and female, lower caste and upper castes and between different states.

Distribution of Income

Country Gini Index	*Poorest 20%*	*II 20%*	*III 20%*	*IV 20%*	*Richest 20%*
India 29.7	9.2	13.0	16.8	21.7	39.3
Pakistan 31.2	9.4	13.0	16.0	20.3	41.2
Bangladesh 28.3	9.4	13.5	17.2	22.0	37.9

WDR: 1999–2000: 238–9.

For India, the income Gini coefficient was 36.8 in 2010–11.

Source: Economic Survey–2013.

National. Sample Survey (NSS) estimates of rural Indian workforce (usual status) shows that share of agriculture in total rural workforce is declining, it declined from 85.6 per cent in 1972–73 to 78.2 per cent in 1993–94. Share of manufacturing, trade and services is widening in rural areas, share of these sectors increased from 12.0 per cent in 1972–73 to 17.2 per cent in 1993–94. However, casual nature of rural labour is increasing. During the last decades, share of casual labour in rural workers has increased from 25.4 per cent in 1972–73 to 35.6 per cent in 1993–94. On the other hand, share of self employed has declined from 65.3 per cent to 58.0 per cent during the period 1972–73 to 1993–94, share of regular workers declined from 9.3 per cent to 6.4 per cent during the same period. During the period 1987–88 to 1993–94 share of casual labour has increased by 2.7 per cent, mainly at the expense of regular workers (share of regular workers declined from 7.7% to 6.4%). Rural households still generate 62.9% of their household income from agriculture sector (55.0% from agriculture and allied activities and 7.9% from agriculture wages). Remaining 37.1 per cent of the rural household income is generated from non-agriculture sector, out of which 6.3 per cent from non-agriculture wages, 16.5 per cent from salaries and remaining 14.3 per cent from other sources. Since agriculture and allied activities is still principal source of income of more than 60 per cent of the population, it is worthwhile to look into the distribution of landholding and areas operated by them.

According to the latest available agricultural census (2000–01), percentage of marginal holdings (area less than 1 hectare) in the country increased from 57.8 per cent in 1985–86 to 59.0 per cent in 1990–91 to 62.88 in 2000–01. It must have increased even further by now, looking at the trend. At the same time percentage of small holdings (1–2 hectares) increased from 18.4 per cent to 19.0 per cent and is still the same in 2000–01, whereas percentage of other holdings (more than 2 hectare) declined from 23.8 per cent to 22.0 per cent and further decreased to 11.69 in 2000–01. The trend explains the already well known fact about the land holdings getting smaller because of division of family property and further leading to the income decline and indebtedness of small and marginal farmers (Agriculture Census 2000–01).

Problem of Governance

The continuing problems of mass poverty, illiteracy and in particular conservative attitudes and interpretations, real or imaginary, of state patronage to one segment of population or the other generate problems of governance as the ruling elite get fragmented into different segments representing various interest groups in the society. The inability of the government to attain a level of economic development or create a system which provide adequate opportunity for the common people to attain the fulfillment of basic needs within the current level of development, leads to mass dissatisfaction. The state of mass scale deprivation create conditions for spreading the contention by the opposition parties that the state was deliberately favouring some and neglecting the other and often settling the issues on the streets through protests which often turn violent, create serious problems of governance. The state in such situations may collapse from within and become totally dysfunctional. There is then, often a tendency to create alternative non-governmental organizations and peoples organizations to take over the functions of the state – creation of a civil society. But so far, little attention has been paid to assess the possibilities whether the markets and civil society combination can effectively perform the functions they are taking over from the state.

Continuation of Absolute Poverty: Economic and Human Dimension

The Planning Commission had been estimating the incidence of poverty at national and state level since the Sixth Five Year Plan. The Economic Survey 1997–98 reported that head count ratio declined from 56.4 per cent in 1973–74 to 37.3 per cent in 1993–94 in rural sector and from 49 per cent to 32.4 per cent in the urban sector, and from 55 per cent to 36 per cent at the all India level. The absolute number of poor however remained same at 320 million on account of increase in population. The survey also noted that there exists wide rural, urban and inter state disparity (Economic Survey, 1997–98: 137–8).

According to Economic Survey, 2013, the Planning Commission has estimated the poverty lines at all India level as an Monthly Per Capita Expenditure (MPCE) of Rs 673 for rural areas and Rs 860 for urban areas in 2009–10. Based on these cut-offs, the percentage of people living below the poverty line in the country has declined from 37.2 per cent in 2004–5 to 29.8 per cent in 2009–10. Even in absolute terms, the number of poor people has fallen by 52.4 million during this period. Of this, 48.1 million are rural poor and 4.3 million are urban poor. Thus poverty has declined on an average by 1.5 percentage points per year between 2004–5 and 2009–10. The annual average rate of decline during the period 2004–5 to 2009–10 is twice the rate of decline during the period 1993–4 to 2004–5. Rural poverty in India is spread over across all the occupation groups. Self-employed in agriculture and allied activities form nearly 38.50 per cent of the rural poor, followed by agricultural labourers (23.32%), non-agricultural labourers (15.80%), self-employed in non-agriculture (15.01%), salaries earners (5.66%) and others (1.71%) (Pant and Patra, 1998). However, there are large interstate variations in distribution of rural poor across occupation groups in Andhra Pradesh, Gujarat, Kerala, Maharashtra and Tamil Nadu. Agricultural labourers have major share of poor as compared to self-employed in agriculture. In Bihar, poor are more or less evenly distributed across self-employed in agriculture, agricultural labourers, non-agricultural labourers and self-employed in non-agriculture. In Haryana, poor are more or less evenly distributed across self-employed in agriculture, agricultural labourers and non-agricultural labourers. Punjab and Kerala have maximum proportion of poor from non-agricultural labourers. Andhra Pradesh, Bihar and north-eastern region has high proportion of poor from self-employed in non-agriculture group (Pant and Patra, 1998).

The Human Development Report (HDR, 2013) claims that to some extent poverty eradication efforts in different countries have succeeded by quoting that first of the eight Millennium Development Goals, to halve the proportion of people living on less than $1.25 a day relative to 1990, was achieved in 2012, three years before that target date. Brazil (where the percentage of the population living on less than 2005 Purchasing Power Parity (PPP) $1.25 a day went from 17.2% to 6.1%), China (from 60.2% to 13.1%) and India (from 49.4% to 32.7%). For example, between 1990 and 2008, China alone lifted a remarkable 510 million people out of poverty.

However this is only one aspect of the picture, the overall gap between rich and poor in these countries have either remained same or has expanded during the same period.

Poverty in India, Pakistan and Bangladesh

Country	*India*		*Pakistan*		*Bangladesh*	
	Rank	*Value*	*Rank*	*Value*	*Rank*	*Value*
Human poverty index 1997	59	35.9	71	42.1	73	44.4
Population below income poverty line %	$ 1 a day	NPL	$1 a day	NPL	$ 1 a day	NPL
	52.5	36.0	11.6	34.0	28.5	48.0

Source: Human Development Report, 1999

IX Five Year Plan, Govt. of India, 1997–2002.

HDR measures inequality in terms of two indicators. The first indicator is the income Gini coefficient which measures the deviation of distribution of income (or consumption) among the individuals within a country from a perfectly equal distribution. For India, the income Gini coefficient was 36.8 in 2010–11. In this respect, inequality in India is lower than many other developing countries, e.g. South Africa (57.8), Brazil (53.9), Thailand (53.6), Turkey (40.8), China (41.5), Sri Lanka (40.3), Malaysia (46.2), Vietnam (37.6), as well as countries like USA (40.8), Hong Kong (43.4), Argentina (45.8), Israel (39.2), Bulgaria (45.3), etc. which are otherwise ranked very high in terms of human development index. The second indicator is the quintile income ratio, which is a measure of average income of the richest 20 per cent of the population to that of poorest 20 per cent. The quintile income ratio for India was 5.6 in 2010–11. To estimate the rural-urban gap, the monthly per capita expenditure (MPCE), defined first at household level to assign a value that indicates the level of living to each individual or household is used. According to the provisional findings of the 68th round (2011–12) of the NSS, average MPCE Uniform Reference Period (URP based) is ₹ 1,281.45 and ₹ 2,401.68 respectively for rural and urban India indicating rural-urban income disparities.

According to the UN Human Development Report (HDR, 2011), which estimates the human development index (HDI) in terms of three basic capabilities: to live a long and healthy life, to be educated and knowledgeable, and to enjoy a decent economic standard of living, the HDI for India was 0.547 in 2011 with an overall global ranking of 134 (out of 187 countries). As per the India Human Development Report (IHDR) 2011, brought out by the Institute of Applied Manpower Research and the Planning Commission. Human Development Index (HDI) between 1999–2000 and 2007–08 has increased by 21 per cent, with an improvement of over 28 per cent in education which is one of the main drivers. India is ranked 129 in terms of the gender inequality index (GII) which captures the loss in achievement due to gender disparities in the areas of reproductive health, empowerment and labour force participation, with values ranging from 0 (perfect equality) to 1 (total inequality). A lot more needs to be done as our GII is higher than the global average of 0.492. Even neighbours like Pakistan (115), Bangladesh (112), and Sri Lanka (74), have performed better in terms of this indicator (Economic Survey, 2013). Many segments of the population like landless agricultural labourers, marginal farmers, scheduled castes (SCs), scheduled tribes (STs) and other backward classes (OBCs) continue to suffer social and financial exclusion.

A number of policy options were used to bring about development or rather social development in the country, which now is known as the new economic policy putting more faith in market forces globally. The rapid urbanization and globalization is promoting consumerist life styles and it is likely to effect the human relationships adversely in the family, in educational institutions at all levels, at the work place and in the community in general. The deterioration of social relationships will result in social tensions in the family, work and in general. The capacities of traditional institutions such as family, neighbourhood groups and older persons to provide support to individual in stress would decline.

Environmental Issues

Future growth and overall quality of life are critically dependent on the quality of the environment. The natural resource base of a country and the quality of its air, water, and land represent a common heritage for all generations. The current trend of expanding needs of huge populations is bound to destroy that endowment indiscriminately in the pursuit of short-term economic goals. It would penalize both our present and future generations. From present information concerning rapid destruction of many of the world's resources it is clear that meeting the needs of a world population which has already crossed 7 billion mark and still growing, would be an impossible task.

It is clear that continuing on our present path of accelerating environmental degradation would severely compromise the ability of present and future generations to meet their needs. A slowing of population growth rates would help ease the intensification of many environmental problems. However, the rate and timing of fertility declines, and thus the eventual size of world population would largely depend on the quality of governance, which is likely to decline as the conflicts within the countries grow and the power of the state to govern in view of rapidly growing corruption and social fragmentation decline.

Rapidly growing population have already created land, water and fuel shortages. In many of the poorest regions of the globe, it is clear that increasing population density has contributed to severe and accelerating degradation of the very resources that these growing populations depend on for survival. To meet expanding needs, environmental devastation would be ignored, the productivity of existing resources would be stretched further so as to benefit more people. Increases in Gross National Product (GNP) and food production are slower than population growth, as a result per capita levels of food production and supply would decline. Ironically, the resulting persistence of poverty would perpetuate high fertility rates, as the poor are often dependent on large families for survival.

Inadequate Health Care

The other aspect the developmental experts highlight is that many people in Third World nations fight a constant battle against malnutrition, disease, and ill health. The well-known indicators of health status are life expectancy at birth, child mortality rates, female mortality rates, births attended by trained manpower, nutritional status, immunization coverage, etc.

In the mid-1970s, more than 1 billion people, almost half the population of the developing world (excluding China), were living on diets deficient in essential calories. In both Asia and Africa, over 60 per cent of the population barely met minimum caloric requirements necessary to maintain adequate health. Moreover, it has been estimated that this caloric deficit amounted to less than 2.0 per cent of the world cereal production. Malnutrition therefore is not due to an imbalance between population and food supplies, it is more due to inequality in world income distribution. Thus malnutrition and poor health in the developing world are more a matter of unequal distribution than of food production. Nearly one third of the world population was without access to health services, 1.33 billion did not have access to safe drinking water, 2.25 billion (more than half the world population) lived without sanitation facilities. Nearly 180 million children under age 5 were malnourished. The percentage for under weight children in all developing countries was 18 per cent compared to 22 in least developed countries and 6 in developed countries Todaro and Smith (2012).

According to Human Development Report, 1999, 28 per cent population in all developing countries, 41 per cent in least developed countries, 50 per cent in Sub Sahara Africa did not have access to safe drinking water. The figure for lack of sanitation facilities is given as 57, 63 and 56 per cent for the respective regions, and figure for under weight children is given as 31, 40 and 32 per cent.

The importance of access to clean drinking water, which is one of the most important measures of health, cannot be overemphasized. The market friendly development efforts have been promoting sale of safe drinking water, soft drinks, and alcohol pouches in these places to combat water-borne diseases, responsible for more than 35 per cent of the deaths of young children in Africa, Asia, and Latin America. The cigarette consumption with 1970–72 = 100 as base had become 160 per adult in case of all developing countries and 156 in case of least developed countries (HDR, 1999: 175). In case of developed countries it is 88 and in South Asia 134.

The data reveal that in 1997, the number of doctors per 1,00,000 people averaged only 14 in the least developed countries, compared with 253 in the developed countries. Most of the medical facilities in developing nations are concentrated in urban areas where only 25 per cent of the population resides. In Bolivia, only one-third of the population lives in cities, but 90 per cent of the health facilities are found there.

Human Rights Violation

Human rights violations have become so routine that the Home Secretary of Government of India was recently at a loss to explain the behaviour of the police force, who perhaps are the worst violators of the human rights. Death in custody, use of third degree methods, entering and searching houses with out proper authorization, detaining women in custody and using force against children are every day occurrences in India and in many developing countries. The trend of human rights violations would grow as the pressure on the police force to maintain law and order grow in view of the rising crime rates and terrorist activities. The growing materialist way of life, continuing mass poverty, ignorance of legal rights, changing attitudes towards sex and more importantly the growing public apathy would further accelerate the human rights violations.

Gender Inequality

Things have changed for the better, but not for all women and not in all domains of gender equality. Progress has been slow and limited for women in very poor countries, and for those who face

Health and Education Related Comparable Data from Four States

	Andhra Pradesh	*Assam*	*Bihar*	*Gujarat*
Male (Life expectancy at birth 2006–10)	63.5	61.0	65.5	64.9
Female (Life expectancy at birth 2006–10)	68.2	63.2	66.2	69.0
Infant Mortality Rates (per 1,000 live births) 2011	43.0	55.0	44.0	41.0
Birth Rate (per 1,000) 2011	17.5	22.8	27.7	21.3
Death Rate (per 1,000) 2011	7.5	8.0	6.7	6.7
Education Related 2010–11				
Girls Enrolment Rate (GER) (6–13 years)	92.0	84.0	102.9	107.2
Pupil-Teacher Ratio (Primary/ Jr.Basic School)	31.0	28.0	76.0	NA
Pupil-Teacher Ratio (Middle/Sr. Basic School)	25.0	21.0	51.0	35.0

Source: Economic Survey, 2013.

other forms of exclusion because of their caste, disability, location, ethnicity, or sexual orientation. Whether for comparisons between men and women in the same country, or absolute comparisons of women across countries, the progress in some domains is tempered by the sobering realities that many women face in other.

Consider the likelihood of women dying during childbirth in Sub-Saharan Africa, which is still comparable to the rate in Northern Europe during the 19th century. Or the difference in school enrolments in Nigeria, where a wealthy urban child averages around 10 years of schooling, while poor rural Hausa girls average less than 6 months. Or the fact that women remain severely disadvantaged in their control over resources and assets in the household. Or that the earnings differentials between men and women have not changed much. Or that women's representation in policy making remains far lower than men's the world over. Or that domestic violence continues to exact a heavy toll on women around the world – regardless of individual or country income, women continue to be the primary victims of violence at home and suffer more severe injuries.

Women and teenage girls in particular would face the brunt of the growing human rights violations in the country. The human rights of women are not only violated in work places and on the streets but inside homes as well, as a NFHS-3 pointed out in India. The women are subjected to sexual harassment by family members themselves and in most cases the women feel powerless to even report such incidences (World Development Report, 2012).

Education of Female Children

The education of female children continues to lag behind at the primary and secondary level of schooling. The participation of girls in school education has been increasing at all stages of education. At the primary level the share of girls in total enrolment increased from 5.4 million in 1950–51 to 47.9 million in 1996–97. At the upper primary level, the same increased from 0.5 to 16.3 million during the same period. The percentages, however, remained below fifty per cent at all the stages. As long as the proportion of girls enrolment does not reach 50 per cent, the disparities in access to education owing to gender difference would continue to persist, resulting in major human rights violation of these female children.

Gender disparities have also lingered among groups that have not benefitted from growth within countries: income poverty widens gender gaps. While the educational attainment of wealthy boys and girls is very similar, gender inequalities are intensified among the poor. In India, the median boy and girl aged 15–19 in the wealthiest fifth of the population reach grade 10, but the median boy in the bottom fifth reaches only grade 6, and the median girl only grade 1 (World Bank Report on Women's Issues, 2012).

Child Abuse

The child abuse refers to violation of basic rights of children. The worst child abuse takes place in their own homes by their own parents in India. The parents of children are not even conscious of the fact that by giving birth to a child, while they are living in abject poverty is a clear case of child abuse. Such children suffer from poor health, often dying within days or months of being born, after suffering hunger and extreme weather conditions. Those who survive become child labours.

The mortality rate of children under five, which is the best indicator of child health of any country, continues to be high. True the rate has shown a consistent decline over the years and is 23.6 for males and 24.2 for females (1994), but the decline is still very slow. The overall percentage of reduction from 1960 to 1980 was 1.4 and from 1980 to 1990 it was 3.1. If we are determined to meet the target of IMR below 60 by 2000 A.D., we need to have 6.5 per cent reduction in the 0–5 years mortality.

Child Labour

The number of full time child workers remains very high despite so much of efforts made during the last few decades. For rural full-time child labour, the absolute number decreased from 13.7 million in 1961 to 11.4 million in 1991 (decrease of 17%). For boys, the number decreased from 8.1 million to 7.4 million (9% decrease) and for girls, from 5.5 million to 4.0 million (decrease of 27%).

Since data on marginal child labour are only available from 1981, it is reported that marginal child labour increased from 2.4 million in 1981 to 10.5 million in 1991 (338% increase). In urban areas, the increase was from 0.08 to 0.62 million (675% increase). For boys, the increase was from 0.032 to 0.22 million (588% increase) and for girls, from 0.048 to 0.40 million (733% increase). In rural areas, an increase is reported from 2.4 million in 1981 to 9.9 million in 1991 (313% increase). For boys, the increase was from 0.64 million to 1.3 million (103% increase) and for girls, from 1.7 million to 8.6 million (405% increase).

It requires a greater maturity on the part of worker to understand the implications of macro practice. The recent examples of movements against corruption, violence against women, etc.

indicate that the opposition and in particular state reactions could be challenging, to say the least. Politicization of macro issues is a normal phenomenon and not many social work scholars are comfortable working with political realities, which in the Indian subcontinent, as also all over the world are beginning to become violent, which goes against the very ethics of social work practice. It is difficult to evolve any consensus on a macro issue since the perspectives on these differ so widely, from one set of people to other. In social work practice, the worker is expected to work with people rather than to address any personal agenda of any kind.

And finally, working on any social issue requires a collective practice model rather than individual worker approaches, again which the social work education does not prepare them well. It requires setting up of independent organization, capable of generating their own resources, keeping their personal life completely public or better still not having any private lives at all. These are realities not easily discussed in routine courses run by institutions and organizations, usually state or corporate funded, both demanding a higher degree of compliance with the status quo.

Therefore, most social work educators were and still are of the view that barring advocacy practice the social workers as professionals may be better of joining any of the social movements in their personal capacity rather than in a professional capacity. The reasons are a social movement is like a wild fire, once it catches on, it is difficult to control and confine it to any kind of ethical framework.

Despite these difficulties the possibility and the need for thinking about wider changes in society has been part of academic discussions in social work, more so in the developing countries, than in developed countries, for obvious reasons. We have, therefore, included it as a method of social work which as a profession, as stated earlier, tries to promote social development both as it is defined in psychology and in somewhat different manner in sociology, social work and in economics. Initiating a movement to mobilize public opinion in society is generally termed as social action in social work. Social action in sociology is defined as any action in society by a person or group of persons. Therefore, for sociologists the social change is a normal phenomenon in society and although they do identify various factors which either facilitate or stall that change, they do not prefer prescribing any strategies for promoting social change or in other words mandating it as a disciplinary obligation for students. It is a fact that society is dynamic and keeps changing but some changes take a long time to happen such as gender relations in developing societies. Education and awareness has been identified as a factor in promoting change and hence social workers have been using it as a strategy for mobilizing change. On the other hand, social movements or attempts at restructuring the thought patterns and values in a society are usually termed as collective behaviour. They are distinguished from other forms of collective behaviour such as groups, which have a clear programme or purpose. They are viewed as forms of collective behaviour nevertheless, because they are large groups and because they arise spontaneously. A social movement, in other words, is defined as a large scale, informal effort designed to correct, supplement, overthrow, or in some fashion influence the social order (Blumer, 1951). A social movement represents an effort by a large number of people, to solve collectively, a problem that they feel they have in common. It is significant to remember here that the mass of persons coming together may at times come together spontaneously but more often an effort is needed to generate awareness first and then motivating them to act and get involved in the process of bringing about change. The possibility for professionals, such as social workers, getting involved thus becomes a necessity to monitor the areas needing change and state response to these. At times state itself advocates the change, but fails as it is not accepted by people in general for a variety of reasons. For example, the minimum age for marriage, dowry prohibition and exploitation of Dalits and other weaker sections continue despite laws in place. Most of these issues arise since persons are unwilling to yield the power they enjoy over others, example gender relations or caste relations in society. It thus becomes an area of facilitating relationships between large communities in a particular society. In social work, this was earlier termed as social action and included as a secondary method of social work. Very few social workers have used this in practice and generally voluntary activists or lawyers have been more active in this field.

For a person to be motivated to join a social movement, he must not only sense a problem, that the change is needed but also (1) feel that something can be done about it and (2) want to do something about it himself. At the very least, he must feel that the status quo is not inevitable, and that change is conceivable. A second stage in the process would be the feeling that a better world is concretely attainable. Davies (1962) has pointed out that people must expect an improvement in conditions before they will embark on revolutions. Ultimately, he feels, it is the dissatisfied state of mind or anger and frustration rather than the tangible provision of 'adequate' or 'inadequate' supplies of food, equality or liberty which produces change small/big revolution.

But even the 'dissatisfied state of mind' is not enough. As a last step, there must be a desire to become involved in the accomplishment of change. The person must feel the need to seek clarification or 'do something.' S/He must embark on what has been called a 'search for meaning' or for 'symbols' that offer to resolve his problem. And s/he must look around for other people with whom s/he can join in attempts at a solution. The person would tend to listen with increasing care to proposals which s/he could view as relating to her/his problem. S/He would be less likely to reject them out of hand or to try to find faults in the solutions that promised her/him a cure. Such a person becomes susceptible, to ideas of collective efforts for change.

A strong increase in susceptibility creates 'gullibility' or 'suggestibility'. A person in this condition may seem to go out of his way to make himself available as a prospective member (Toch, 1966).

On a behavioural dimension, susceptibility may range from passive to active. Many susceptible persons simply wait with an air of quiet expectancy for the answer to present itself. Susceptibility, in these cases, is no more than a readiness to accept; or – in other words have a 'will to believe.' A person's educational level, the social influences that operate on him, the kinds of past experiences he has had, and other factors that determine his outlook on life are also likely to enter into his selective susceptibility. An individual with a college education, for example, would be much less prone to adopt an oversimplified economic programme than would a person who has never been to school. An intensely religious upbringing can lead one to prefer religious to secular solutions (when these are otherwise equivalent). And younger men may be more likely to become involved in radical activities than are men of middle age.

Social movements must show that they can respond to the needs of their clients. They must demonstrate their ability to furnish solutions which make it worth expending time, energy, and dedication. They must promise offerings which people can find useful and desirable. Social movements search of a mass following frequently follow a saturation method, and try to present a 'cafeteria' of appeals, catering to a diversity of needs. The most important appeals of a social movement are contained in its ideology. The term 'ideology' denotes a set of related beliefs held by a group of persons. The ideology of a social movement is a statement of what the members of the movement are trying to achieve together, and what they wish to affirm jointly. Such a statement points out the direction in which the social movement is moving and specifies the principles and objectives that guide its journey.

When a self-change movement claims to be effective, this claim comprises three separate assumptions. The first of these is that a person is not able to solve a problem. The second claim is that the movement in question can solve the problem. The third proposition is that the specific techniques of the movement are the best or the only techniques which can accomplish the job.

The social movement's claim that it can help its members is provable, and frequently proved. Although the assumption that the movement's techniques are the best means to this end is usually false, it is a useful assumption, because it increases the confidence of members. What could be correctly claimed is that every social movement which enables its members to solve their problems must incorporate features that are essential to its effectiveness.

Social movements also retain their members on the road toward the goal. They accomplish this through incentives and encouragement. Members are made aware of their progress through concrete indications of achievement (such as news coverage they receive, letters of support from other organizations, endorsements, etc.). It is also a general practice to rebuke, more or less sympathetically, any member who strays. Lastly, the progress of the whole group provides each member with norms against which she/he can gauge her/his own achievement.

The conditions in slums had progressively deteriorated to the point where all reasonable avenues of personal development had been closed. Given a realistic frame of mind and a clear sense of proportion, the average slum dweller would be forced to conclude that 'there is nothing to aim for, except death through starvation in a country which has no place for me.' S/He would be forced to recognize the pointlessness of her/his existence, and to become aware of her/his exclusion from any social pattern or sequence of advancement. This is a psychological option that cannot be exercised, because of the obvious discomforts it would bring. Like the psychotic patient who is driven into a fantasy world by the increasing intolerability of his real existence, the member of society who finds himself in a corner, must adopt low probability solutions to avoid facing the hopelessness of his fate. Miracles provide prospects of change in situations that are objectively hopeless and offer comfort and a basis for enduring situations that are objectively intolerable.

It is almost impossible to make a scientific study of large group behaviour. Collective behaviour is not institutionalized, but collective behaviour demands a reasonable consensus on some issue, goal or objective (Mc Caughan, 1977). Smelser (1963) identified certain conditions for collective behaviour. His analysis includes both sociological and psychological determinants.

Structural-conduciveness: this means that certain social conditions must exist such as institutionalized forms of segregation, for instance castes in India.

Structural strain: dissonance in societal values should exist. People feel that they are forced to live in slums, or that villages are low-priority areas of development on the government's agenda.

Growth and spread of a generalized belief: for example, suspicion, doubt and rumour may mobilize collective behaviour more easily than information.

A precipitating factor: an incidence of natural disaster may, for example, easily mobilize people to collective action, rather than appeals to prevent it.

Emergence of leadership: a leader capable of generating an emotional appeal can facilitate collective action.

Social control: the possibility of collective behaviour is greater in the absence of formal institutions of social control.

Smelser worked out the factors contributing to collective behaviour in the context of mob violence and not positive collective behaviour of the kind the community worker has in mind. But this does not negate the importance of the findings of the study. For example, apathy on the part of poor people towards their own situation can be countered, by propagating a different set of values and questioning existing social norms, which perpetuate poverty. Smelser was therefore right in suggesting that the possibility of collective action will be greater if the group of people concerned perceives others as their enemy or competitor.

The need for understanding the importance of institutionalized means of social control has been noted by several authors. Durkheim (1964) perceived the constraints, obligations and meaning provided by religion, marriage and parenthood as important determinants of an orderly and effective life and sociological evidence continues to support many of these positions (Gove, Style and Hughes, 1990; Gove, 1994). The importance of religion, in providing an explanation of both life and the meaning of life, needs particularly to be understood. The socialization process in institutions of family, caste and religion, helps in developing social solidarities around these institutions. The greater the control exercised by these institutions, the lesser the chances of any collective thought emerging, which can cut across these boundaries. The chance of mobilizing people around any issue would be very limited in a community, where such loyalties have a strong hold on its members. Prevailing inter-caste tensions and rivalry between different religious groups are examples of such a situation, despite the fact that these divisions apply to people, who share the same neighbourhood (see West, 1995).

De Swan (1990) suggests that in the process of collectivization, problems can occur. But these can be resolved at a higher level of integration. Thus the neighbourhood organization, as an example of locality based corporate actor, can only overcome collective problems by introducing solutions which involve external changes. These solutions can be found in the interplay between local organizations and actors from outside, adding global dimensions to the debate that force all actors to reconsider and rethink preferences, attitudes and information. All these are the kinds of changes in attitudes and information that lead to the vital, proactive, caring social figurations.

Nowadays such a process can be fuelled by the dynamism of collective action as interplay across locality boundaries, of local and global actors, against rigid and evasive local state authorities (Rees, 1991).

The potential threats of today and tomorrow lie in the current decisions of the new elites to do away with the once civilized and functional notion of collectivization as the result of interdependency between rich and poor, powerful and powerless. Forty-four million poor in Europe, 'bag people' in all the major cities, and regions and 16 million unemployed bear witness to the growth of the dual society, the rejection of collectivization and the illusion of individual responsibility for welfare (Rees, Wim Van, 1991). From De Swaan's historical perspective, it becomes clear that the development dynamics of the collectivization process, were fueled by territorial conflict and was doomed from the start.

Political Participation

In a study of political participation, the American public was divided into three broad categories of participation intensity: (1) apathetic, persons who are withdrawn from the political process (about one-third of the American adult population); (2) spectators, persons who are minimally involved in politics (about 60% of the American adult population); and gladiators, persons who are active combatants (5 to 7%).

In more recent studies, this conceptualization of political participation has been modified by acquiring much richer data sets. In one study, teams of researchers from Austria, India, Japan, the Netherlands, Nigeria, Yugoslavia and the United States collaborated in a cross-national comparative study of political participation under the leadership of Sidney Verba and Norman Nie (Verba, Nie and Kim, 1971; Verba and Nie, 1972). The second study was conducted by Lester Milbrath, Everett Cataldo, Richard Johnson, Lyman Kellstedt, and Albert Somit in the Buffalo, New York area from 1966 to 1968 (Milbrath, 1968, 1971). Both these studies took a much broader view of political participation, and through cluster and factor analysis, discovered 'modes' or 'styles' of political participation. Fundamental to this discovery is the notion that political participation is multi-dimensional. Political acts are distinguished not only in terms of how difficult they are, but also in that they represent different styles by which citizens attempt to relate to government and politics. It is suggested that these modes really are quite similar in the two studies even though they are different in format and content. The modes of participation first reported in Verba, Nie, and Kim (1971) held for all the countries where their collaborators were conducting similar studies: Austria, India, Japan, the Netherlands, Nigeria and (with some modifications) Yugoslavia. This similarity across national cultures increases our confidence that these modes characterize participation in most democratic political systems.

The Advocacy Process

Efforts to deal with deficiencies in the establishment have, throughout history amused, astonished, puzzled, irritated, challenged and at times horrified the common man/spectators. If they are small-scale, they are viewed as ridiculous amateur attempts; when they grow big and create history, they are perceived as lawful change (see Toch, 1966).

Advocacy practice requires a conviction about the issues which are relevant in a current social context and are crucial in ensuring and holding the human rights of a significant section of the population in a society. There are no strict rules for advocacy work, except non-use of violence, no matter what the goal or its use by the opposition. Its approaches must be culturally, socially and politically specific. Widespread participation of common man, in an advocacy campaign is generally a precondition for success.

Planning an advocacy campaign is a dynamic process. It involves identifying the issue, developing solutions, building support and bringing issues, solutions and political will together to ensure that the desired change takes place. Finally, it involves monitoring and evaluating the entire process. The effectiveness and success of any advocacy process depends, amongst other factors, on how well the following steps are implemented:

- Identifying and stating the issue
- Collecting the relevant information
- Conducting a stakeholder analysis
- Mobilizing public opinion
- Mobilizing and managing the necessary resources
- Networking
- Monitoring and evaluation

It may be necessary to revisit and revise these steps in different contexts. Successful advocacy does not proceed in a straight line and rarely unfolds exactly according to plan. Be prepared for unforeseen events and consequences and it helps to be flexible.

Advocacy Tools

In advocacy practice, each issue demands a different approach and use of different strategies, partners, tactics, methods, resources, materials and so on. In embarking upon an advocacy campaign, it is important to assess the capacity of the organization, existing social conditions and public opinions favouring or opposing different issues, the available options and strategic choices, etc. It is a long process and the progress may be slow and gradual, needing patience.

The following are considered the 'tools' of advocacy. Skilled use of these tools help in creating a favourable public opinion for the cause a worker is trying to focus.

- *Information:* Most of the time the people in general are either not aware of or do not know the details about many of the issues which require policy interventions. Hence gathering, managing and disseminating information lays the basis for determining the foundation of an advocacy campaign. Research is considered one important and authentic way of gathering information.
- *Research:* Conducting research and policy analysis has emerged as a potential social work practice areas which uses the information from various sources and develops it into policy options which become the key content of an advocacy campaign.

- *Media Networking:* Social work practitioners or other socially conscious persons even though may be able to collect information, but lack the capacity to disseminate the information among all stakeholders. Networking and collaborating with various media is thus used to communicate the campaign's message(s) to the different stakeholders.
- *Social Mobilization:* In a democracy, use of wide public support is essential for getting the attention of policy makers. Therefore, enlisting the broadest possible support from a wide range of stakeholders, including the public at large, is essential to influence the policy making bodies.
- *Lobbying:* The lobbying is also known as making friends in different places to support your cause. This is done by meeting different members of the policy making body cutting across political parties and feeding them relevant information regarding the issue at hand. Convincing the decision-makers, who have the power to make the desired change, requires an ability to develop special knowledge and presentation skills, to argue your case effectively without offending them.
- *Public Litigation:* Public interest litigation is by now an established way of using the legal system to challenge a policy or law to either bring about a change or prevent a change. The social worker here works with other professionals such as lawyers or other experts to convince the judiciary.

To conclude, the task of promoting social development is a task where different professions have to come together and collaborate in highlighting its implications before the policy makers. The social worker as a professional can initiate or collaborate in social development programmes.

12

Skills of Facilitating Relationships

The term 'skill', refers to the special ability that a person has in carrying out a particular task. All professional workers learn specific skills relevant to their professional work. There are however, different ways to identify skills. For example, some scholars identify specific activities such as communicating, attending to feelings, conflict solving, planning, recording and so on whereas others may concentrate on, what we shall refer to as core skills such as communication, listening, analytical thinking, self-control and so on. These core skills enable a person to carry out a number of tasks listed above with ease.

In identifying the skills a reference to tasks is made to highlight the skills by giving details of the actual practice situation. For example, Corey (2000) identified the following: active listening, restating, clarifying, summarizing, questioning, interpreting, confronting, reflecting feelings, etc. as leadership skills. It is obvious that Corey is identifying the tasks that a counselor has to carry out. A closer examination of these tasks reveal that listening, restating, clarifying, summarizing, questioning, interpreting in particular and some other tasks in general will require an ability on the part of counselor to be able to communicate well – therefore the skill a counselor needs to have is communication. But as is obvious there are other abilities, for example, thinking which will help the leader to analyse and understand the persons and their behaviour objectively. Therefore, it is obvious that skill is an ability which helps you to carry out a task or a variety of tasks. Still, if you develop the ability to question people, you can be called a skilled interrogator, and interrogation is identified as a skill.

The skills of facilitating relationships identified below are based on experience of working with people, theory of human behaviour and on logical reasoning.

- Rapport Building
- Communication
- Listening
- Observation
- Analytical Thinking
- Empathy
- Self-Control

Skills in Rapport Building

Though some indication of how to go about developing a relationship with the people has already been provided earlier, during the discussion on process and principles, it may be helpful to discuss this again briefly. The key to developing a healthy and purposeful relationship, lies in the worker's understanding of human behaviour, including her/his own. When the worker is able to use her/his knowledge, to control her/his own behaviour in specific situations, in such a way that the worker elicits the desired response, from people s/he is dealing with, s/he has mastered the skill of developing relationships. This requires a sound understanding of her/his own self, coupled with the capacity to check her/his normal response, to produce a desired response. This requires an understanding of the client and knowledge to change or deal with it which includes accepting a response during any interaction, without being judgmental. Checking personal emotions, or expressing them to elicit a desired response, constitutes an important part of the skill in human relationships.

The key is acceptance or rather warm acceptance and empathy, conveyed by person's facial and verbal gestures. For example, s/he at least understand, what it means to be poor, out of a job or a single mother and how harassed one could get in these situations. Further, the ability to use different cultural symbols, such as linguistic expressions, body language, facial gestures, in conversation with clients, is crucial to genuine acceptance. To take yet another example, people can be irritating and have irrational attitudes, but the social workers do not condemn them for holding such attitudes, but help them over time to review and change these to their advantage. The professional or logical code of ethics guides a worker's behaviour, rather than personal values or biases.

Facilitating relationships needs using referrals and working in partnership with many professionals. Deciding professional boundaries and controlling professional rivalries and jealousy is a complex phenomenon, which can ruin relationships between colleagues. The only way to avoid this is to concentrate on self-development strategies, rather than try to curb the growth of others, or to feel humiliated by the success of others. A positive attitude towards success is to accept and acknowledge strong points and try to improve upon weak points, in a conscious and determined manner. This helps in maintaining a healthy relationship with other professional colleagues.

Communication Skill

Communication is an important area of facilitating the relationships process. It is therefore necessary for us to look at some common problems faced by social workers while communicating with their clients. Social workers and other professionals engaged in helping services use communication as a skill to accomplish their professional goals. Communication generally refers to the process of conveying ideas, facts, fiction and feelings to others. The effectiveness of the communication depends on the degree of its clarity, extent of reduction in the possibility of distortion from the sender to the receiver. In other words, the message conveys, what it is expected to convey. If the message is not conveyed effectively, (to be discussed later why did this happen) in order to rectify the situation, the social worker has to restate or re-communicate the message. The ability to restate or use the appropriate words is an important part of the communication skill. The purpose of an effective communication is to convey the message in such a way, that it is understood and accepted by the receiver as being logical and to be acted upon or taken note of seriously. It has to be communicated, that it is not seen as an instruction or an order or even a request, and certainly not as a threat.

It may be helpful for a person planning to take facilitation work to attend a training programme to assess her own communication skills and gain more control over her communication, during the facilitation work. A social worker helps the clients with their communication skills as well. It is not necessary for a social worker to do everything, the clients can be referred to a communication consultant or training programme, but in Indian sub continent such facilities are still not easily available. It may be more practical to run a training workshop for your clients with your own resources. You can train a group of clients to improve their communication skills.

Silence is a very effective form of communication, so is the body language. Some other components of the communication process are content, feelings and symbols. Communication serves four major functions in any interaction; control, motivation, emotional expression and exchange of information (see Robins, 1997). For example, the content of communication can decide who is in control. It is normal for communication to arouse feelings. Excess of emotions during communications is a clear indication of the weakness of the actor. However, some communications may be for the very purpose of release of emotions. Professionals often make the mistake of communicating their frustrations with their clients. A professional communicator is very careful in selecting the right words and tone to accomplish the purpose of the communication. Many a times the silence accomplishes much more, which words can't. The silence with focus on clients conveys patience, lack of anxiety and sincerity, all of these goes to help the client, to trust the social worker.

Corey thinks a social worker has to listen, restate, clarify, summarize, question, interpret, confront, support, empathize, facilitate, give feedback, suggest, disclose information about self and so on (see Corey, 2000). These are tasks an effective communicator will perform during a session and should be useful for a professional to practice these. It makes it clear that we should pay more attention to the components of communication during the facilitation process. It may therefore be helpful to see what other factors can facilitate communication.

Factors Facilitating Communication

- Focus
- Diversity
- Objectivity
- Time and Content Management
- Eye Contact
- A Relaxed Pace

Focus

In communication, losing focus while communicating happens all the time including with very experienced communicators. Focus means the communicator is aware where one is heading, in other words, is clear about what is to be communicated, how it is affecting the client and the outcome is what s/he has planned and expected. Focus, along with knowledge of content to be communicated, helps social worker to anticipate its impact on client. It is normal that the message may not be accepted in the first instance or misinterpreted and people may want to know more. The knowledge of the communicator, gives authenticity to the message. For example, the interpretation of a particular behaviour and its consequences for the client, explained by a doctor. The client is aware of the expertise of the social worker. The knowledge makes it clear to communicate since the communication then is specific and to the point and not manipulated or superficial. The social worker's communication, helps the client to relax and share or forces them to go in a shell to protect themselves. Either way it can lead to a loss of focus, if the social worker is not monitoring the outcome. A very relaxed client becomes too talkative and hence gets distracted from the main theme.

Diversity

The tendency to evaluate and approve, is considered a major human barrier in communication (Monappa and Saiyadain, 1979). The problem referred to suggests that even before you communicate, you have either condemned or accepted the audience and that is likely to reflect in your communication. In order to remain objective and in control during the communication, the personal likes and dislikes, have to be kept in control. Personal biases must not be allowed to interfere with your communication. It is by no means an easy task, just the fact that we have received some education and training about diversity, does not mean that we have done away with our values. A social worker is only human, has earlier life experiences with different kinds of people and has been groomed by a particular culture. A value framework at a personal level, is likely to remain in place and is perfectly normal, just be aware of it and make sure it does not affect your professional communication.

Knowledge about Other Cultures

It is quite common in working with people to notice that some are easily able to accept and trust persons from other cultures, while others take a much longer time. Many clients from a higher caste background, may consider a social worker from a lower caste as incompetent. It takes a considerable time for many to take actual facts rather than preset notions into account, before passing a judgment on others. A social worker who knows about the upper caste practices and values, would be in a far better situation to handle such clients. It is obvious, an individual will not benefit from a facilitation process till this happens. Labelling or passing a judgment in interpersonal communication is simply ruled out. According to communication theory, this may happen on account of a number of factors. The social worker's lack of familiarity with the culture or the language of the client, can often result in causing an emotional hurt, by the tone or body language of the communicator.

For example, using a high pitch tone is quite common in some cultures while addressing youngsters, or a particular body language, like use of hand or facial expression is consider normal, while other cultures may disapprove it. An inappropriate gesture can cause the communication to break either temporarily or permanently. The key lies in understanding the reaction of the person and rephrasing either whole or part of the communication. These are just a few observations, to indicate, how simple ignorance about people different from us can cause problems. In interpersonal communication it is extremely important to be aware of the significance of tone, symbols, body language, each single word and pause and how it is likely to be interpreted by the receiver.

Objectivity

A major requirement for mastering the art of communication is, to be able to observe facts objectively and analyse them logically. It is quite common to interpret and assign motive to behaviour, and very common to see thing as we want to see. A smile can be interpreted as mocking or a welcome sign. A professional sees it as smile, knows what it means by remaining cool. It is normal for clients to seek guidance for a number of things. A professional helps them to find their own answers by encouraging them to think. Emotional involvement distorts communication invariably. Emotional involvement of the communicator can lead to manipulation of the impact of communication. In communication terminology, it is called filtering. Filtering refers to a sender manipulating information so that it will be seen more favourably. It is common to see actors dramatizing a communication, in a drama, to generate emotions among the audience. It is significant to remember here that the objectivity means, that the end results are not manipulated but anticipated. For example, a social worker is not using communication to please or hurt the client. The social worker is simply stating a fact, for example, the client behaved in a particular situation and social worker explains its implications, how it is likely to be interpreted by others. In some cases the clients may like what they hear from the social worker, while sometimes it may be painful for them. The social worker's conveying the facts is important and so is the manner of communication.

Time and Content Management

In a facilitation session the social worker should keep a good record of the time and content of the session. It helps to analyse who said what, what is the progress during a session. A common problem in interpersonal communication is over communication and under communication. In over communication, one person dominates the communication and the other/s do not get sufficient space to participate, hence the results are rather unsatisfactory. A professional social worker, uses a very carefully selected content and style of communication suited for a specific situation. A professional never gives sermons, or long speeches. Usually it consists of a precise comment or a question to either get more information or provide an explanation. Over-communication including repetition, reflects anxiety and inability to focus on facts. A specific content has to be covered during a session, for example, exploring a client's perception of a particular event in their life. Professional worker should keep the communication short and focused. Learn to encourage the other to speak but guide them to come to the point by crisp observations.

Eye Contact

Maintaining proper eye contact is essential in successfully responding to the clients. By proper eye contact, does not mean staring at the client all the time. At times, it may be useful to look elsewhere to allow some space to the client, before we focus on the face again. In Indian culture, the females find it difficult to maintain regular eye contact with a male adult, who is not intimately related to them or is not within the permissible degree of informal relationship. It may be helpful to give her some privacy. Lack of proper eye contact can be interpreted as avoidance or not paying enough attention as well. A client never trusts the prescription of a doctor, who never looked up, while the patient was describing the symptoms of the problem.

A Relaxed Pace

Any anxiety on the part of social worker to hurry up the proceedings can prove disastrous. A relaxed pace is always helpful in interpersonal communications. It requires proper planning to avoid other matters to interrupt the maintenance of a feeling of no hurry or anxiety, to just move on. Never give your client the impression that they are not important for you.

Listening

Listening is an important skill in communication process, as it helps one to receive and interpret verbal communications, but very few of us make full use of it. A professional listener gets the content of what is said along with reasons for that particular communication. The professional by using the interactive listening skills, interprets the entire communication immediately, by looking at it in a holistic framework. The skill of listening, therefore, has to be developed by sharpening analytical skills of content, tone and the body language or facial expressions of the speaker. Listening skills require the development of sensitivity in the listener, to pay attention to the speaker and to respond periodically in an appropriate manner, to encourage or convey the fact that you are following and understanding the message clearly. The body language has also to reflect that you are paying attention to the speaker. At times, a proper eye contact and a nod, is adequate response, to convey that you are following the speaker. A professional listener learns to focus, on the conversation and the actor all the time. The cultural understanding of body language is important, for example in Hyderabad (South India), a person nods his head from side to side while showing agreement, while in North India, same gesture is seen as a sign of disagreement. The term 'Baai' is considered a respectable term in Gujarat and Rajasthan, while it is considered a derogatory term elsewhere for women. Many rural and tribal terms and symbols convey quite different meanings.

Non-Verbal Cues

Non-verbal cues are to note and interpret what is not said. Some important non-verbal cues are facial expressions, head movements, posture, body and hand movements, self and other touching, leg positions and movement, etc. Quality of tone, speed of delivery, pauses, hesitation, clothing, hair style, and other items of personal adornments are also considered non-verbal cues.

Due precautions are needed while interpreting the non-verbal cues as it is subjective and difficult to verify, as most non-verbal cues have ambiguous meaning. Non-verbal cues are good indicators of a person's emotional state and the ability to control emotions. Non-verbal cues are used by persons to project a certain self-image, such as honest or a brave person. At the same time non-verbal cues, can indicate what the communicator thinks of the recipient. For example, a warm smile indicates trust and a silent pensive person non-trust (see Hall, 2007).

Observation

Observation is also an important part of the communication process as it refers to the ability of a person to understand things by using simple observation techniques. A keen observer is able to observe small and simple facts, which others ignore or consider unimportant. In facilitating relationships the ability to observe the thinking, feelings and actions of clients, helps the social worker to understand them and respond to these, without questioning. Feelings are difficult to hide and facial expressions and eyes are gateways to understanding the feelings. A keen observer can tell, if a person is feeling tense, happy or uninterested through keen observation skills. Similarly, the body gestures are good indicators of a person's mood and thinking as well.

Points to remember in developing observation skills:

- Pay attention to details;
- Concentrate on the finer points rather than generalizing;
- Keep your emotions in check;
- Be patient.

Analytical Thinking

The interpretation by a social worker of the statements, emotions and actions of clients, requires an ability on the part of professional social worker, to analyse these and to explain it to clients. The professional social worker acquires, through their training, knowledge and theories, the experience of applying these in real life situations. In facilitating to change people's response to situations and persons, worker has to analyse the client's response to specific situations. The framework of self and other or other theories are used to assess this. The goal is to help the client's conscious of reasons and be able to control their own behaviour. The social worker in a session with families or other groups, is often required to intervene to explain, that members have deviated from the task at hand. This frequently happens in meetings of the groups, to discuss their relationships and its implications. It is not uncommon to see people forget the purpose and start indulging in blaming others or mocking each other. The session of the group may thus generate a lot of heat or merry making or both, which are likely to distract the group from its task at hand. The ability of social worker to analyse the situation and to take corrective measures, requires analytical thinking. The social worker may summarize, restate, interpret, clarify, question or confront the members, to accomplish the focus. The task of summarizing similarly requires the skill on the part of the social worker, to state what the gist of the session was.

We have still not stated in very specific terms, what is analytical thinking. The analytical skill simply refers to what is happening, why it is happening and how it is impacting different persons, in a coherent manner. It also refers, to being able to perceive a particular social reality from various perspectives. For example, selecting an appropriate situation from a case study, reflects on the various factors constructing the event. A client is not able to control her/his emotions in a situation, if her/his integrity is questioned. The analytical skill of the social worker lies in, being able to explore person's view, the stress s/he faces and then exploring various possibilities for rectifying it. The social worker should be able to see, the feasibility of achieving the objective, in terms of current capacity of the client, the time frame and the external environment. Analytical thinking can also be described as raising pertinent questions, regarding the problem and solutions both. Some scholars would simply refer to the skill as the capacity to think straight. The social workers also have to learn to control their emotions as we suggested earlier to develop good analytical skills.

Empathy

Empathy can simply be defined as the ability to correctly read the emotional state of other. It is a complex and difficult task. A common person views emotional reactions and evaluates these as natural or unnatural. For example, the level of frustration a person should exhibit faced with failure or the level of joy in case of success, the appropriate level of sadness or anger, in cases of betrayal by a spouse and so on. The fact is that there is no standard reaction, we assume it is there and expect everybody to follow an illusion. A professional thinks otherwise, and looks at 'the' client, rather than using general standards. Nothing can hurt the process of gaining the trust of the client more, than giving an impression that you do not understand the emotional state of the person concerned.

In other words, empathy refers to the capacity of a person to put oneself in some body else's situation and understand the feelings and emotions involved. It is often referred to as an intuitive feeling of others' emotions and feelings. A social worker should be skillful, in anticipating how individuals express themselves, deal with, tension and conflict, defend themselves when threatened, etc. In dealing with children in difficult circumstances and women in particular, this skill is most often tested. The problems and tensions, that a child on the street in India goes through, in places like Mumbai, Delhi, Chennai, Colombo, Karachi or Dhaka, cannot be easily understood by a person who has never faced such a situation personally. Similarly, the fear and trauma of sexual harassment and abuse faced by females, irrespective of socio economic strata, is difficult to understand by a male social worker. The anxiety of females in a group, for example in a Panchayat (village level local body organization in India) meeting or Gram Sabha (village general body) meeting, can only be understood, through empathy. The worker needs an intuitive understanding of the torture and exploitation of Dalits in India. Empathy is a real test of our ability to realize the sufferings of others, the dilemmas and tensions and uncertainty, others have faced and are still facing, in countries like India, Pakistan, Bangladesh, Sri Lanka and many others.

The skill of empathy can be developed, first by becoming aware of the differences that are characteristic of the life of people of different strata in a society. The next step is accepting and respecting these differences. Accepting the fact that people are different is easy, but accepting that we are equal and have no right to impose our superiority is, difficult. For example, an urban educated person finds it so hard to accept, that tribal and rural people are human and have same civil rights. The male superiority syndrome is very real despite years of social struggles, legal reforms and education and training efforts. Same is true for caste and class differences. An empathetic understanding begins with an awareness that not all people think, feel and act uniformly. Similarly, not all people possess capabilities considered normal. In Indian context, where cultural differences are so much in evidence, a social worker should be careful in making a remark like, ' you can't even understand such a simple thing or how could you be so ignorant'. These reactions convey a tendency to impose personal standards on others.

A response indicating understanding many a times is a sympathetic nod, or some other non-verbal cues. A genuine appreciation of other's emotions conveys itself to the others, all that you need is not to pretend.

Self-Control

A common human weakness is, to be guided by emotions rather than mind. People are quite prone to feel annoyed, happy, violence prone or depressed, in a variety of situations. The first symptom of a person loosing self-control is, the degree of stress reflected in your behaviour. Expression of anger, irritation, frustration, are symptoms of expectations not realized, reflecting preconceived notions about others. The stress begins with expectations and increases with failure. This is a symptom of lack of self-control. A family starts fighting among themselves, as soon as a session begins, the social worker feels the stress. The need to handle a situation is obvious, but the social worker is primarily there to help the clients to do things on their own and try and find ways of finding solutions to their problems. Inviting suggestions from a client or a group of clients to deal with such situations, is a normal professional reaction displaying anxiety to control events and behaviour, indicates loss of self-control. A professional is always in control over emotions and feelings, to act objectively and efficiently.

Steps to Develop Self-Control

The development of professional self is an important aspect of professional training programme.

Review Your Own Behaviour

The first step is to differentiate personal from professional. All human beings develop specific values about different aspects of life situations. It is a natural process of our growing up. Cultures play an important part in developing these value preferences. We therefore, are accustomed to treat certain behaviours as desirable and others in varying degrees of either tolerable or to be denounced. As an individual we have the freedom to practice these, but as a professional, we are guided by professional values, where a deliberate attempt is made, to keep a non-judgmental stance to the extent possible. However, exercising more control on our behaviour requires that we become aware of our weaknesses.

Address Some Simple Queries

- Do I believe in religious, caste, class or any other kind of superiority?
- Do I believe in a gender hierarchy?
- What are my moral ethics and how passionately I want them to be followed?
- Are these impacting my behaviour during my professional interactions with clients?
- And with others in general?

Do remember that even if we try to hide our true feelings and reactions, our eyes and other non-verbal clues can leak out the truth. It is common, to get swayed by our need to talk, to control things, to be hurt by criticism or opposition to our ideas and so on. A review of our own behaviour after sessions is helpful in making us aware of the areas which may need change and modification. Awareness to control expectations to a desired level, an objective assessment of situations and a determined effort to achieve professional competence, through continuous reviews and practice, is a good way to bring about improvements.

- *Calmness:* shows confidence and portrays that any unsolvable problem is solvable.
- *Curiosity:* implies that you don't have the answer to every question.
- *Empathy:* gives the impression that you know what they are going through.
- *Respect:* treating clients as equals and not patronizing them. Being honest to them is part of our professional ethics. It is extremely essential that we work out our code of ethics and keep reviewing our behaviour periodically to make sure that we are following it.

13

Techniques of Facilitating Relationships

In modern day practice the keyword for a successful and effective practice is a precise, focused and scientific approach, not leaving things to chance. In social work till recently, not many precise tools were available for practice. The problem still persists, many new ways have evolved over the years, to look at both the problems and the ways to resolve them. Well, the days of explanations for failures are over; the success is simply rated by what a practitioner delivers. Use of scientific tools, to know the specific details about the client/s, and their problems under investigation are routine. The medical sciences are able to use more precise tools, as they are dealing with more measurable characteristics of individual and symptoms of problems, whereas behavioural professionals are still struggling with developing adequate tools. Measuring personality or stress or anxiety levels are far more complicated than measuring blood pressure. Reliable tools are not easily accessible to all practitioners, though there is a direct relation, between stress level and some medical problems. Yet, we have to collect facts to give a factual base to our facilitating process to avoid mistakes. Construction of own tools has to be culture specific, as it plays an important part in designing our data collection process. Secondly, we have to use multiple sources, to get the same data to avoid subjectivity, which is a major problem in both collection and interpretation of data, with respect to human behaviour.

Assessment is a critical thread running through the development of social work and other professionals dealing with behavioural change. Assessment of individuals, groups, families, communities and organizations, therefore, pose many challenges. In practice, assessment and intervention are transactional and non-linear. As a general rule assessment precedes intervention (Germain, 1968). Yet, there may be situations where further assessment may be needed after the intervention.

It is inevitable therefore, to discuss the process and the procedures of assessment techniques used for various purposes at various levels of interventions, to help the practitioners to collect relevant indices to make a tentative diagnosis, but they are free, to make modifications if need be, based on their own cultural and social context. Some attempts at developing assessment tools have been made and handbooks of psychological tools for measuring personality, leadership styles, stress level and various other behaviours are readily available. Many online sites are also available on the internet and one can use these, but the problem of checking the cultural relevance and content or validity remains to be taken into account. Content or validity refers to checking the claims of what the tool is trying to measure and its authenticity.

A social worker needs to be familiar with the following:

1. Assessment of Individuals
2. Assessment of Groups
3. Assessment of Families
4. Assessment of Communities
5. Assessment of Organizations
6. Computerized Assessment

Assessment of Individuals

We have to ask a simple question before we start using or constructing an assessment tool or at least a guideline. What do we want to assess? For example, do we want to assess the personality type or do we want to know a particular personality trait such as whether a person is outgoing or reserved and so on. A social worker can work in collaboration with other professionals, to get the assessment done, as is the case with medical practitioners. But one must know the basics of assessment process and its uses. In the Indian sub continent the social service agencies and professionals are not well organized and are not very resource rich either. Hence the current practice and future possibilities of using services of other professionals is rather dismal, yet it can certainly improve the quality of professional practice, if qualified practitioners are associated to do it. In the delivery of social services, for example, many a times the legal or medical implications are not fully taken into account, in assessment of a client's problem.

Secondly, it is important to be clear about the framework a professional is using to arrive at a diagnosis, to decide the nature and scope of assessment. For example, a person is facing problems in the spousal relationship. A framework refers to a professional's diagnostic tool for determining the possible causes of problems, in spousal relations. In practice, the social worker generally may resort to a simple plan of study-diagnosis-and treatment. A framework is still needed to provide a guideline for the study stage, to know the facts, the social worker considers significant for arriving at an understanding of problems in the relations. For example, if the client is wife and her preliminary statement refers to domestic violence, what facts we need to know? Should the focus of assessment be wife, husband or both? What facts we need to know about one or both, depends on whether we are using a Freudian or Rogerian perspective. Do keep in mind that the factors causing problems in spousal relations, are class specific, (rich or poor), location specific,(rural, urban-small town or metropolis), as well as culture specific (Indian or American). The framework being used in this book to explain relationships, the difficulties and dealing with these, has been dealt within detail in the chapter on theories. The assessment according to this framework, will focus on how self or other's oriented spouses are, the history of psychosocial development and dependence level, etc. to determine what needs to be done, to facilitate the relationship. The assessment will include, the awareness level about the problem and its implications, the emotional energy, anxiety level, the social skills, the willingness to change, the self-concept including self-confidence level, etc.

Sources of Assessment

Self-report known as client's written descriptions of their feelings, behaviour and thoughts (Kopp, 1993), is an important source of assessment used by professionals. Usually an individual is expected to fill up a questionnaire. The questionnaire can be closed ended, where answers are also provided or it may be a mixed one where some are left open for the individual to provide a more descriptive response. Self-report may be a record of occurrence of certain behaviours, such as extreme anger resulting in violence, emotional breakdown or use of certain words or phrases such as 'stupid', 'bastard' or 'you are an idiot'. It is also known as self-monitoring, defined as a two-step process: (1) the individual recognizes the occurrence of the event, and (2) systematically records it (Thorensen and Mahoney, 1974).

Description of events and surrounding circumstances help in a much better assessment of the individual and may even help identify specific objectives, in terms of areas of new behaviours to be addressed. Providing an individual, an opportunity to freely narrate an event may result in some spontaneous behaviour, which can be very revealing, particularly revealing the relationships or perception of others in general and significant others in particular.

Advantages and Disadvantages of Self-report

It is obvious that a person is in a far better situation to know the nature of a crisis situation, its impact and the severity of feelings, etc. and therefore can provide an authentic account of these. Yet, when it comes to a self-assessment, the subjectivity can also easily creep in and distort facts. Self-report can lead to self-realization and help in dealing with identification of area of change. It can also lead to self-confidence on the part of client, having discovered the ability of not only identifying the problem, but also the possibility of being able to deal with it.

Significant Factors in the Client's Life Space

Collecting facts from the many person's constituting the life space of the client is routine in social work, while others do not directly tap this source primarily because of ethical reasons. Social workers believe in the right to confidentiality of the individual, but help the client to realize the social responsibility towards family and society. Further, following a theoretical perspective of client-social network dependence in creation and resolution of relationship issues, makes it inevitable to have a look at the entire eco-map of the life space of the client. It may or may not be necessary to secure the cooperation of others, in the resolution of the problem, but some modifications in the life-space, cannot be altogether ruled out. Objective facts are essential, in assessment of social networks, around the client (see Tracy and Whittaker, 1993). Some facts cannot be accessed through the client, as the person may not be aware of these, for example, events at birth and during early childhood. Antecedents are events that occur prior to a behaviour and affect its probability of occurrence, often by signaling the likelihood of various consequences. For example, a child may behave differently, in a peer group or school than at home, because of experiencing different consequences. The consequences of earlier behavioural responses, are thus important for the recurrence of behaviour. Such facts may not be adequately provided by the client.

Observation by the Social Worker

A good source of collection of facts is social worker's own observation of client, family members and others constituting the eco-map of client's life space. The first hand observations can provide many insights about the client's relationships and the behavioural responses including the communication pattern. These facts provide a more objective basis for analysing the facts provided by the client and others.

Assessment of Individuals

Use two sets of tests, one which test their general notions without going into details and the second where you spell out different aspects in more detail. Both formulations are given below:

Self-Concept

Source: Self-report

Intelligence

(a) Better than others
(b) Better than my father?
(c) Brother
(d) Friend
(e) Colleague
(f) Superior

Social Hierarchy

Who are you (open ended let the respondent use a term to describe)?

Social Skills

(a) Meeting people
(b) Maintaining relationships
(c) Attending social functions
(d) Inviting people home
(e) I like looking after children/parents
(f) I have no problem communicating with others

Note: you can use a five point or three point scale

Emotional Intelligence

You can measure the emotional intelligence consisting of the following points by asking some questions given here as examples. You can add more questions if you find it necessary.

Self-awareness

(a) I know why I get irritated
(b) I do not know
(c) Not sure.

Do you over react to when irritated

(a) I never over react
(b) Sometimes I do
(c) Not sure

Self-regulation, (mood or feelings)

(a) I can control my feelings
(b) Cannot control feelings
(c) Not sure
(d) I undergo frequent mood changes
(e) Not very frequently
(f) Not sure

Self-motivation

(a) I have a set routine of work
(b) I work when I have to
(c) I postpone it often

Empathy

(a) I can understand my wife's frustration when I do not treat her well
(b) I don't know why she gets so upset
(c) Not sure
(d) I can understand my mother's anxiety when I come home late
(e) I don't know why she gets so upset
(f) My boss gets upset when I am not punctual
(g) Can't understand why he gets so upset
(h) Not sure

Self-Other orientation

(a) I take all decisions without consulting anyone
(b) I always consult others
(c) I give everyone space to take their decisions

Bar-On, conceptualizes EI as consisting of five main factors: intrapersonal, interpersonal, stress management, adaptability, and general mood. The intrapersonal component is based on an individual's self-awareness and expression. This requires individuals to be aware of their emotions and effectively express them to others. The interpersonal component involves an individual's social awareness and adeptness at social relationships. A key aspect here is the ability to empathize with how others experience social situations and the feelings they experience, as well as the ability to build and maintain relationships. Stress management deals with a person's ability to manage and regulate his or her emotions. Individuals high on this dimension control their emotions instead of allowing emotions to control them. Adaptability revolves around a person's capacity to adjust, his or her feelings in order to effectively deal with emotional situations, whether internal or external. The last dimension, general mood, is based on a person's degree of happiness or overall feeling of well-being. This dimension has been described as a key social work, emotionally intelligent behaviour.

An Exercise in Self-Exploration

This is an exercise to clarify my thinking about the decisions I take and its implications for me and other people I care for.

Before answering please think and then answer.

Implications for Change of Job

How the decision will impact my family

(1) My spouse will lose her/his job
(2) I wont live close to my parents
(3) Children will have to change school
(4) Will my spouse be happy
(5) Will my mother be happy
(6) Will my brother be happy
(7) How about my children

What is it about the job that I do not like?

(1) Working conditions
(2) Intellectual satisfaction
(3) Very stressful
(4) The working hours are too long
(5) My colleagues are not very nice
(6) The salary is not good

Who should decide about what I should do?

Identify the others who will be affected.

Note: This is just an illustration to guide, how to create a hypothetical situation depending on the client's profile to assess the self others position of the client.

Individual Assessment: Source Worker

During the interaction with the client make your own assessment about the client on all indicators on which s/he has given a self-report. You can then make notes on where you agree or disagree with the self-assessment. This will help the worker to factually know the self-awareness level of the client. In other words the points from where the counseling session can commence. For example, a person who reports a high level of others orientation, is not aware of how others will be affected by his/her decisions. Further, a professional will take adequate steps, to recheck his/her conclusions about the client. It is always advisable, to discuss these in supervisory conferences or team meetings. A better way is to refer the client to other professionals to make sure.

Individual Assessment: Other Sources

It is always good to get information about the client from other sources, such as close family members, friends, work colleagues, etc., if the client is comfortable about that. But sometimes the clients are not open to this process, which makes things difficult. If possible help them to accept such findings, as it will help in clarifying many issues, relating to their relationship problems. There are other professionals, such as clinical psychologists and psychiatrists, who can also be used for getting assessment of the individual client done.

Family Intervention

One of the earliest programmes specifically designed to reduce conflict between parents and children, has proven to be one of the most effective: Problem-solving communication training, an integration of family systems and cognitive-behavioural approaches, encourages constructive parent-child communication in a manner that reduces the escalation of a conflict (Laursen, Brett, 2006).

Family Assessment

The family assessment refers to screening all relationships in the family, including all family members individually, to assess their current capacities for contributing to family well-being or otherwise, etc. The assessment takes into account number of current family members living together, their education, employment and economic status along with level of social development, etc. Obviously, a family assessment is done when one or more members end up facing problems, and help is needed to put them back on track. The examples are children showing symptoms of abuse, women facing domestic violence, a member becoming drug addict or alcoholic and so on. Such incidences are a reflection of a mal functioning family or in other words, the family is not able to provide care and support, members need for healthy growth, and development or coping with specific stresses in their life situation. The assessment has to come up with a number of answers, such as the source of the malfunctioning, the seriousness of the problem, the possible intervention approaches and so on.

Comprehensive family assessment begins with the first contact with a family and continues until the 'case' is closed. It must be carried out in partnership with families and in collaboration with others in the community, subject to the consent by the client group. The general objective is to identify individual and family strengths and factors impacting the interpersonal relationships in the family. It is a process and has to be updated when major changes in family circumstances occur and at the points of key decision-making in a case. Although professionals working with different objectives such as protection of children, prevention of domestic violence, and family counsellors, will focus on different factors, yet by and large they are likely to cover all aspects of family and all factors impacting upon its functioning. Professionals working with children, for example, are interested in assessing the risk of child abuse and the chances of family breakdown, while the professional working with domestic violence issues, will focus on alcohol and drug abuse, economic resources and in general behavioural aspects of partners. But it is obvious that many factors, including some outside the family, impact the functioning of the family. The approaches to family assessment have taken different routes to arrive at their destination but three basic patterns dominate the discussion. As Parke Ross D. et al. (1988) in their study suggested, it is the cognitive, behavioural and affective domains of family functioning, that we are all concerned with and trying to understand. In other words, values, notions and concepts, impacting the family norms and the socio-economic context of the families, including their geography and the patterns of behaviour that emerge. It is advisable to focus on all three to arrive at a comprehensive understanding in our assessment process.

Approaches to Family Assessment

1. Ecological perspective
2. Behavioural perspective
3. Institutional perspective

The Ecological Perspective

The family ecology can be defined as the interpersonal relationship among members and the various constituents that surround them at any point of time. It is visible and felt by all visiting it. You feel relaxed and happy or you experience the tension and an urge to escape. Its like the constituents of an orchestra producing music or a jarring note. The ecological perspective builds on systems theory and is concerned with relations among living entities and aspects of their environment (Germain, 1979). The life model developed using ecological perspective suggests four hypotheses to explain family stress;

1. life transitions involving developmental changes such as onset of puberty,
2. status role changes and crisis events,
3. unresponsive social and physical environments, and
4. communication and relationship difficulties (Germain and Gitterman, 1980).

The ecology of the family includes the following:

- The members currently living together
- The family of husband
- The family of wife
- The family friend circle
- The work place of both
- The school/college of children
- The religious practices and contacts
- The neighbourhood
- The reference groups of all members
- Other significant actors or organizations

We will discuss each of these in detail to analyse the emergence of the family ecology.

The Members

The members of the family living together constitute the core of the family. As the numbers and the age of the members change, it impacts the ecology of the family in subtle ways, at times impacting members' interpersonal relationships immediately, while at other times, the impact produces change manifesting itself much later. For example, relationship in a family is affected when a new member is added in the family, the birth of a child or a parent or sibling of either spouse joining the family. It definitely gets affected, when any member develops a romantic relationship, either for the first time in the case of children or an additional one in the case of spouses. The birth of subsequent children or addition of new members on any account will similarly bring about changes in the ecology.

There are numerous studies of large families resulting in economic deprivation for members and short families resulting in emotional imbalance of different kind.

As the children grow, the relationship in the family continue to be impacted, along with other members aging. The member's values, self-concepts and expectations from each other, are constantly changing, thereby producing changes in the ecology.

Work out all the details regarding members such as:

- Male spouse: Age/Education/Occupation/Income
- Relationship with female spouse: caring/dominating/equal/ subservient, etc.
- Female spouse: Age/Education/Occupation/Income
- Relationship with male spouse: caring/dominating/equal/ subservient, etc.

For all other members:

- Relationship with male spouse: Example son
- Age/Education/Occupation/Income
- Explore all relationships and make a note

Family of Husband

Explore the following details:

- Total members.
- Age/Education/Occupation/Income of all.
- Explore the main relationship between parents.
- Explore the parent-child relationship.
- Explore the sibling relations.

Family of Wife

- Repeat the same as in case of husband's family.

Finally explore the relationship between the husband and wife's family. Which family seems to be having closer ties, with the family under assessment with what implications for all relationships.

Friend Circle

Explore the friend circle of all members and make a note about its impact on relationships in the family.

Work Relationships

Analyse the work relationships of all working members and its impact on family relations.

School/College Relations

Find out the details of school/college relationships and its impact on family relations.

Religious Practices

Prepare a note about religious practices of all members including parents of the spouses. Identify significant similarities or differences among members' religious practices and its impact on relations.

Neighbourhood

Identify the friendly neighbours and their impact on family.

Reference Group

Identify the reference groups of all members and check the similarities or differences. Role assignment in families is a function of gender and normative expectations of reference groups (Walsh, 1982).

Identify any other individual/family/organization impacting family relations currently; NGO/lawyer/government welfare agency/ social worker, etc.

Behavioural Perspective

The family assessment from a behavioural perspective takes a clinical view of all the members, identifies specific personality traits of each member, tries to identify any abnormalities impacting the relationships. The behaviour of all members towards each other, is the focus of assessment, the issues are identified based on the analysis. The behavioural perspective refers to the analysis of actual behaviour patterns, within the family. For example, the parents' communication styles, frequency and feelings involved. The behavioural assessment scans the actual happenings in the family, its impact on different members, the resultant environment for members to meet their needs. It helps in understanding the nature of bonds with each other and the rivalries in groups.

Institutional Perspective

Institutional perspective looks at the standard practices of the family such as allocation of power between members and their respective roles, in short, the family structure. It explains the malfunctioning of the family, in terms of lack of clarity about role/s, or inability of members to accept and perform role/s such as an alcoholic father or an ailing mother or wife. The conflict in the family is explained, generally as the non-acceptance of current power structure. It becomes dysfunctional as members do not understand or perform their roles. This could happen on account of a number of factors, such as growth of children, economic empowerment of women, aging of the parents or loss of job and so on, resulting in a changed structure, causing problems of both understanding and acceptance. Very often, a change in personal power over others, is difficult to accept such as an educated and working wife and grown up educated children. The institutional perspective as Nagy and Spark, (1973) pointed out, the families develop a hierarchy of obligations, or a multigenerational balance sheet of merit and indebtedness, which has tremendous impact on individual members, since any move toward differentiation may imply disloyalty. The family assessment scans the traditional family practices, structures and roles and members' commitment to these and so on, in the context of contemporary social changes. This perspective relies on individual assessment of members and their self concepts and value preferences including their position on self-other orientation. In interpersonal terms, differentiation of self with others, acceptance of it objectively, refers to the relationship between intellect and goal achievement, on the one hand and feelings or emotions on the other. The family mal-function is explained, in terms of members caught between the two and the resulting stress. The within 'Gotra' and inter caste marriages are a case in point.

Case Example

The social worker is approached by a woman aged 38 years, having three children; a son aged 6 years, daughters aged 8 and 10 years; having problem with her alcoholic and violent husband.

Note: How has the woman approached the social worker? Has she approached the social worker on her own or she has been persuaded by others to seek help. It is important to ascertain her commitment to do something about the problem. If she has been persuaded by others to come, the social worker should help her, to decide what she wants to do. The social worker cannot approach her problem, unless s/he has some idea about the strength and weaknesses, of the client. Helping her to decide, taking her own situation into account, whether she wants to do anything about it. It is important since it is she who will have to suffer the hardships and pain, to accomplish the change.

A professional social worker by using assessment technique, would get a good idea what she can do and if she needs capacity building and support, to carry her through the ordeal. Yet a constant firm message, that she can help herself, while others will offer support, is helpful. Give her time to think and to reflect and decide. Check the nature of help she identifies and seek. She might prefer a change in husband's behaviour towards the family, rather than a clear break. The need for assessment becomes obvious yet again. The worker would assess the possibility of change as far as husband is concerned, before being able to guide her about the approach. The process will go on, till a resolution of the problem. The process of facilitation may go on monitoring the changes, helping her to review her situation and providing further insights to carry on her life. Do not rush her into any decision, let her take as much time she needs to want to seek a change on her own accord.

A common mistake committed by social workers in the Indian sub continent is, to show concern and anxiety about her situation and offer sympathy. The social workers often are guided by their own values, to urge her to act immediately, to rectify the situation, takes the problem in her stride, as not much could be done about it, given the situation. Both these approaches have to be avoided. A careful assessment will reveal the capacity of the client to act, or incorporate some changes to handle the situation. That should provide the guideline for action. The social worker should know, the legal implications of the case, such as Domestic Violence Act, Divorce laws, Child Labour Act and so on.

Generally, all users of social work services will be experiencing anxiety, a normal phenomenon in a situation generating uncertainty and stress. It will help the users effectively, if the social worker is able to assess whether it is a state anxiety or a trait anxiety. As is clear from the term itself, a state anxiety is one which a person encounters in specific situations, whereas a trait anxiety is a characteristic of one's personality. There are different techniques which have evolved over the years, to test both of these. It is also necessary to be able to measure the intensity level of anxiety.

Table 1

Anxiety Assessment Techniques

Anxiety	*Assessment Technique*
State anxiety	Self-report
	Behavioural
	Cognitive
	Physiological
Trait anxiety	Self-report

Assessment Techniques

The use of questionnaires has been the primary assessment technique for trait anxiety. There are multiple techniques, that can be used for the assessment of state anxiety. The assessment techniques are shown in Table 1 and include self-report, behavioural, cognitive and physiological measures. The most comprehensive method of assessing state anxiety is, through a combination of the available techniques, as there are individual differences in the experience of anxiety.

Self-Report Measures

The majority of individual assessment is based on self-report measures, despite the fact that personality theory states, that behaviour can easily be observed. Self-report questionnaires, have the following advantages: they are easy to administer, results are easy to analyse, results can be compared to normative data and results can be subjected to factor analysis, for greater clarity. One of the earliest, self-report anxiety measures is the Taylor Manifest Anxiety Scale (Taylor, 1953). Another commonly used self-report measure of anxiety is, the State-Trait Anxiety Inventory (STAI; Spielberger, 1989). The STAI assesses both state and trait anxiety.

The Endler Multidimensional Anxiety Scales (EMAS) assesses both state anxiety and trait anxiety as multidimensional constructs and assesses the perception of the situation (Endler, Edwards and Vitelli, 1991). Cognitive-worry and autonomic-emotional state, are the two components of state anxiety assessed by the EMAS-State measure. The EMAS-Trait measures assess a predisposition to experience anxiety in the following four situational domains: social evaluation, physical danger, ambiguous situation, and daily routines. Recent research has resulted in the addition of the following two situational domains: self-disclosure (to family or to friends) and separation anxiety (Endler and Flett, 2002).

The Anxiety Sensitivity Index consists of 16 items and assesses the fear of experiencing anxiety (Reiss, Peterson, Gursky and McNally, 1986).

Another self-report instrument commonly used to assess anxiety is the Beck Anxiety Inventory (BAI; Beck, Epstein, Brown and Steer, 1988). The BAI consists of 21 items representing two factors: somatic symptoms and subjective anxiety symptoms. A weakness is that the BAI does not distinguish between state and trait anxiety. Respondents are asked to report the degree to which they have been bothered by the symptoms assessed over the past week.

Table 2

Inventories

The Scales	*Author/year*
Anxiety Sensitivity Index	Reiss et al. (1986)
Beck Anxiety Inventory	Beck et al. (1988)
Endler Multidimensional Anxiety Scales (EMAS)	Endler et al. (1991)
EMAS-Social Anxiety Scales (EMAS-SAS)	Endler and Flett (2001)
State-Trait Anxiety Inventory (STAI)	Spielberger (1983)
Taylor Manifest Anxiety Scale	Taylor (1953)

Behavioural Measures

Another anxiety assessment technique is the measurement of various behaviours. The presence and frequency of certain behaviours are rated by others (e.g. clinicians, experimenters). The behaviours indicating the level of anxiety an individual is experiencing, depends upon the situation. For example, measures of social anxiety include measurement of the maintenance of eye contact, communication style and frequency during a social function, body language and fidgeting (see Leary, 1986). Some of these behaviours will not figure in other situations. Behaviours are often recorded in role-play situations, due to the impracticality of rating people in naturalistic environments. Behavioural observation techniques are less subjective on the part of the examinee, than the use of self-report measures. However, the presence of the examiner in an evaluative role, may affect the level of anxiety. Further in an interaction situation, the behaviour of a person may represent a confound. S/he may respond differently to different participants, depending on variables such as the social skill level of the other participants (Arnkoff and Glass, 1989), yet behavioural assessment techniques for performance situations, have been shown to be highly reliable.

Cognitive Measures

Anxiety also has a cognitive component. Cognitive measures examine, the thoughts an individual has. This can be done through thought-listing procedures (Cacioppo and Petty, 1983) or via a questionnaire approach. Thought-listing techniques ask participants to record thoughts, in paper and pencil format, while they are in an anxious situation (Cacioppo and Petty, 1983). Participants are asked, not to concern themselves with spelling or grammar, and not to edit the thoughts as they arise. The list of thoughts is, analysed according to such indices, as content or frequency. Variations of this technique include: (i) having participants state their thoughts aloud rather than recording them and (ii) having participants watch a video of their performance and state their thoughts during the viewing.

Physiological Measures

Anxiety has a physiological component, thus allowing for the assessment of anxiety through physiological means. Among the physiological measures are measurement of heart rate, twitching of fingers, sweating and difficulty in breathing or an accelerated breathing. Additionally, blushing has been used to assess social anxiety. The different physiological measures do not, however, correlate well with one another or with self-report measures (Leary, 1986). Respiration rate has been shown to be positively related to self-reported anxiety.

The trait anxiety, the predisposition to be anxious in different situations, is generally assessed through self-report instruments. There are differences to be found among individuals, in terms of intensity and frequency, and therefore the assessment of trait anxiety, should be multi-dimensional to cover various facets (see Norman S. Endler and Nancy L. Kocovski, 2005).

Assessment of Groups

The relationships in group, for example in play group, work group and peer group, can become stressful because of a number of factors. A primary factor is, the discord in values and an unsettled power structure. If members are not in agreement about their own relationship and their relationship with the leader, everyone would become equally confused about their roles in the group. A basic requirement for a normal functioning of the group, is a minimum level of compatibility among group members, in terms of values, an understanding of group norms, leadership and frequent communications to sort out issues. The worker should screen these to begin with. This would help the worker to see the group functioning objectively, identify the short comings, share these with members and help them to discuss what they want to do about improving it. Barring some very difficult situations, for example, where one or more than one conditions of normal functioning are missing, frequent focused group meetings, to explain individual reactions and support to modify them can bring about considerable change.

Indicators for Assessment

Group goals: In assessing goals, focus on how the goals were decided, feasibility, the group development level, resources, structure and leadership and duration.

Group power structure: it refers to who has what status and role in a group.

Leadership: style and assessment of performance of leaders, current and past.

Decision-making processes: refers to style of decision-making, e.g. democratic and participatory, autocratic and sub group dominated and so on.

Degree of differences among members: refers to differences in age, experience, education, class and caste status, economic, etc.

Nature of conflicts: refers to issue based conflicts or person centered, egoistic or caste or class centered.

Communication patterns: open and friendly, or stressful and critical, person or issue centered. No clear pattern generally chaotic and unguided, etc.

Degree of openness or sharing issues: good, limited, none, very closed.

Financial position and transparency: financial resources available, sources and transparency in financial matters.

Group bonding: very strong, developing, weak, no bonding, etc.

Growth oriented groups can continue for longer duration as experiences in the group will go a long way in increasing communication skills, confidence level, and others-orientation of members.

Assessment of Communities

Community assessment should begin with understanding what the term is being used for in the first place. Is it a locality, interest group such as farmers, workers etc., or gender, caste group, tribe, or religious group or any other? In social work the worker is dealing with a locality, hence the boundaries are important to take note off, where it begins and ends.

Population of the Community

Historical details and nature of migration patterns or population growth or decline are important features to be recorded and analysed. What is the total number of people involved? It is helpful to know the number of children, the number of teenagers, the number of adult women and adult men and the number of older people. What major religious and caste groups reside in the community and their mutual relationships and interaction pattern are? Are there regional and occupational divisions as well which either unite or divide the community?

Economic Profile

The formulation of an economic profile would require collecting information about the following matters. What do most of the people do for a living? The size and nature of their income and spending pattern, the shortfall in income and household expenditure and the pattern of consumption. The class they belong to, the existing disparity among them in terms of resources and so on. The number of earning members in a family. The kind of assets they own. An important part of analysis should be the possibility of any effort, individually and collectively for making improvements, increasing livelihoods and stabilizing the economic status, to increase need fulfillment.

Social Profile

The nature of social relationships in the community, if at all a relationship among people exist. Are there any dominant groups, or major conflict among people on religious, caste, regional or economic basis etc. What do most of the women do, how educated they are and their participation level in household and community life. How many children go to school? What do the other children do? What do the teenagers do? An assessment of change reflecting in different levels of formal schooling among generations in the community is very helpful. How many years of schooling have they had? Current access to schools, details of schools and functionaries in schools. Relationship between teachers and children, between children and between community members and school staff etc., Perceptions of people about education, gender differences in access and levels etc.

What languages are usually spoken in the community? Which one is used most? What language (s) can the people read and write? How many people can read and write well enough to use simple instructional material? Gender differences in roles and social participation at current levels and possibility of its increase should be carefully assessed along with strategies helpful in achieving this. The relationship between gender thus comes to fore and the worker must do an objective analysis of the same, so that undue conflict and tension is avoided. The nexus between religion and social prescriptions and roles should be carefully assessed. Psychological readiness or difficulties of women in resorting to change is yet another area needing careful analysis in the community.

The social service scenario is equally important in assessing the community such as, transport and communication facilities, places of worship, a meeting place, health care facilities, market and shops, parks and open spaces etc.

Seasonal Patterns

Do community activities depend on weather patterns, such as rainy or dry seasons, winter or summer.

Physical Facilities

Types of housing, water supply, roads, electricity, etc.

Local Bodies and Significant Actors

Identify the local bodies and offices providing services to the community, such as health, education, water, roads, electricity etc. Identify the traditional system of administration and decision-making in the community. The actors involved, a local government officer, a community committee, or a group of elders\elites. The way decisions are made, and who are the prime beneficiaries. And are they carried out? The centers of dissents and how the, dissent is dealt with?

Programme Participation and Impact Assessment

The overall assessment about the possibility of programme participation on the part of people and likely impact of programmes in a time schedule are other important aspect of community assessment.

Assessment of Organizations

Assessment of an organization can be done from different perspectives, such as a financial perspective would reveal its financial strength and weaknesses. In social work terminology, the organization refers to only organizations providing welfare services to the people, as the framework for assessment of organizations (see Julie et al., 2011) seem to suggest. They suggest carrying out an internal assessment followed by an external assessment. The internal assessment will cover legal basis, administrative structure, programmes and services provided, personnel policies, and resources; while the external environment will cover relationship with funding agencies, with clients, other organizations and political leaders. In India, an organization refers to an organized effort to carry out any work, having a number of people. The objective of social work, in working with an organization in India, is to facilitate the relationships in the organization, at all levels to increase its efficiency, on the one hand and to promote employee welfare and development on the other. This practice in reality is a unique role that social work plays generally in developing countries and more specifically India. Therefore, social workers are interested in assessing the relationships in an organization and would use, what is generally known as an organizational behaviour perspective. An assessment of an organization will consist of assessment of human relationships at different levels in an organization, the leadership quality and style, the communication system and personnel satisfaction with organization policies, etc. Some aspects will require self report measures, while others can be covered by observation and organizational data available about various matters in the organization such as employee record of absenteeism, performance evaluation, promotion, productivity graph, wastage, etc. The focus should be:

- How people feel when they come to work?
- Are they experiencing happiness and growth along with the organization?
- Are they planning to achieve new goals?
- Is the organization experiencing growth?

These four dimensions will help in assessing the current state of different stakeholders in an organization, their relationship with each other and with the organization as a whole. Other questions can be added if need be.

Exploring Feelings

The employee of an organization on a given day on being asked, 'how are you feeling today', is likely to give a variety of responses beginning from good to lousy. It however does not indicate how the employee feels about the organization. In order to discover that look up the following facts:

- The attendance record
- The arrival and departure time
- Any attempts to leave the organization
- Time spent in an organization
- Any record of innovative contribution
- Satisfaction level in general

The complaint record of the employee, that is history of any complaints filed by the employee or filed by others against the employee, is also a good indicator of his/her relations in the organization.

The attendance record of an employee is a simple indicator of how committed s/he is to her/his work. Difficulties and other preoccupation occur, as normal routine in a person's life, but the responses of persons to these differ, when seen in the background of their work. These differences are reflected in the attendance records. An experienced professional is able to see the pattern.

Along with the attendance record, there is another clue to be found in the arrival and departure records of employees, helping an experienced person to see the pattern emerging as a clear indicator of loyalty of a person to her/his work and perhaps colleagues or supervisor as well.

Departure time in particular, in case of some employees, on a regular basis, particularly from a group of employees, is a clear indication of their bonding. This reflects their commitment to organization and to their group. Further exploration will help in assessing the group bonding. A high turnover rate is an indicator of no bonding with the organization or the colleagues.

Consequently, if persons are spending a long time with an organization and a group within an organization, this is a reflection of bonding. It is not easy for everyone to create something new, particularly in some categories of work, but if they do it, for example, no wastage, never missing a target or dead line, can easily be defined as an important contribution and is a reflection of their bonding.

In higher categories; giving new directions to different processes, achieving different results, changing goals and strategies; are a reflection of bonding within the team and with the overall work scenario. It is also a reflection of focus and achievement-motivation, of individual members.

The history of conflicts is a revealing document, in terms of inter personal interactions and the resultant feelings. It also reflects the group vs individual dynamics, as a frequent conflict record reflects absence of group bonding, whereas no record of any conflict suggests strong group bonding.

Finally taking into account various indices given above, a general satisfaction level of persons with their work environment can be worked out, summarizing the feeling level or bonding patterns in an organization. However, the human relationships and organizational relationships, that is relationships between various groups, should be analysed separately, from the one that exists within a group, to arrive at an assessment of human relationships in an organization.

Computerized Assessment

Computerized assessment refers to the technique of arriving at an assessment by feeding the data collected through various tests in the computer and using a software to analyse the data. For example, many behaviour related tests use computer assessment techniques to arrive at the final analysis.

14

Rethinking Social Work in India

Social Work Education has completed seventy seven years of its existence in India. The number of schools and university departments offering courses in social work has registered a phenomenal increase during this period. There are more than three hundred schools of social work throughout the country, with a large number of students on their rolls. The number of social work practitioners must now be running into thousands. Yet, despite the growth of social work education and practice, the growth of social work literature produced in the country has been rather slow. Consequently, reliance on social work literature, produced in the West was inevitable. In many seminars, the problem of acquiring literature on time, its cost and relevance and the fact that it was produced in a socio-economic milieu at extreme variance with our own, was stressed. The problem was found to be more acute in the case of literature dealing with methods of working with people.

The growth of literature dealing with methods of social work continues to be precarious for a number of reasons. Unlike the trend in the West, where social work practitioners have made a significant contribution to the growth of social work literature, practitioners in India have left the job entirely to social work educators. Similarly, the trend of interchange from practice to teaching and vice-versa is rather weak in India, as people tend to stick to either practice or teaching. This led to the creation of a wide gulf between social work educators and practitioners. The practitioners possess valuable experience, but they lack the research and writing skills necessary for producing literature. Educators, on the other hand, do not possess the grassroots experience needed to modify their understanding of methods, grounded in literature produced in the West. Recently another disturbing trend has emerged. A number of books have appeared published in India, particularly as an introductory text. Most of these are written by authors, who have not studied social work and neither have worked in the field. Therefore, what they write has largely been borrowed from literature produced in the West.

It is time that we start some rethinking about the nature and practice of social work in India. The universal validity of social work formulations, conceptualized in western world, has been debated for a long time, without any conclusion. For example, the six methods of social work conceptualized by Friedlander (1980) are still taught in many departments/schools of social work, from Kerala to Kashmir, since the beginnings of social work in India. Perhaps it is time to wake up and do some rethinking about it. The first method, earlier known as case work, now rechristened as, 'working with individuals' refers to, dealing with individual problems in various settings. The general purpose is to help the individuals, aware of the causative factors for their problems, strengthen self-confidence by providing care and support, capacity building to take appropriate decisions to deal with the problems and issues. In India some support at environment modification is provided by the worker. The second method which has almost become non-existent in USA and seldom used in India (see Siddiqui, 2008), is group work to use both programme activities and relationships in groups and relationship with the worker, to accomplish group goals as well as individual development.

Working with group as a method of helping people emerged as an independent professional activity and only later merged with the social work profession. It was since then incorporated as a method of social work in the USA. There are mixed reactions among those, who were associated with its growth since its inception, about merger with social work and its development, and its current status as a social work method in USA. As Andrews suggests, group work's identification with social work was motivated by a desire to professionalize and to find a place in the university. She after interviewing a number of early practitioners concluded that according to some, this merger blunted the radical spirit of group work (see Andrews C., 2001). Klein, (1972) suggests, that the numerical strength of group workers was small compared to case workers in US, the influence by the clinical approach of these workers, diluted their own emphasis in group work practice on social action and prevention. Glasser and Mayadas (1986) were more emphatic, when they concluded that the merger of group work with social work, was the death knell of group work, as a unique methodology. In USA, the group work's focus thus gradually shifted to individuals, instead of being on group and its potential (Middleman, 1981). This is still the case in social work practice in general in the west, where individual problems, in particular mental health issues, dominate the practice and group work is no exception. Group work, however, is an accepted method of intervention, though its focus is on individual needs and problems. But that should not lead one to think, that that is the only objective, which group work as a method can be used to achieve.

The use of groups in developing countries like India, has been somewhat different than that of the west. Yet, as is the case in USA, but perhaps for a very different set of reasons, it has not been very popular in social work education and practice. Group work has been a part of social work curriculum, since the beginning of social work education in India. In practice, however, the social workers have not made full use of the potential of the method. Social workers working with children, youth and women, either in government organizations, such as children's institutions, prisons, family welfare organizations or non-governmental organizations, focused more on social development, i.e. relationship and values of members or community problems, can use group work to help facilitates relationships both in groups and in communities. The social work practice in the beginning mainly dealt with psychological problems of individuals and the work with individual cases was the preferred approach. The potential of group and its influence on individual values and relationships was not acknowledged. In the early forties the research on groups was in a very nascent stage of its development. It has not made much progress even now in the developing countries. Social work has not been able to demonstrate, either then or now, the potential of group work practice in India, though one of the most popular programmes of women empowerment and poverty alleviation, in recent times, has emerged in the form of self-help groups. Social work can develop a model of designing self-help groups, methods of capacity building of the members and financial strategies for sustaining these groups, to achieve the objectives of these groups. Such helping interventions are very different from the practice models of group work in the west. However, such practice wisdom is still not fully developed, learned or used in actual practice. Another practice model though talked about but seldom used in practice is the integrated social work practice model. Since the main focus in practice is, either individual or community, the work is seen as case work or community work. However, in both cases the worker has to work with groups, but that is not seen, as the main objective or method of intervention. Still, unless the worker is fully familiar with using group as a medium and using its potential to achieve the practice objectives, the practice competence will remain inadequate. Using the practice skills of different methods, to achieve the larger objective, is yet a different practice reality, generally found in developing countries. In developed countries, the social work education is generally method based, so it trains you as a counselor, group worker or community worker. The generic courses are debated but seldom used. In India, the trend is to use generic courses, followed by more specialized inputs to increase the professional skills of the workers.

Ironically when the worker is working with a group, such as family, it is not seen as group work practice either. Such interventions are generally termed as family social work or social work with families. Friedlander has not elaborated whether he treated family also as a group, and therefore group work also meant dealing with families. The process of dealing with family issues is termed family therapy, and is different from the general process of group work. It is, therefore, obvious that working with families requires a different expertise and should be identified as a different method of social work, as many scholars, including a recent text dealing with the generalist practice of social work (Julie Birkenmaier et al., 2011) has already done and be taught as a separate course. Working with family, therefore, should be considered a separate method of social work. It can be argued that working with organization can also be considered a separate method, yes it can be and a large number of social workers are working with organizations, but so far the approach used, or the objective of such practice has not followed social work philosophy and professional ethics. The social worker working with organizations, surrenders her/his objectivity, as s/he is employed by a particular party, s/he is thus not able to maintain her/his neutral role, in facilitating relationships. The other problem is, the context becoming too large for a social worker to achieve desirable outcomes.

The method of working with a community is a method where a social worker works with a community and again for obvious reasons, the method has not been very popular in the developed world. Community work is a method, now widely used by a variety of practitioners, in India and other developing countries, by social workers. Social workers are specifically trained in the use of the method. Though our practice realities differ substantially from that of the west, an indigenous model has not been developed to define our practice. It is, therefore, not surprising to find many practitioners having doubts, about the relevance of knowledge to practice, leading to poor competence levels. Lack of practice based research to build indigenous knowledge base continue to haunt educators and practitioners.

Community work is essentially concerned with initiating change, through a process of analysing social situations, forming relationships with different groups and developing a core group to sustain the initiative. It has three main objectives. The first is the democratic process of involving people in thinking, deciding, planning and playing an active part in the development and operation of services that affect their daily lives. The second relates to promoting the value of belonging to a community. The third is concerned with the need for integration of community planning efforts, to think of community and meeting its needs instead of launching a series of separate programmes for needs and problems. This means working under constant tensions between people's needs and the scarce resources available to meet them, between the conflicting demands of different groups and different ideas about the kind of change that is desirable.

The core expertise needed is the ability to facilitate human relationships. In working with individuals, groups and families, caring and functional relationships can make all the difference in their life. It can only be achieved by a caring worker. If s/he succeeds first in establishing her/his own relationship with the community and gain their respect and trust, s/he has covered half the ground. If s/he has developed a good understanding of the relationship issues in a community, s/he can achieve her/his objective with greater confidence and a clear mind.

Irrespective of the competence level of the worker, working with community is a method of social work since it involves relationships. The other three methods that Friedlander mentioned in his introductory text, namely social action, social welfare administration and social work research, though are included in the curriculum of social work training, are treated as supportive methods. Many authors dealt with social action as part of community work (see Siddiqui, 1984) which can be treated as a separate method, since its scope is to cover the macro issues beyond the communities. The macro social work practice, as it is termed (see Denis D. Long et al., 2006), makes use of social action to a large extent to achieve its goals in India. However, as the authors point out, it is difficult to define what it means, since it includes as diverse goals as war on poverty to a war on terrorism, at the same time respect for consumers and concern for environment. They also admit that before 1970, the term macro practice was nonexistent in the developed world. In India however, the setting up of the first school of social work has debated the issue. It debated focusing the curriculums on service delivery or a radical reduction of poverty, deciding on service delivery. The debate is still on with a variety of options to include, courses on Human Rights, Environment and Consumer Protection, to work for Economic and Social Justice, etc. Social Action is however, a method of social work, which attempts to bring about change at the macro level for advocating change, at the policy level or preventing change, for example, continuation of pro-poor policies, despite its poverty, in countries like India.

All professions carry out research, regularly for enhancing their knowledge base. Research, therefore, cannot be called an exclusive domain of social work. Most of its methods and techniques rely on knowledge developed by social scientists and other disciplines. Social work curriculum can include some content on research methods, relevant to the practice in its content. Considering social work practice trends in India and other developing countries, not many have made a serious use of research methods, in practice. The research on social work related issues by social work educators and scholars have been rather disappointing compared to other disciplines in social sciences. Social Work Research cannot be treated as an exclusive method of social work.

Coming to the last method of social work, known as Social Work Administration also at times referred to as Social Administration in UK and Social Welfare Administration by some authors, can hardly be called a method. It cannot be considered a method, since there is no particular methodology involved to achieve its objective. Further, there is hardly any consensus on its definition, objective or scope. According to definitions provided by authors, it refers to social policy issues, in other words, administration of social issues. Such a vast area has resulted in exclusive courses dealing with Social Policy and Social Services. Sydney and Beatrice Webb were interested in finding the reasons for social disorganization rather than offering curative services to the victims. They founded the London School of Economics to achieve this goal, leading to development of Economics, Sociology and Political Science (see Kendall, 2000). The social work curriculum will have to include some part of it in its content to strengthen the knowledge base, particularly for macro practice, but it again cannot be termed as a method of social work. The other definitions of welfare administration, refer to the general content of administration, referring to the management of welfare policy objectives, within the framework of given resources, which is no different from business management or any other kind of management.

Julie (Julie, Birkenmaier, et al., 2011) has talked about working with organizations, treating it as a method, along with individual, group, family and community. However, as pointed out, in India the practice is different from the one suggested by Julie et al., as our objectives are different. However, there are some curriculums, containing content on Management of NGOs, where it can be helpful. However, the reality of organizations providing welfare services, particularly non-governmental organizations, is very different from that of similar organizations in the developed countries, hence it cannot be considered as a method of social work intervention, in the Indian context.

The social work can therefore be defined as a profession of facilitating human relationships at all levels, such as individual, group, family, community and society, to facilitate social development. It has following methods;

- Working with Individuals
- Working with Groups
- Working with Families
- Working with Communities, and
- Social Action

Social work believes in human rights, social justice, non-violence and sustainable social development, to ensure a better life for all children of the world. Its vision is, respect the poor and help the poor to become independent of all helpers. Its core expertise is human relationships. It firmly believes in achieving all goals through peaceful and of non-violent strategies.

References

Abercombie, Nicholas, Hill, Stephen and Turner, Bryan S. (1994). *Dictionary of Sociology*. UK: Penguin.

Adams, R. and Laursen, B. (2001). The Organization and Dynamics of Adolescent Conflict with Parents and Friends. *Journal of Marriage and Family*, 63: 97–110.

Ainsworth, M., Blehar, M., Waters, E. and Wall, S. (1978). *Patterns of Attachment*. Hillsdale, NJ: Erlbaum.

Ainsworth, M.D.S. (1968). Object Relations, Dependency, and Attachment: A Theoretical Review of the Infant-Mother Relationship. *Child Development*, 40: 969–1025.

—— (1982). Attachment: Retrospect and Prospect. In C.M. Parkes and J. Stevenson-Hinde (Eds), *The Place of Attachment in Human Behavior*, New York: Basic Books, pp. 3–30.

—— (1989). Attachments Beyond Infancy. *American Psychologist*, 44: 709–716.

Allen, J.P. and Land, D. (1999). Attachment in Adolescence. In J. Cassidy and P. Shaver (Eds), *Handbook of Attachment Theory and Research: Theory, Research, and Clinical Applications*, New York: Guilford Press.

Allport, Gordon (1937). *Personality: A Psychological Interpretation*. New York: Holt, Rinehart & Winston.

Amato, Paul R. and Booth, Alan (1996). A Prospective Study of Divorce and Parent-Child Relationships. *Journal of Marriage and Family*, 58 (2): 356–365.

Andrews, C. (2001). Group Work's Place in Social Work: A Historical Analysis. *Journal of Sociology and Social Welfare*, XXVIII (4): 45–65.

Arnkoff, D.B. and Glass, C.R. (1989). Cognitive Assessment in Social Anxiety and Social Phobia. *Clinical Psychology Review*, 9: 61–64.

Asia Forest Network (2002). *Participatory Rural Appraisal for Community Forest Management*. Santa Barbara, CA: Asia Forest Network.

Austin, D.M. (1998). *A Report on Progress in the Development of Research Resources in Social Work*. Washington, D.C.: Institute for the Advancement of Social Work Research.

Baccus, Jodene R. and Baldwin, Mark W. (2007). Interpersonal Cognition. *Encyclopaedia of Social Psychology*, New Delhi: Sage.

Baldock, Peter (1974). *Community Work and Social Work*. London: Routledge and Kegan Paul.

Baldwin, M.W. and Fehr, B. (1995). On the Instability of Attachment Style Ratings. *Personal Relationships*, 2: 247–261.

Bales, Robert Freed (1950). *Interaction Process Analysis: A Method for the Study of Small Groups*. Cambridge: Addison-Wesley.

Bandura, Albert (2002). Social Foundation of Thought and Action: A Social Cognitive Theory. In David F. Marks (Ed.), *The Health Psychology Reader*, London: Sage.

Bar-On, Reuven (2007). *Educating People to be Emotionally Intelligent*. Westport: Praeger.

Barrett, Richard A. (1984). *Culture and Conduct*. Belmont: Wadsworth.

Bartholomew, K. and Horowitz, L.M. (1991). Attachment Styles among Young Adults: A Test of a Four-Category Model. *Journal of Personality and Social Psychology*, 61: 226–244.

Bartlett, H. (1970). *The Common Base of Social Work Practice*. Washington, D.C.: National Association of Social Workers.

Baxter, L.A. (1984). Trajectories of Relationship Disengagement. *Journal of Social and Personal Relationships*, 1: 29–48.

—— (1994). Thinking Dialogically about Communication in Personal Relationships. In R. Conville (Ed.), *Uses of Structure in Communication Studies*, New York: Praeger.

Beck, A.T., Epstein, N., Brown, G. and Steer, R.A. (1988). An Inventory for Measuring Clinical Anxiety: Psychometric Properties. *J Consult Clin Psychol*, 56 (6): 893–897.

Berscheid, E. and Peplau, L.A. (1983). The Emerging Science of Relationships. In H.H. Kelley (Ed.), *Close Relationships*, New York: W.H. Freeman & Company, pp. 1–19.

Birkenmaier, Julie, Berg-Weger, Marla and Dewees, Marty (2011). *The Practice of Generalist Social Work*. New York: Routledge.

Blakely, T.J. and Dziadosz, G.M. (2009). Community Treatment and Rehabilitation: One Agency's Model of Case Management. *Care Management Journals*, 4 (3): 129–135.

Blumer, H. (1951). The Field of Collective Behavior. In A.M. Lee (Ed.), *Principles of Sociology*, New York: Barnes and Noble.

Boehm, W. (1958). The Nature of Social Work. *Social Work*, 3 (2): 5–8.

Bogaert, A.F. and Sadava, S. (2002). Adult Attachment and Sexual Behavior. *Personal Relationships*, 9: 191–204.

Bogardus, E.S. (1925). Measuring Social Distance. *Journal of Applied Sociology*, 9: 299–308.

Bose, A.B. (1995). *Social Welfare at the Crossroads* (Mimeograph). Hersey-Saiyaddain Memorial Lecture, Delhi: Delhi School of Social Work.

Bowlby, J. (1969/1982). *Attachment and Loss, Vol. 1: Attachment*. New York: Basic Books.

—— (1973). *Attachment and Loss, Vol. 2: Separation*. New York: Basic Books.

—— (1979). *The Making and Breaking of Affectional Bonds*. London: Tavistock.

—— (1980). *Attachment and Loss, Vol. 3: Loss*. New York: Basic Books.

—— (1988). *A Secure Base*. New York: Basic Books.

Bowlby, J. and Ainsworth, Mary (1992). *The Origin of Attachment Theory*. London: Routledge.

Bracht, N. (Ed.) (1990). *Health Promotion at the Community Level*. New York: Sage.

Brennan, K.A. and Shaver, P.R. (1995). Dimensions of Adult Attachment, Affect Regulation, and Romantic Relationship Functioning. *Personality and Social Psychology Bulletin*, 21: 267–283.

Brennan, K.A., Clark, C.L. and Shaver, P.R. (1998). Self-Report Measurement of Adult Attachment: An Integrative Overview. In J.A. Simpson and W.S. Rholes (Eds), *Attachment Theory and Close Relationships*, New York: Guilford Press.

Bretherton, I. (1985). Attachment Theory: Retrospect and Prospect. In I. Bretherton and E. Waters (Eds), *Growing Points in Attachment Theory and Research: Monographs of the Society for Research in Child Development*, Serial No. 209, 50 (1–2): 3–38.

—— (1987). New Perspectives on Attachment Relations: Security, Communication, and Internal Working Models. In J. Osofsky (Ed.), *Handbook of Infant Development*, 2nd edition, New York: Wiley.

—— (1992). The Origins of Attachment Theory: John Bowlby and Mary Ainsworth. *Development Psychology*, 28: 759–775.

Brody, Gene H. (1998). Sibling Relationship Quality: Its Causes and Consequences. *Annual Review of Psychology*, 49 (1): 1–24.

Brody, Gene H. (Ed.) (1996). *Sibling Relationships: Their Causes and Consequences*. Westport, CT: Alex Publishing.

Brooks-Gunn, Jeanne, Duncan, Greg J., Klevanov, Pamela Kato and Sealand, Naomi (1993). Do Neighborhoods Influence Child and Adolescent Development? *American Journal of Sociology*, 99: 353–395.

Brown, P. (1967). *A Biography*. CA: California University Press.

Bryan, Robert (1973). *Organizing Strangers: Poor Families in Guatemala City*. Texas: University of Texas Press.

Burghardt, Steve (1982). *Organizing for Community Action*. New Delhi: Sage.

Burkitt, Ian (1991). *Social Selves: Theories of Social Formation of Personalities*. Thousand Oaks, CA: Sage.

Burnham, J.B. (1986). *Family Therapy*. London: Routledge.

Butcher, Hugh (1992). Community Work: Current Realities, Contemporary Trends. In Pam Carter, Tony Jeff and Mark K. Smith (Eds), *Changing Social Work and Welfare*, Buckingham: Open University Press.

Byrne, D. (1961). Interpersonal Attraction and Attitude Similarity. *Journal of Abnormal Social Psychology*, 62: 713–715.

Cacioppo, J.T. and Petty, R.E. (1981). *Attitudes and Persuasion: Classic and Contemporary Approaches*. Dubuque, Iowa: William C. Brown.

—— (1982). *Perspectives in Cardiovascular Psychophysiology*. New York: Guilford Press.

—— (1983). *Social Psychophysiology: A Sourcebook*. New York: Guilford Press.

Cafferty, T.P., Davis, K.E., Medway, F.J., O'Hearn, R.E. and Chappell, K.D. (1994). Reunion Dynamics among Couples Separated during Operation Desert Storm: An Attachment Theory Analysis. In K. Bartholomew and D. Perlman (Eds), *Advances in Personal Relationships, Vol. 5: Attachment Processes in Adulthood*, London: Jessica Kingsley.

Campbell, J.D., Trapnell, P., Heine, S.J., Katz, I.M., Lavallee, L.R. and Lehman, D.R. (1996). Self-Concept Clarity: Measurement, Personality Correlates, and Cultural Boundaries. *Journal of Personality and Social Psychology*, 70 (2): 141–146.

Carnelley, K.B., Pietromonaco, P.R. and Jaffe, K. (1996). Attachment, Caregiving, and Relationship Functioning in Couples: Effects of Self and Partner. *Personal Relationships*, 3: 257–278.

Carr, E.G. and Durand, V.M. (1985). Reducing Behaviour Problems through Functional Communication Training. *Journal of Applied Behaviour Analysis*, 18 (2): 111–126.

Cartwright, D. and Zander, A. (Eds) (1968). *Group Dynamics*. New York: Harper & Row.

Cassidy, J. (1994). *Emotion Regulation: Influences of Attachment Relationships*. CA: Sage.

Cattell, R.B. (1971). *Abilities: Their Structure Growth and Action*. Boston: Houghton-Mifflin.

Cattell, R.B. and Nesselroade, J. (1967). Likeness and Completeness Theories Examined by Sixteen Personality Factor Measures on Stably and Unstably Married Couples. *Journal of Personality and Social Psychology*, 7: 351–361.

Chambers, Robert (1994). The Origins of Participatory Rural Appraisal. *World Development*, 22 (7): 953–969.

Chandra, Sushil (1967). *Sociology and Deviance in India*. Bombay: Allied Publishers.

Chatterjee, P. (1975). Towards a Typological Paradigm of Community Organization. *Indian Journal of Social Work*, 36 (1): 1–14.

Chatterjee, Pranab and Koleski, Raymond (1970). The Concept of Community and Community Organization: A Review. *Social Work*, 15 (3): 82–92.

Checkoway, Barry (1995). Six Strategies of Community Change. *Community Development Journal*, 30 (1): 2–20.

Cheyne, Alice (1926). *Nature and Scope of Social Work* (Mimeograph). New York: American Association of Social Workers.

Christensen, A. and Heavey, C.L. (1990). Gender and Social Structure in the Demand/Withdraw Pattern of Marital Conflict. *Journal of Personality and Social Psychology*, 59: 73–81.

Clarke, Helen I. (1947). *Principles and Practice of Social Work*. New York: Appleton Century.

Cohn, D.A., Silver, D.H., Cowan, C.P., Cowan, P.A. and Pearson, J. (1992). Working Models of Childhood Attachment and Couple Relationships. *Journal of Family Issues*, 13: 432–449.

Collins, N.H. and Feeney, B.C. (2000). A Safe Haven: An Attachment Theory Perspective on Support Servicing and Caregiving in Intimate Relationships. *Journal of Personality and Social Psychology*, 7.8: 1053–1073.

Collins, N.L. and Read, S.J. (1990). Adult Attachment, Working Models, and Relationship Quality in Dating Couples. *Journal of Personality and Social Psychology*, 58: 644–663.

—— (1994). Cognitive Representations of Attachment: The Structure and Function of Working Models. In K. Bartholomew and D. Perlman (Eds), *Advances in Personal Relationships, Vol. 5: Attachment Processes in Adulthood*, London: Jessica Kingsley.

Conn, Steve R. and Rieke, Mark L. (1994). *The 16PF Technical Manual*. Champaign, IL: Institute for Personality and Ability Testing.

Cooke, P. (1989). *Localities*. London: Unwin.

Cooley, C.H. (1902). *Human Nature and Social Order*. New York: Scribner's.

—— (1909). *Social Organization*. New York: Scribner's.

Cooper, M.L., Shaver, P.R. and Collins, N.L. (1998). Attachment Styles, Emotion Regulation, and Adjustment in Adolescence. *Journal of Personality and Social Psychology*, 74: 1380–1397.

Corey, G. and Corey, M. (2006). *Groups: Process and Practice*. Belmont: Thompson.

Corey, Gerald (2000). *Theory and Practice of Group Counseling*. Belmont: Thompson.

Cowen, Phillip A. and Hetherington, Eileen M. (Eds) (1991). *Family Transitions*. London: Routledge.

Crane, Jonathan (1991). Effects of Neighborhoods on Dropping Out of School and Teenage Childbearing. In Christopher Jencks and Paul E. Peterson (Eds), *The Urban Underclass*, Washington, D.C.: Brookings Institution, pp. 299–320.

Crowell, J.A. and Owens, G. (1996). *Current Relationship Interview and Scoring System* (Unpublished Manuscript). State University of New York at Stony Brook.

Crowell, J.A., Fraley, R.C. and Shaver, P.R. (1999). Measurement of Individual Differences in Adolescent and Adult Attachment. In J. Cassidy and P.R. Shaver (Eds), *Handbook of Attachment: Theory, Research, and Clinical Applications*, New York: Guilford Press.

Crowell, J.A., Treboux, D., Gao, Y., Pan, H., Fyffe, C. and Waters, E. (in press). Secure Base Behavior in Adulthood: Measurement, Links to Adult Attachment Representations, and Relations to Couples' Communication Skills and Self-Reports. *Developmental Psychology*.

Darling, Nancy and Steinberg, L. (1993). Parenting Styles as Context: An Integrative Model. *Psychological Bulletin*, 113: 487–496.

Das, Gurcharan (2000). Nation of Thieves. *Times of India*, January 23.

Davies, James C. (1962). Towards a Theory of Revolution. *American Sociological Review*, 2: 6.

Davies, Martin (1981). *The Essential Social Workers*. London: Heinemann Educational Books.

Davies, W.K.D. and Herbert, D.T. (1993). *Communities within Cities: An Urban Social Geography*. London: Belhaven Press.

Davila, J. and Bradbury, T.N. (2001). Attachment Insecurity and the Distinction between Unhappy Spouses Who Do and Do Not Divorce. *Journal of Family Psychology*, 15: 371–393.

Davila, J., Burge, D. and Hammen, C. (1997). What Does Attachment Style Change? *Journal of Personality and Social Psychology*, 73: 826–838.

Davila, J., Karney, B.R. and Bradbury, T.N. (1999). Attachment Change Processes in the Early Years of Marriage. *Journal of Personality and Social Psychology*, 76: 783–802.

De Swan, Abram (1990). *The Management of Normality: Critical Essays in Health and Welfare*. London: Routledge.

Deckard, K.D. and Dodge, K.A. (1997). Externalizing Behaviour Problems and Discipline Revisited: Nonlinear Effects and Variation by Culture, Context and Gender. *Psychological Inquiry*, 8 (3): 161–175.

Denton, K. and Zarbatany, L. (1996). Age Differences in Support Processes in Conversation between Friends. *Child Development*, 67: 1360–1373.

DeYoung, Colin G., Peterson, Jordan B. and Higgins, Daniel M. (2009). Sources of Openness/Intellect: Cognitive and Neuropsychological Correlates of the Fifth Factor of Personality. *Journal of Personality*, 78 (4): 825–858.

Dickson, F.C. (1995). The Best is Yet to Be: Research on Long-Lasting Relationships. In J.T. Wood and S. Duck (Eds), *Understanding Relationship Processes: Off the Beaten Track*, Beverly Hills, CA: Sage, pp. 22–50.

Dixon, Jane (1995). Community Stories and Indicators for Evaluating Community Development. *Community Development Journal*, 30 (4): 327–336.

Duck, Steve (2007). *Encyclopaedia of Social Psychology*. CA: Sage.

Dunn, J. (1996). Brothers and Sisters in Middle Childhood and Early Adolescence: Continuity and Change in Individual Differences. In J.H. Brody (Ed.), *Sibling Relationships: Their Causes and Consequences*, Norwood, NL: Ablex.

Dunn, J., Slomkowski, C., Beardsall, L. and Rende, R. (1993). Adjustment in Middle Childhood and Early Adolescence: Links with Earlier and Contemporary Sibling Relationships. *Journal of Child Psychology and Psychiatry*, 35 (3): 491–504.

Durkheim, E. (1964). *The Division of Labour in Society*. New York: Free Press.

Economic Survey of India (1997, 1998, 2013). Delhi: Government of India.

Endler, N.S. and Flett, G.L. (2002). *EMAS Social Anxiety Scales (EMAS-SAS)*. Los Angeles, USA: Western Psychological Services.

Endler, N.S., Edwards, J.M. and Vitelli, R. (1991). *Endler Multidimensional Anxiety Scales (EMAS)*. Los Angeles, USA: Western Psychological Services.

Endler, Norman S. and Kocovski, Nancy L. (2005). Personality Disorders at the Crossroads. *Journal of Personality Disorders*, 16 (6): 487–502.

Epstein, N.H., Baucom, D.H. and Daiuta, A. (1977). Cognitive-Behavioral Couples Therapy. In W.K. Halford and D.H. Markman (Eds), *Clinical Handbook of Marriage and Couples Interventions*, New York: Wiley.

Erikson, Erik H. (1951). *Childhood and Society*. New York: W.W. Norton & Co.

—— (1997). *Life Cycle Completed*. New York: W.W Norton &Co.

Etzioni, A. (1995). Nation in Need of Community Values. The Second Times/Demos Lecture, *The Times*, London, February 20.

Eysenck, H.J. (1990). Genetic and Environmental Individual Differences: The Three Major Dimensions of Personality. *Journal of Personality*, 58 (1): 245–261.

Eysenck, M.W. and Calvo, M.G. (1992). Anxiety and Performance: The Processing Efficiency Theory. *Cognition and Emotion*, 6 (6): 409–434.

Ezzamel, M. and Willmott, H. (1998). Accounting for Team Work: A Critical Study of Group Based Systems of Organizational Control. *Administrative Society Quarterly*, 43: 358–396.

Feeney, B.C. and Collins, N.L. (2001). Predictors of Caregiving in Adult Intimate Relationships: An Attachment Theoretical Perspective. *Journal of Personality and Social Psychology*, 80: 972–994.

Feeney, B.C. and Kirkpatrick, L.A. (1996). Effects of Adult Attachment and Presence of Romantic Partners on Physiological Responses to Stress. *Journal of Personality and Social Psychology*, 70: 255–270.

Feeney, J.A. (1996). Attachment, Caregiving, and Marital Satisfaction. *Personal Relationships*, 3: 401–416.

—— (1998). Adult Attachment and Relationship-Centered Anxiety: Responses to Physical and Emotional Distancing. In J.A. Simpson and W.S. Rhodes (Eds), *Attachment Theory and Close Relationships*, New York: Guilford Press.

—— (1999). Adult Romantic Attachment and Couple Relationships. In J. Cassidy and P.R. Shaver (Eds), *Handbook of Attachment: Theory, Research, and Clinical Applications*, New York: Guilford Press.

Feeney, J.A. and Noller, P. (1990). Attachment Style as a Predictor of Adult Romantic Relationships. *Journal of Personality and Social Psychology*, 58: 281–291.

Feeney, J.A., Noller, P. and Callan, V.J. (1994). Attachment Style, Communication and Satisfaction in the Early Years of Marriage. In K. Bartholomew and D. Perlman (Eds), *Attachment Processes in Adulthood*, Vol. 5, London: Jessica Kingsley.

Feeney, J.A., Noller, P. and Patty, J. (1993). Adolescents' Interactions with the Opposite Sex: Influence of Attachment Style and Gender. *Journal of Adolescence*, 16: 169–186.

Festinger, L. (1954). A Theory of Social Comparison Processes. *Human Relations*, 7: 117–140.

Fincham, F.D. and Bradbury, T.N. (1991). Cognition in Marriage: A Program of Research on Attributions. In W.H. Jones and D. Perman (Eds), *Advance in Personal Relationships*, Vol. 2, London: Kingsley, pp. 159–203.

Finkel, Eli J. (2007). Betrayal. *Encyclopedia of Social Psychology*, Thousand Oaks, CA: Sage.

Fischer, J. (1973). Is Social Work Effective? A Review. *Social Work*, 18: 5–20.

Fletcher, Garth (2007). Close Relationships. *Encyclopedia of Social Psychology*, Thousand Oaks, CA: Sage.

Foa, U.G. and Foa, E.B. (1974). *Societal Structures of the Mind*. Oxford: Charles C. Thomas.

—— (1976). Resource Theory of Social Exchange. In J.W. Thibaut, J.T. Spence and R.C. Carson (Eds), *Contemporary Topics in Social Psychology*, Morristown, NJ: General Learning Press.

Forgas, J.P. (2001). Affective Influences on Communication and Attribution in Relationships. In V. Manusov and J.H. Harvey (Eds), *Attribution, Communication Behavior, and Close Relationships*, New York: Cambridge University Press, pp. 3–20.

Fox, Suzy and Spector, Paul (Eds) (2004). *Counter Productive Work Behaviour: Investigation of Actors and Targets*. Washington, D.C.: American Psychological Association.

Fraenkel, P. (1997). Systems Approaches to Couple Therapy. In W.K. Halford and D.H. Markman (Eds), *Clinical Handbook of Marriage and Couple Interventions*, New York: Wiley.

Fraley, R. Chris (2007). Attachment Theory. *Encyclopedia of Social Psychology*, CA: Sage.

Fraley, R.C. and Shaver, P.R. (1997). Adult Attachment and the Suppression of Unwanted Thoughts. *Journal of Personality and Social Psychology*, 73: 1080–1091.

—— (1998). Airport Separations: A Naturalistic Study of Adult Attachment Dynamics in Separating Couples. *Journal of Personality and Social Psychology*, 75: 1198–1212.

—— (2000). Adult Romantic Attachment: Theoretical Developments, Emerging Controversies, and Unanswered Questions. *Review of General Psychology*, 4: 132–154.

Fraley, R.C., Garner, J.P. and Shaver, P.R. (2000). Adult Attachment and the Defensive Regulation of Attention and Memory: Examining the Role of Preemptive and Postemptive Defensive Processes. *Journal of Personality and Social Psychology*, 79: 1–11.

Freud, Sigmund (1962). *Three Essays on the Theory of Sexuality*. Trans. James Strachey, New York: Basic Books.

Friedlander, W.A. (1980). *Introduction to Social Welfare*. New York: Prentice Hall.

Fuller, T.L. and Fincham, F.D. (1995). Attachment Style in Married Couples: Relation to Current Martial Functioning, Stability Over Time, and Method of Assessment. *Personal Relationships*, 2: 17–34.

Furnham, A. (2005). *The Psychology of Behaviour at Work: The Individual in the Organization*. London: Psychology Press.

Gale Group (2001). *Gale Encyclopedia of Psychology*. 2nd edition, Gale Group: The University of California.

Gellner, Ernst (1986). *Positivism and Relativism in Social Sciences*. Cambridge: Cambridge University Press.

George, C. and Solomon, J. (1996). Representational Models of Relationships: Link between Caregiving and Attachment. *Infant Mental Health Journal*, 17 (3): 198–216.

—— (1999). Attachment and Caregiving: The Caregiving Behavioral System. In J. Cassidy and P.R. Shaver (Eds), *Handbook of Attachment: Theory, Research, and Clinical Applications*, New York: Guilford Press.

George, C., Kaplan, N. and Main, M. (1985). *Adult Attachment Interview* (Unpublished Manuscript). 2nd edition, Berkley: University of California.

Gergen, K.G. and Gergen, Mary M. (1981). *Social Psychology*. New York: Harcourt, Brace & Jovanovich.

Germain, C.B. (1968). Social Study: Past and Future. *Social Case Work*, 49: 403–409.

Germain, C.B. (Ed.) (1979). *Social Work Practice: People and Environments*. New York: Columbia University Press.

Germain, C.B. and Gitterman, A. (1980). *The Life Model of Social Work Practice*. New York: Columbia University Press.

Giddens, Anthony (1989). *Sociology*. Oxford: Polity Press.

—— (1991). *Modernity and Self-Identity*. Cambridge: Polity Press.

Glasser, P. and Mayadas, N. (1986). *Group Workers: Theory and Practice in the 80s*. NJ: Rowman and Littlefield.

Glick, G.C. and Ross, Amanda (2013). *Mothers Influence on Adolescent Behaviour* (Unpublished). Department of Psychology, Missouri University.

Glueck, S. and Glueck, E. (1959). *Predicting Juvenile Delinquency*. USA: Harvard University Press.

Goldfarb, W. (1943). Effects of Institutional Care on Adolescent: An Approach to Personality. *Journal of Experimental Education*, 12: 106–129.

Goleman, D. (1995). *Emotional Intelligence*. New York: Holt, Reinhart and Winston.

Gore, M.S. (1981). The Scope of Social Work Practice. In T.K. Nair (Ed.), *Social Work Education and Practice in India*, Madras: ASSWI.

Gottman, J.M. (1994). *What Predicts Divorce? The Relationship between Marital Processes and Marital Outcomes*. Hillsdale, NJ: Lawrence Erlbaum.

Gove, Walter R. (1994). Why We Do What We Do: A Bio-Psychosocial Theory of Human Motivation. *Social Forces*, 73 (2): 363–394.

Gove, Walter R., Style, Carolyn Briggs and Hughes, Michael (1990). The Effect of Marriage on the Well-Being of Adults: A Theoretical Analysis. *Journal of Family Issues*, 11: 4–35.

Goverment of India (1987). *Encyclopaedia of Social Work in India*. Ministry of Finance, New Delhi: Government Press.

Government of India (2007–08). *Economic Survey*. Ministry of Finance, New Delhi: Government Press.

Graham, Mekada (2002). *Social Work and African-Centered Worldviews*. Birmingham: Venture Press.

Green, Lawrence W. and Ottoson, Judith M. (1994). *Community Health*. St. Louis: Mosby.

Greenberg, Leslie S. and Johnson, Susan M. (1988). *Emotionally Focused Therapy for Couples*. New York: Guilford Press.

Greenwood, E. (1957). The Attributes of a Profession. *Social Work*, July.

Gudykunst, W.B. and Kim, Y.Y. (1997). *Communicating with Strangers: An Approach to Intercultural Communication*. New York: McGraw-Hill.

Guthrie, D.M. and Noller, P. (1988). Married Couples' Perceptions of One Another in Emotional Situations. In P. Noller and M.A. Fitzpatrick (Eds), *Perspectives on Marital Interaction*, Cleveland and Philadelphia: Multilingual Matters, pp. 153–181.

Hagan, John (1985). *Modern Criminology: Crime, Criminal Behaviour, and its Control*. New York: McGraw-Hill.

Hall, Judith A. (2007). Nonverbal Cues and Communication. *Encyclopedia of Social Psychology*, Thousand Oaks, CA: Sage.

Harre, R. (1989). Language Games and Texts of Identity. In J. Shotter and K.J. Gergen (Eds), *Texts of Identity*, Thousand Oaks, CA: Sage.

Hatfield, E., Utne, M.K. and Traupmann, J. (1979). Equity Theory and Intimate Relationships. In R.L. Burgess and T.L. Huston (Eds), *Social Exchange in Developing Relationships*, New York: Academic Press.

Hatfield, Elaine and Rapson, Richard L. (2007). Equity Theory. *Encyclopaedia of Social Psychology*, Thousand Oaks, CA: Sage.

Hazan, C. and Shaver, P.R. (1987). Romantic Love Conceptualized as an Attachment Process. *Journal of Personality and Social Psychology*, 52: 511–524.

Hazan, C. and Zeifman, D. (1999). Pair Bonds as Attachment: Evaluating the Evidence. In J. Cassidy and P. Shaver (Eds), *Handbook of Attachment: Theory, Research, and Clinical Applications*, New York: Guilford Press.

Hecht, M.L. (1993). A Research Odyssey: Toward the Development of a Communication Theory of Identity. *Communication Monographs*, 48: 201–216.

Herzberg, F. (1976). *The Managerial Choice: To be Efficient and to be Human*. IL: Dow Jones.

—— (1987). One More Time: How Do You Motivate Employees? *Harvard Business Review*, 65 (5): 109–120. Originally published in 1968.

Herzberg, F., Mausner, B. and Snyderman, B. (1959). *The Motivation to Work*. New York: Wiley.

Hillery, G. (1995). Definitions of Community: Areas of Agreement. *Rural Sociology*, 1: 117.

Hinde, R. (1995). A Suggested Structure for a Science of Relationships. *Personal Relationships*, 2: 1–15.

Hoegel, Martin and George, Hans (2001). Team Work Quality and the Success of the Innovative Projects. *Organization Science*, 12 (4): 435–449.

Hollis, Florence (1964). *Case Work: A Psychosocial Therapy*. New York: Random House.

Howe, David (1995). *Attachment Theory for Social Work Practice*. London: Palgrave Macmillan.

—— (1996). Surface and Depth in Social-Work Practice. In N. Parton (Ed.), *Social Theory, Social Change and Social Work*, London: Routledge.

—— (1998). Relationship Based Thinking and Practice in Social Work. *Journal of Social Work Practice*, 12 (1): 45–56.

Howe, David, Trinder, L. and Feast, J. (2002). *The Adoption Reunion Handbook*. New York: Wiley.

Howe, N., Aquan-Assee, J., Bukowski, W.M., Rinaldi, C. and Lehoux, P.M. (2000). Sibling Self-Disclosure in Early Adolescence. *Merrill-Palmer Quarterly*, 46 (4): 653–671.

Human Development Reports (1998, 1999, 2013). New York: Oxford University Press.

IASSW (International Association of Schools of Social Work) (2002). *Social Work Definition*.

—— (2013). *Model Social Work Definition*.

Ickes, W. and Simpson, J.A. (1997). Managing Empathic Accuracy in Close Relationships. In W. Ickes (Ed.), *Empathic Accuracy*, New York: Guilford Press, pp. 218–250.

Jacob, K.K. (1994). *Social Work Education in India*. Udaipur: Himanshu Publications.

Jacobson, N.S. and Christensen, A. (1996). *Acceptance and Change in Couple Therapy*. New York: Norton.

Kapadia, K.M. and Pillai, S.D. (1971). *Young Runaways*. Bombay: Popular Prakashan.

Karve, Irawati (1993). The Kinship Map of India. In Patricia Oberoi (Ed.), *Family, Kinship and Marriage in India*, Delhi: Oxford University Press.

Kelley, H.H. (Ed.) (1983). *Close Relationships*. New York: W.H. Freeman & Company.

Kelley, H.H. and Thibaut, J.W. (1978). *Interpersonal Relationships and Theory of Interdependence*. New York: Wiley.

Kendall, Katherine A. (2000). Worldwide Beginning of Social Work Education. *The Indian Journal of Social Work*, 61 (2): 141–156.

Khinduka, S. (1965). *Social Work in India*. Allahabad: Kitab Mahal.

Kirchler, E., Rodler, C., Holzl, E. and Meier, K. (2001). *Conflict and Decision Making in Close Relationships*. Hove, UK: Psychology Press.

Kirkpatrick, L.A. and Davis, K.E. (1994). Attachment Style, Gender, and Relationship Stability: A Longitudinal Analysis. *Journal of Personality and Social Psychology*, 66: 502–512.

Kirkpatrick, L.E. and Hazan, C. (1994). Attachment Styles and Close Relationships: A Four-Year Prospective Study. *Personal Relationships*, 1: 123–142.

Kitzmann, K.M., Cohen, R. and Lockwood, R.L. (2002). Are Only Children Missing Out? Comparison of the Peer Related Social Competence of Only Children and Siblings. *Journal of Social and Personal Relationships*, 19 (3): 299–316.

Klein, Allan F. (1972). *Effective Group Work*. New York: Association Press.

Kobak, R. and Hazan, C. (1991). Attachment and Marriage: Effects of Security and Accuracy of Working Models. *Journal of Personality and Social Psychology*, 60: 861–869.

Kobak, R.R. and Sceery, A. (1988). Attachment in Late Adolescence: Working Models, Affect Regulation, and Representations of Self and Other. *Child Development*, 59: 135–146.

Konrath, Sara (2009). Self-Expansion Theory. *Encyclopedia of Social Psychology*, Thousand Oaks, CA: Sage.

Kopp, Judy (1993). Self Observation: An Empowerment Strategy in Assessment. *Social Casework*, 70 (5): 276–284.

Kunce, L.J. and Shaver, P.R. (1994). An Attachment-Theoretical Approach to Caregiving in Romantic Relationships. In K. Bartholomew and D. Perlman (Eds), *Advances in Personal Relationships*, Vol. 5, London: Jessica Kingsley.

Kuppuswamy, B. (1961). *An Introduction to Social Psychology*. Bombay: Asia Publishing House.

Kurdek, L. and Blisk, Derience (1983). Dimensions and Correlates of Mother's Divorce Experiences. *Journal of Personality and Social Psychology*, 6 (4): 1–24.

Lal Das, D.K. and Bhaskaran, Vanila (2008). *Research Methods for Social Work*. Jaipur: Rawat.

Langer, Ellen J. (1997). *The Power of Mindful Learning*. Cambridge, MA: Da Capo Press.

Larson, R.W. and Richards, M.H. (1994). Family Emotions: Do Young Adolescents and Their Parents Experience the Same States? *Journal of Research on Adolescence*, 4 (4): 567–583.

Larsson, B. and Frisk, M. (1999). Social Competence and Emotional Behaviour: Problems in 6–16 Year-Old Swedish School Children. *European Child and Adult Psychiatry*, 8 (1): 24–33.

Laursen, B. (1993). The Perceived Impact of Conflict on Adolescent Relationships. *Merrill-Palmer Quarterly*, 39: 535–550.

—— (2006). Conflict. *Encyclopedia of Human Development*, Thousand Oaks, CA: Sage.

Law, J. (1986). On the Methods of Long-Distance Control: Vessels, Navigation and the Portuguese Route to India. In J. Law (Ed.), *Power, Action and Belief: A New Sociology of Knowledge*, London: Routledge & Kegan Paul.

Leary, M.R. (1983). *Understanding Social Anxiety: Social, Personality, and Clinical Perspectives*. Beverly Hills, CA: Sage.

Lecky, Prescott (1994). *Self-Consistency: A Theory of Personality*. New York: Island Press.

Leder, Jane Mersky (1993). Adult Sibling Rivalry. *Psychology Today*, January–February.

Leonard, P. (1977). The Contribution of the Social Sciences: Ideology and Explanation. In C. Briscoe and D.N. Thomas (Eds), *Community Work: Learning and Supervision*, London: George Allen and Unwin.

Levitas, Gloria B. (1967). *Culture and Consciousness: Perspectives in Social Sciences*. New York: George Braziller.

Levy, David (1941). The Hostile Act. *Psychological Review*, 48: 356–361.

Lewin, K. (1946). Action Research and Minority Problems. *Journal of Social Issues*, 2: 34–46. Reprinted in Kurt Lewin (1997), *Resolving Social Conflicts and Field Theory in Social Science*. Washington, D.C.: American Psychology Association.

Lewis, H.B. (1971). *Shame and Guilt in Neurosis*. New York: International University Press.

Long, Denis D., Tice, Caroline J. and Morrison, John D. (2006). *Macro Social Work Practice: A Strength Perspective*. Belmont, CA: Thomas Brooks/Cole.

Lowenstein, L. (Ed.) (2010). *Creative Family Therapy Techniques: Play, Art and Expressive Therapies to Engage Children in Family Sessions*. Toronto: Champions Press.

Lyon, D. (1984). Community as Ideology and Utopia. University Quarterly, *Culture Education and Society*, 38 (3), Summer.

Madan, T.N. (1993). The Structural Implications of Marriage in North India: Wife-Givers and Wife-Takers among the Pandits of Kashmir. In Patricia Oberoi (Ed.), *Family, Kinship and Marriage in India*, Delhi: Oxford University Press.

Madan, T.N. (2009). *Modern Myths and Locked Minds: Secularism and Fundamentalism in India*. Delhi: Oxford University Press.

Magana, Lynette C., Myers-Walls, Judith A. and Love, Dee (2006). *Different Types of Parent-Child Relationships, Provider-Parent Partnership*. Purdue University at their website http:www.ces.purdue.edu/provider/parent/

Main, M., Kaplan, N. and Cassidy, J. (1985). Security in Infancy, Childhood, and Adulthood: A Move to the Level of Representation. In I. Bretherton and E. Waters (Eds), *Growing Points of Attachment Theory and Research*, Monographs of the Society for Research in Child Development, 50: 66–106.

Maine, Henry Sumner (1897). *Village Communities in the East and West.* London: John Murray.

—— (1972). *Ancient Law*. London: Everyman Edition.

Makari, George (2008). *Revolution in Mind: The Creation of Psychoanalysis*. New York: Harper Collins.

Malatesta, C.Z. and Haviland, J.M. (1982). Learning Display Rules: The Socialisation of Emotion in Infancy. *Child Development*, 53: 990–1003.

Malitz, M. (1960). *Psycho-Cybernetics*. New York: Basic Books.

Maniaci, M.R. and Reis, H.T. (2010). The Marriage of Positive Psychology and Relationship Science. *Journal of Family Theory*, 2: 47–53.

Maslow, A.H. (1943). A Theory of Human Motivation. *Psychological Review*, 50 (4): 370–396.

—— (1954). *Motivation and Personality*. New York: Harper Collins.

—— (1962). *Towards a Psychology of Being*. New York: Nostrand.

Mayo, Elton (1933). *The Human Problems of an Industrial Civilization*. MA: Harvard.

Mayr, Ernst (1970). *Population, Species and Evolution: An Abridgement of Animal Species and Evolution*. US: Harvard University Press.

McCarthy, D. (1954). Language Development in Children. In L. Carmichael (Ed.), *Manual of Child Psychology*, London: Wiley.

McCaughan, Nano (1977). Group Behaviour: Some Theories for Practice. In C. Briscoe and D.N. Thomas (Eds), *Community Work: Learning and Supervision*, London: George Allen and Unwin.

McClelland, David (1987). *Human Motivation*. New York: Cambridge.

McGoldrick, M. and Hardy, K.V. (2008). *Revisioning Family Therapy: Race, Culture and Gender in Clinical Practice*. New York: Guilford Press.

McGoldrick, M., Giordano, Joe and Garcia-Preto, Nydia (1996). *Ethnicity and Family Therapy*. New York: Guilford Press.

Mcleod, Saul (2007). Carl Rogers. www.simly psychology.org/perspective.html

McMillan, D.W. and Chavis, D.M. (1986). Sense of Community: A Definition and Theory. *Journal of Community Psychology*, 14: 6.

Mead, George H. (1934). *Mind, Self and Society*. Chicago: University of Chicago Press.

Middleman, R. (1981). The Use of Programme. In S. Abels and P. Abels (Eds), *Social Work with Groups* (Mimeograph), Proceedings of the Advancement of Social Work with Groups, Louisville.

Mikulincer, M. and Arad, D. (1999). Attachment Working Models and Cognitive Openness in Close Relationships: A Test of Chronic and Temporary Accessibility Effects. *Journal of Personality and Social Psychology*, 77: 710–725.

Mikulincer, M. and Nachshon, O. (1991). Attachment Styles and Patterns of Self-Disclosure. *Journal of Personality and Social Psychology*, 61: 321–331.

Milbrath, Lester W. (1968). The Nature of Political Beliefs and the Relationship of the Individual to the Government. *American Behavioural Scientist*, 12 (2): 28–36.

—— (1971). A Paradigm for the Comparative Study of Local Politics. *Politico*, 36: 5–35.

Milbrath, Lester W. and Goel, M.L. (1977). *Political Participation*. Lanham: University Press of America.

Moller, Arlen C. and Deci, Edward L. (2007). Control. *Encyclopedia of Social Psychology*, CA: Sage.

Monappa, A. and Saiyadain, Mirza S. (1979). *Personnel Management*. New Delhi: Tata McGraw-Hill.

Montemayor, R. (1986). Family Variation in Parent-Adolescent Storm and Stress. *Journal of Adolescent Research*, 1: 15–31.

Montgomery, B.M. (1988). Quality Communication in Personal Relationships. In S.W. Duck (Ed.), *Handbook of Personal Relationships*, New Jersey: John Wiley & Sons.

Morales, Armando T. and Sheafor, Bradford W. (1995). *Social Work: A Profession of Many Faces.* Boston: Allyn and Bacon.

Murray, Sandra L. (2007). Dependence Regulation. *Encyclopedia of Social Psychology*, CA: Sage.

Nadkarni, Vimla and Desai, K.T. (2012). *Report of National Consultation on National Network of Schools of Social Work for Quality Enhancement of Social Work Education*. Mumbai: TISS.

Nagy, B. and Spark, G.M. (1973). *Invisible Loyalties: Reciprocity in Intergenerational Family Therapy.* New York: Harper & Row.

Naik, R.K. and Siddiqui, H.Y. (Eds) (1989). *Social Work and Social Development.* New Delhi: Geetanjali.

Nair, T.K. (Ed.) (1981). *Social Work Education and Social Work Practice in India.* Madras: Association of Schools of Social Work in India.

Napier, A.Y. and Whitaker, C.A. (1978). *The Family Crucible.* New York: Harper & Row.

Narayan, Lata (2008). Contextualising Social Work Practice in India. *Indian Journal of Social Work*, Special Issue, 69 (2): 107.

Newcomb, T. (1943). *Personality and Social Change.* New York: Dryden.

Newman, J. (1994). Conflict and Friendship in Sibling Relationships: A Review. *Child Study Journal*, 24 (2): 119–148.

NFHS–3 (2005–06). *Gender Equality and Women Empowerment in India*. National Family Health Survey, Government of India.

Nieuwenhuize, C.A.O. Van (1982). *Development Begins at Home: Problems and Prospects of the Sociology of Development.* Oxford: Pergamon Press.

Oberoi, Patricia (Ed.) (1993). *Family, Kinship and Marriage in India.* Delhi: Oxford University Press.

Offe, Claus (1975). The Theory of the Capitalist State and the Problem of Policy Formation. In Leon N. Lindberg et al. (Eds), *Stress and Contradiction in Modern Capitalism*, Lexington: Heath.

—— (1996). *Varieties of Transition: The German and East European Experience.* Cambridge: MIT Press.

Olson, Mancur (1965). *The Logic of Collective Action: Public Goods and the Theory of Groups.* New York: Harvard University Press.

Orbach, I. (1995). Attachment Styles and Repressive Defensiveness: The Accessibility and Architecture of Affective Memories. *Journal of Personality and Social Psychology*, 68: 917–925.

Osgood, C.E. (1962). *An Alternative to Surrender*. Urbana: University of Illinois Press.

Osgood, Mary H. (1977). Rural and Urban Attitude Toward Welfare. *Social Work*, 22: 41–47.

Oskamp, S. (1977). *Attitudes and Opinions*. Englewood Cliffs, NJ: Prentice Hall.

Pahl, J. (1995). Friendly Society, Parents and Friends. *Journal of Marriage and the Family*, 63: 97–110.

Pant, Devendra Kumar and Patra, Kakali (1998). Rural Poverty in India in an Era of Economic Reforms. Paper Presented in the NCAER-IDRC Workshop on Micro Impact of Macro Adjustment Policies in India (MIMAP-India), NCAER, New Delhi.

Parikh, K.S. and Shah, Ajay (1999). Second Generation Reforms. In Kirit S. Parikh (Ed.), *India Development Report: 1999–2000*, Delhi: Oxford University Press.

Parke, R.D. (1988). *Family and Peer Relationships*. London: Routledge.

Parke, R.D., MacDonald, K., Beitel, A. and Bhavnagri, N. (1988). The Role of the Family in the Development of Peer Relationships. In R. Dev Peters and R.J. McMahan (Eds), *Marriages and Families: Behavioural Treatments and Processes*, New York: Brunner/Mazel.

Pathak, S.H. (1989). Social Development and Social Work: Some Unresolved Issues. In R.K. Naik and H.Y. Siddiqui (Eds), *Social Work and Social Development*, New Delhi: Geetanjali.

Pathak, S.H. (2000). Social Work Educators as Scholars: Some Animadversions. *The Indian Journal of Social Work*, 61 (2): 212–220.

—— (2012). *Social Work and Social Welfare*. Bangalore: Niruta Publications.

—— (2014). In a Personal Correspondence with Author.

Patterson, G.R. and Capaldi, D.M. (1991). Anti-Social Parents: Unskilled and Vulnerable. In Phillip A. Cohen and Eileen M. Hetherington (Eds), *Family Transitions*, London: Routledge.

Patton, R.D. and Cissell, W.B. (Eds) (1990). *Community Organization: Traditional Principles and Modern Applications*. Johnson City: Latchpins.

Perlman, M. and Ross, H.S. (1997). Who's the Boss? Parents' Failed Attempts to Influence the Outcomes of Conflicts between Their

Children. *Journal of Social and Personal Relationships*, 14: 463–480.

Perner, Josef, Ruffman, Ted and Leekam, Susan R. (1994). Theory of Mind is Contagious: You Catch it from Your Sibs. *Child Development*, 65: 1228–1238.

Peterson, James and Zill, Nicholas (1986). Marital Disruption, Parent-Child Relationships and Behaviour Problems in Children. *Journal of Marriage and Family*, 48 (2): 295–307.

Piaget, Jean (1997). *The Moral Judgement of the Child*. New York: Free Press.

Pietromonaco, P.R. and Barrett, L. (1997). Working Models of Attachment and Daily Social Interactions. *Journal of Personality and Social Psychology*, 73: 1409–1423.

Pilgrim, D., Rogers, A. and Bentall, R. (2009). The Centrality of Personal Relationships in the Creation and Amelioration of Mental Health Problems: The Current Interdisciplinary Case. *Health*, 13 (2): 235–254.

Pistole, M.C. (1989). Attachment in Adult Romantic Relationships: Style of Conflict Resolution and Relationship Satisfaction. *Journal of Social and Personal Relationships*, 6: 505–510.

Punekar, S.D. and Rao, Kamala (1962). *A Study of Prostitutes in Bombay*. Bombay: Allied Publishers.

Raffaelli, M. (1997). Young Adolescents' Conflicts with Siblings and Friends. *Journal of Youth and Adolescence*, 26: 539–558.

Rahman, M. Anisur (1990). The Case of Third World: People's Self-Development. *Community Development Journal*, 25 (4): 307–313.

Ramchandran, P. (1968). Research in Social Work. *Encyclopaedia of Social Work in India*, Vol. 2, pp. 386–394.

—— (1975). Review of Social Work Research in India. In S.D. Gokhale (Ed.), *Social Welfare: Legend and Legacy*, Bombay: Popular Prakashan, pp. 220–230.

Ranade, S.N. (1972). *Social Work Research in India* (Mimeograph). New Delhi: Indian Council of Social Science Research.

Redfield, Robert (1947). The Folk Society. *American Journal of Sociology*, 52 (4): 293–308.

Rees, Wim Van (1991). Neighbourhood, the State, and Collective Action. *Community Development Journal*, 26 (2): 96–102.

Reimer, E.W. (1971). *School is Dead*. Harmondsworth, UK: Penguin.

Reiss, S., Peterson, R.A., Gursky, D.M. and McNally, R.J. (1986). Anxiety Sensitivity, Anxiety Frequency and the Prediction of Fearfulness. *Behaviour Research and Therapy*, 24: 1–8.

Revell, B. (1997). Using Play and Art Therapy to Work with Families. In B. Bidwell (Ed.), *Hand in Hand: A Practical Application of Art and Play Therapy*, London: Thames River Publishing.

Richman, N. and Lansdown, R. (Eds) (1988). *Problems of Preschool Children*. Oxford, England: John Wiley & Sons.

Richmond, Mary (1917). *Social Diagnosis*. New York: Russell Sage.

Rivera, Felix G. and Erlich, John L. (Eds) (1995). *Community Organizing in a Diverse Society*. Boston: Allyn and Bacon.

Robins, Stephen P. (1997). *Essentials of Organizational Behaviour*. NJ: Prentice Hall.

Rogers, C. (1951). *Client-Centered Therapy: Its Current Practice, Implications and Theory*. London: Constable.

—— (1959). A Theory of Therapy, Personality and Interpersonal Relationships as Developed in the Client-Centered Framework. In S. Koch (Ed.), *Psychology: A Study of a Science, Vol. 3: Formulations of the Person and the Social Context*, New York: McGraw-Hill.

Roloff, M.E. (1981). *Interpersonal Communication: The Social Exchange Approach*. CA: Sage.

Roopnarine, J., Johnson, J. and Hooper, F. (1994). *Children's Play in Diverse Cultures*. Albany, New York: State University of New York Press.

Ross, P. (1996). The Influence of Significant Others on Learning about Relationships. In S. Duck (Ed.), *Handbook of Personal Relationships*, New York: Wiley, pp. 343–359.

Rothman, Jack (1969). Three Models of Community Organisation Practice. Proceedings of National Conference on Social Welfare, Social Work Practice, New York: Columbia University Press.

Rotter, J.B. (1954). *Social Learning and Clinical Psychology*. New York: Prentice Hall.

Rubin, Allen (2000). Social Work Research at the Turn of the Millennium: Progress and Challenges. *Social Work Practice Research*, 10: 9.

Rubin, Zick (1970). Measurement of Romantic Love. *Journal of Personality and Social Psychology*, 16 (3): 265–273.

Ruch, Gillian, Turney, Danielle and Ward, Adrian (Eds) (2010). *Relationship Based Social Work*. London: Jessica Kingsley.

Rutter, M. (1993). Resilience: Some Conceptual Considerations. *Journal of Adolescent Health*, 14 (8): 626–631.

Salisch, Von M. (2001). Children's Emotional Development: Challenges in Their Relationships to Parents, Peers, and Friends. *International Journal of Behavioural Development*, 25: 310.

Sayer, Jennifer (1986). Ideology: The Bridge between Theory and Practice. *Community Development Journal*, 21 (4): 294–303.

Scherer, K.R., Wallbott, H. and Summerfield, A.B. (Eds) (1986). *Experiencing Emotions: A Cross-Cultural Study*. Cambridge, MA: Cambridge University Press.

Seligman, Martin (1993). *Learned Helpless*. New York: Oxford University Press.

Sen, Amartya (1999). *Introduction to Human Development Report 1999*. New York: Oxford University Press.

Seymour, S. (1993). Socio-Cultural Contests: Examining Sibling Roles in South Asia. In C.W. Nuckolls (Ed.), *Siblings in South Asia: Brothers and Sisters in Cultural Context*, New York: Guilford Press.

Sharma, Ursula (1993). Dowry in North India: Its Consequences for Women. In Patricia Oberoi (Ed.), *Family, Kinship and Marriage in India*, Delhi: Oxford University Press.

Sheldon, Brian and Macdonald, Geraldine (2009). *A Textbook of Social Work*. London: Routledge.

Sherif, M. (1936). *The Psychology of Social Norms*. Oxford: Harper.

—— (1966). *Group Conflict and Cooperation: Their Social Psychology*. London: Routledge and Kegan Paul.

Sherif, M., Harvey, O.J., White, B. Jack, Hood, William K. and Sherif, Cavolyn W. (1988). *The Robbers Care Experiment: Inter-Group Conflict and Cooperation*. Middletown: Wesleyan University Press.

Siddiqui, H.Y. (1984). *Social Work and Social Action*. New Delhi: Harnam Publications.

—— (1987). Towards a Competency Based Education in Social Work. *Indian Journal of Social Work*, April.

—— (1989). Rethinking Social Work Education. In R.K. Nayak and H.Y. Siddiqui (Eds), *Social Work and Social Development*, New Delhi: Geetanjali.

—— (2005). *Social Development in the Indian Sub-Continent*. Jaipur: Rawat.

—— (2008). *Group Work: Theories and Practices*. Jaipur: Rawat.

—— (2011). *A Sociological Analysis of Distance Education* (Mimeograph).

Sillars, A., Roberts, L.J., Leonard, K.E. and Dun, T. (2000). Cognition during Marital Conflict: The Relationship of Thought and Talk. *Journal of Social and Personal Relationships*, 17: 479–502.

Sillars, A.L. (1995). Communication and Family Culture. In M.A. Fitzpatrick and A.L. Vangelisti (Eds), *Perspectives on Family Communication*, Thousand Oaks, CA: Sage.

Simmel, G. (1955). *Conflict*. New York: Free Press.

Singh, J.P. (2004). Contemporary Indian Family. In Bert N. Adams and Jan Trost (Eds), *Handbook of World Families*, CA: Sage, pp. 126–166.

Singh, S. and Srivastava, S.P. (2005). *Teaching and Practice of Social Work in India*. Lucknow: New Royal Book Co.

Sivaramakrishnan, K.C., Dasgupta, B. and Buch, M.N. (1993). *Urbanization in India: Basic Services and Peoples Participation*. New Delhi: Institute of Social Sciences.

Skidmore, R.A., Thackeray, M.G. and Farley, O.W. (1988). *Introduction to Social Work*. New York: Prentice Hall.

Smelser, Neil J. (1963). *Theory of Collective Behaviour*. New York: Free Press.

Smith, Greg (1996). Ties, Nets and an Elastic Bund: Community in the Postmodern City. *Community Development Journal*, 31 (3): 250–259.

Sori, C.F. (2006). *Engaging Children in Family Therapy: Creative Approaches to Integrating Theory and Research in Clinical Practice*. New York: Routledge.

Specht, Harry (1986). Social Support, Social Networks, Social Exchange and Social Work Practice. *Social Service Review*, 60 (2): 218–240.

Spielberger, C.D. (1989). *State-Trait Anxiety Inventory: Bibliography*. 2nd edition, Paulo Alto, CA: Consulting Psychologists Press.

Steinberg, Laurence (2001). We Know Some Things: Parent-Adolescent Relationships in Retrospect and Prospect. *Journal of Research on Adolescence*, 11 (1): 1–19.

Stern, D. (1986). *The Interpersonal World of the Infant*. New York: Basic Books.

Stocker, C.M., Lanthier, R.P. and Furman, W. (1997). Sibling Relationships in Early Adulthood. *Journal of Family Psychology*, 11 (2): 210–221.

Taibbi, R. (2007). *Doing Family Therapy: Craft and Creativity in Clinical Practice*. New York: Guilford Press.

Tajfel, P. (1970). *Human Groups and Social Categories*. London: Cambridge University Press.

Taylor, J.A. (1953). A Personality Scale of Manifest Anxiety. *J Abnorm Soc Psychol*, 48: 285–290.

Thomas, H. (1967). *I am OK You are OK*. New Delhi: Sterling.

Thompson, Neil (2010). *Theorizing Social Work Practice*. UK: Palgrave Macmillan.

Thorensen, C.E. and Mahoney, M.J. (1974). *Behavioural Self-Control*. New York: Rinehart and Winston.

Thyer, Bruce A. (2000). A Decade of Research on Social Work Practice. *Research on Social Work Practice*, January: 5–8.

Tidwell, M.O., Reis, H.T. and Shaver, P.R. (1996). Attachment, Attractiveness, and Social Interaction: A Diary Study. *Journal of Personality and Social Psychology*, 71: 729–745.

Timms, Noel (1970). *Social Work: An Outline for Intending Student*. London: Routledge and Kegan Paul.

Toch, Hans (1966). *The Social Psychology of Social Movements*. London: Methuen.

Todaro, Michael P. and Smith, S.C. (2012). *Economic Development*. Delhi: Pearson.

Toseland, R.W. and Rivas, R.F. (2001). *An Introduction to Group Work Practice*. Boston: Allyn and Bacon.

Tracy, Elizabeth M. and Whittaker, James K. (1993). The Social Network Map: Assessing Social Support in Clinical Practice. In Julia B. Raunch (Ed.), *Assessment*, Milwaukee: Family International Inc.

Trecker, H.B. (1948). *Social Group Work: Principles and Practice*. New York: Women's Press.

Uchino, B.N., Cacioppo, J.T. and Kiecolt-Glaser, J.K. (1996). The Relationship between Social Support and Physiological Processes: A Review with Emphasis on Underlying Mechanisms and Implications for Health. *Psychological Bulletin*, 119: 488–531.

Vangelisti, A.L. (Ed.) (2004). *Perspectives on Family Communication*. London: Routledge.

Verba, Sidney and Nie, Norman H. (1972). *Participation in America: Political Democracy and Social Equality*. New York: Harper & Row.

Verba, Sidney, Ahmed, Bashir and Bhatt, Anil (1971). *Caste, Race and Politics: A Comparative Study of India and the United States*. CA: Sage.

Verba, Sidney, Nie, Norman H. and Jae-on Kim (1971). *Modes of Democratic Participation: A Cross-National Comparison*. Beverly Hills, CA: Sage.

Vetere, A. and Dowling, E. (2005). *Narrative Therapies with Children and Their Families: A Practitioner's Guide to Concepts and Approaches*. London: Routledge.

Vroom, Victor H. (1964). *Work and Motivation*. New York: Wiley.

Wadsworth, Barry J. (1996). *Piaget's Theory of Cognitive and Affective Development: Foundations of Constructivism*. 5th edition, New York: Longman.

Wallerstein, J.S. (1991). The Long-Term Effects of Divorce on Children: A Review. *Journal of American Academy of Child and Adolescents*, 30 (3): 349–360.

Wallerstein, Judith S. and Kelly, Joan Berlin (1980). *Surviving the Break-Up: How Children and Parents Cope with Divorce*. New York: Basic Books.

Walsh, F. (Ed.) (1982). *Normal Family Processes*. New York: Guilford Press.

Waters, E. and Crandall, V.J. (1964). Social Class and Observed Maternal Behaviour from 1940–1960. *Child Development*, 35: 1021–1032.

Weisner, T. (1993). Overview: Sibling Similarity and Differences in Different Cultures. In C. Nuckolls (Ed.), *Siblings in South Asia: Brothers and Sisters in Cultural Context*, New York: Guilford Press, pp. 45–70.

Weisner, T.S. (1993). Siblings in Cultural Place: Ethnographic and Ecocultural Perspectives on Siblings of Developmentally Delayed Children. In Z. Stoneman and P. Berman (Eds), *Siblings of Individuals with Mental Retardation, Physical Disabilities, and Chronic Illness*, Baltimore: Brooks, pp. 51–83.

Weiss, R.S. (1982). Attachment in Adult Life. In C.M. Parkes and J. Stevenson-Hinde (Eds), *The Place of Attachment in Human Behavior*, New York: Basic Books.

West, Elizabeth (1995). Organization Building in the Wake of Ethnic Conflict. *Social Forces*, 73 (4): 1333–1364.

Whitaker, D.S. (1995). *Using Groups to Help People*. London: Routledge.

Whiting, B. and Whiting, J. (1975). *Children of Six Cultures: A Psychocultural Analysis*. New York: Wiley.

Wilmot, W.W. (1995). *Relational Communication*. New York: McGraw-Hill.

Wilmot, W.W. and Hocker, J.L. (2001). *Interpersonal Conflict*. 6th edition, New York: McGraw-Hill.

Witmer, Helen L. (1942). *An Analysis of Social Institutions*. New York: Farrar and Rinehart.

Wood, J.T. and Duck, S. (Eds) (1996). *Confronting Relationship Challenges, Vol. 6: Understanding Relationship Processes: Off the Beaten Track*. Thousand Oaks, CA: Sage.

World Development Report (2012). *Gender Inequality and Development*. New York: Oxford University Press.

World Development Report (1999–2000). New York: Oxford University Press.

Worsley, Peter (1970). *Introducing Sociology*. Harmondsworth: Penguin.

Xyrichis, A. and Ream, A. (2008). Team Work: A Concept Analysis. *Journal of Advance Nursing*, 61 (2): 232–241.

Zimbalist, Sidney (1977). *Historic Themes and Landmarks in Social Welfare Research*. New York: Harper & Row.

Index

activists/leaders, communities, 138
advocacy process, 179–181
  tools, 180–181
ambivalent parent-child relationship, 91
analytical thinking, 190–191
Ancient Law (Maine), 77
anxiety, 53, 188
attachment theory, 49–52
avoidant parent-child relationship, 91

BCT. *see* behavioural couples therapy (BCT)
behavioural couples therapy (BCT), 59–60
betrayal, 14, 53–54, 109
  and conflict, 100–101
Bonilla, Frank, 138
Bowlby, John, 49, 50

case studies
  social work, 34–38
caste hierarchies, 68
change, conflict and, 55–56
child abuse, 172–178
child labour, 172–178
children, pro-social behaviours, 7
class background, and spousal relationship, 81
client, assessment of, 116–123
  based on interpretation of facts, 121–122
  questionnaire for, 117
  Self-Assessment of Strengths and Weaknesses (assessment form), 117–121
Close Relationships (Kelley), 15
closeness, 56
cognition, defined, 60
cognitive behavioural couples therapy, 60
communication gap, and conflict, 100
communication skills, 184–185
  analytical thinking, 190–191

empathy, 191–192
listening, 189
observation, 190
self-control, 192–194
communication
and conflicts, 102–106
distortion, 105–106
factors facilitating, 185–188
in families, 108
skills (*see* communication skills)
communities, 133–154
activists/leaders, 138
assessment of, 212–214
boundaries of, 146–147
concepts relating to, 134–136
concerns, 138–141
conflicts, 142
defined, 135
environment of, 136–138
methods of entry into, 144–146
needs, determination of, 147–148
people's participation in, 148–154
profile, development of, 146–147
programme planning, 147–148
small, 135
computerized assessment, 217
Concept of Self Actualization (Rogers), 74
conflict management, 56
conflicts, 14–15, 96–106
and change, 55–56
betrayal and, 100–101
communication and, 102–106
communication gap and, 100
communities, 142
difference in values and, 102
factors causing, 98–102
in groups, 131–132
in parent-child relations, 90
interpersonal, 14, 97
intervention strategies, 21–22
intrapersonal, 14, 54–55, 97
lack of self-control and, 101–102
perceptual distortion and, 99
strong self-orientation and, 98–99
contract, establishment of, 115–116
control, 56–57
culture, 77
culture, and spousal relationship, 78–79

dependence regulation, 57–58
depression, 58
disagreements, in relationships, 56
disengaged families, 108
disorganized parent-child relationship, 91
diversity, and communication, 186
domestic violence, in families, 108–109
dyadic conflict, 55

economy, globalization of, 160–162
education
and human relationships, 39–40

and spousal relationship, 79–80
emotional aspect, self-concept, 67
emotional energy, 52
emotional intelligence, 52–53
emotionally focused therapy, 60
empathy, 191–192
enmeshed family, 108
Erikson, Erik, 55
ethical issues, families, 109
extramarital affairs, 109
eye contact, 188
Eysenck, M.W., 71

family systems therapy, 61–62
family(ies), 2–3, 76–95, 107–108
affairs and betrayals, 109
assessment of, 202–212
communication in, 108
domestic violence in, 108–109
ethical issues, 109
failing, 3–4
gender roles in, 109
parent-child relationship, 85–92
patriarchal, 77–78
sibling relations, 92–95
spousal relationship, 76–84
structure of, 108
working with, 109–113
Family, Kinship and Marriage in India (Oberoi), 76
Freud, Sigmund, 54, 97
full literacy, 138–139

gender inequality, 170–172
gender roles, in families, 109
generation gap, 90
globalization of economy, 160–162
group conflict, 55
groups, working with, 127–132
conflicts in, 131–132
monitoring, 128–130
relationship patterns in, 130–131
setting up routine, 127–128
terms of contract and, 127

Hatfield, Elaine, 9
Hill, Octavia, 2
Human Development Report (HDR), 161–162
human relationships, 1, 39–62
and mental health, 18
and productivity, 5
behaviour pattern consistency and, 8
conflicts in (*see* conflicts)
defined, 10–12
dimensions of, 6–9
education and, 39–40
examples of, 11–12
importance of, 1–2, 15–18
law of, 12–15
nature of, 10–12
paradigmatic views, 47–48
social work and, 30
techniques of facilitating (*see* techniques, of facilitating relationships)
theories (*see* theories, human relationships)
human rights violations, 170

IASSW. *see* International Association and Schools of Social Work (IASSW)
IFSW. *see* International Federation and Social Workers (IFSW)
individuals, process of facilitating relationships, 114–126
  client, assessment of, 116–123
  contract, establishment of, 115–116
inferiority feelings, 72
information, as tool of advocacy, 180
integrative behavioural couples therapy, 60
intelligence, 45
interdependence theory, 43–45
  components of, 44–45
  intelligence and personality, 45
International Association and Schools of Social Work (IASSW), 24
International Federation and Social Workers (IFSW), 24
interpersonal cognition theory, 48–49
interpersonal conflict, 14, 97
intrapersonal conflict, 14, 54–55, 97

Johnson, Susan, 60

Kelley, Harold, 15, 43
Kurt, Lewin, 55

law of relationship, 12–15
Lecky, Prescott, 67
Levitas, Gloria, 136–137
Levy, David, 93
listening, 189
lobbying, as tool of advocacy, 181
long-term relationships, 5–6
Lyon, David, 135

marriage, 77
Mead, G.H., 27
media networking, as tool of advocacy, 181
mental abilities, self-concept, 66–67
mental health, human relationships and, 18
Minnesota Multiphasic Personality Inventory (MMPI), 42
MMPI. *see* Minnesota Multiphasic Personality Inventory (MMPI)
monitoring, of groups, 128–130
morphological phenotype, 40–41
mutual expectations, and human relationships, 12–13

National Sample Survey (NSS), 163
Nieuwenhuis, Van, 31
non-verbal cues, 189

objectivity, and communication, 187

observation, 190, 199
organizations, assessment of, 214–217

parent-child relationship, 85–92
  factors affecting, 88
  individual differences and, 92
  stages of, 87–89
  types of, 91
parenting style, 58–59
participatory rapid appraisal (PRA), 146
patriarchal family, 77–78
perceptual distortion, and conflict, 99
personal power, 72
personality development, 40
personality factors, and spousal relationship, 81–82
personality tests, 41–42
  MMPI, 42
physical aspect, self-concept, 65–66
Piaget, Jean, 55, 97
political participation, 178–179
positional power, 72
positive relationship, 5
positive self-concept, 45–46
poverty, 2, 165–167
PRA. *see* participatory rapid appraisal (PRA)
primary inferiority feeling, 72
productivity, human relationships and, 5
profile, community, 146–147
programme planning, 147–148
public interest litigation , as tool of advocacy, 181

questionnaire, for assessment of individual, 117

rapport building, skills in, 183–184
Redfield, Robert, 135
reflected appraisal, 69
research, as tool of advocacy, 180
Richmond, Mary, 2, 29
Rogers, Carl, 63
Rubin, Zick, 15

secondary inferiority feeling, 72
secure parent-child relationship, 91
Self-Assessment of Strengths and Weaknesses (assessment form), 117–121
self-awareness, 70–71
self-concept, 63–75
  emotional aspect, 67
  importance of, 63
  mental abilities, 66–67
  of mentally healthy person, 64
  physical aspect, 65–66
  social aspect, 67–69
  theories of (*see* theories, self-concept)
self-confidence, 71–73
self-control, 192–194
self-discipline, 101

self-esteem, 71
self-orientation, 129–130
self-other relationship, 47–48
self-report, 197–198
self-respect, 71
self-view of relationships, 9–10
Seligman, Martin, 57
'selling model' approach, 144
Sherif, Muzafer, 70
sibling relationships, 92–95
sibling rivalry, 14, 93–94
silence, 185
skills, of facilitating relationships, 182–194
  in rapport building, 183–184
social action, 155–181
  absolute poverty, 165–167
  advocacy process, 179–181
  child abuse, 172–178
  environmental issues, 168
  gender inequality, 170–172
  globalization of economy, 160–162
  growth of social iniquities, 163–164
  human rights violations, 170
  inadequate health care, 168–169
  marginalization of state, 162–163
  political participation, 178–179
  problem of governance, 164
social aspect, self-concept, 67–69
social change, in human societies, 2
social comparison, 69–70
social competence, 7
social exchange theory, 43
social functioning, 27–28
  individual and, 29
social iniquities, growth of, 163–164
social mobilization, as tool of advocacy, 181
social norms, and spousal relationship, 78–79
social work, 23–27
  and human relationships, 30
  beginnings of, 28–29
  case studies, 34–38
  definition of, 27–34
  in medical setting, 37–38
Social Work: A Profession with Many Faces (Morales and Sheafor), 23
spousal relationship, 2, 76–84
  class background and, 81
  culture and, 78–79
  education and, 79–80
  personality factors and, 81–82
  problems in, 82–84
  social norms and, 78–79
  work status, 80–81
state-anxiety, 53
strong self-orientation, and conflict, 98–99
superiority complex, 73

techniques of
  community assessment, 212–214
  computerized assessment, 217
  facilitating relationships, 195–217

family assessment, 202–212
individuals, assessment of, 196–202
organizations, assessment of, 214–217
theories, human relationships
attachment theory, 49–52
interdependence theory, 43–45
interpersonal cognition theory, 48–49
personality tests, 41–42
social exchange theory, 43
theory of self and others orientation, 45–48
theories, self-concept, 69
reflected appraisal, 69
social comparison, 69–70
theory of self and others orientation, 45–48
self-other relationship, 47–48
total surrender, 46–47
therapies
behavioural couples therapy, 59–60
cognitive behavioural couples therapy, 60
emotionally focused therapy, 60
family systems therapy, 61–62
integrative behavioural couples therapy, 60
Thibaut, John, 43
total surrender, 46–47
trait-anxiety, 53
Traupmann, Jane, 9

Ultra Non-Directive Approach, 144
Utne, Mary, 9

Webb, Beatrice, 2
Webb, Sydney, 2
work status, and spousal relationship, 80–81
World Development Report (WDR), 162–163